How to
Cook

Publisher's Note: Raw or semi-cooked eggs should not be consumed by babies, toddlers, pregnant or breast-feeding women, the elderly or those suffering from a recurring illness.

Publisher & Creative Director: Nick Wells
Senior Project Editor: Catherine Taylor
Art Director: Mike Spender
Layout Design: The Urban Ant Ltd.
Digital Design & Production: Chris Herbert
Production Controller: Digby Smith

Special thanks to Gina Steer for her continued help and contributions.

This is a **FLAME TREE** Book

FLAME TREE PUBLISHING
Crabtree Hall, Crabtree Lane
Fulham, London SW6 6TY
United Kingdom
www.flametreepublishing.com

Flame Tree is part of The Foundry Creative Media Company Limited

First published 2010

Copyright © 2010 Flame Tree Publishing

12 14 13 11
3 5 7 9 10 8 6 4 2

ISBN: 978-1-84786-962-3

A copy of the CIP data for this book is available from the British Library.

Printed in China

All images © The Foundry Creative Media Co., except the below.
Courtesy of Shutterstock and © the following photographers: 4l Indigo Fish; 14l & 79, 44 Elena Elisseeva; 14r & 46l, 26l, 28l, 41l, 84l, 138r l Robyn Mackenzie; 15 & 174 Forster Forest; 158l & 160 Taratorki ; 16t, 21l mates; 16b Mike Flippo; 17 DRGill; 18r Aga & Miko (arsat); 18l erkanupan; 19 Paul Cowan; 22r ZTS; 23r arenacreative; 23l & 88, 46r Joe Gough; 27 Viktor1; 29 Steve Lovegrove; 30 RookCreations; 31r Dewitt; 31l HomeStudio; 32 Svetlana Lukienko; 33l Sandra Cunningham; 33r, 48, 52, 98, 119, 126, 133, 125l & 127, 138l, 154l & 157, 169b, 169t Monkey Business Images; 34 silabob; 35 Natalia Klenova; 36l Colour; 36r & 40 Birdy68; 37b Justin Paget; 38 3445128471; 39 Khorkova Olga; 41r fotogiunta; 42r Andi Berger; 42l Zamula Artem; 43 Eugene Berman; 50 msheldrake; 53 efka; 54t anlogin; 54b, 156r Tatuasha; 59r Robert Anthony; 63l Eaststeel; 63r RexRover; 65r Worytko Pawel; 72 Burak Can Oztas; 73b Girish Menon; 73t & 77 Alister G Jupp; 74 Andre Bonn; 75 MikeE; 78 Magone; 80 Coprid; 81l Kateryna Dyellalova; 81r Paul Turner; 82 olszphoto; 83 Elena Schweitzer; 84r viki2win; 85r moonbeam; 97 NicolasMcComber; 107r ilker canikligil; 108 Richard Griffin; 111 Newton Page; 112b Terence Mendoza; 114 Nic Neish; 118l Kruglov_Orda; 120 LockStockBob; 125r Valentyn Volkov; 129 Martin Darley; 130 matka_Wariatka; 135l Brett Mulcahy; 136 PeterKikta; 137 Heidi Hart ; 144 Christopher Elwell; 149 Dewayne Flowers; 150 a9photo; 152 Norma Cornes ; 175 StockLite; 176r David W Hughes; 176l Ilike; 177 zkruger. Courtesy of Cephas Picture Library and © the following photographers: 87 Dean Skip; 93 James Jackson; 96 Jean-Paul Boyer. Courtesy of Fotolia/Monkey Business: 102b.

How to
Cook

Ingredients • Techniques • Recipes

**FLAME TREE
PUBLISHING**

Contents

The **first half** of this book is intended to set you up – whether you are a complete beginner or a more experienced cook. From **essential equipment** and **handy conversions** to a wealth of **key methods** and recipes for **cooking meat** and **making sauces** and more, it contains what you need to learn '**how to cook**'. Read from start to finish or dip in to remind yourself of the basic recipe for mayonnaise – either way, it will be an **invaluable companion** in the kitchen.

Meal Suggestions

The **second section** of the book offers a tempting **selection of recipes** for you to try out your newly honed skills. To help inspire you further, we have grouped them into meal suggestions of **starter**, **main course** and **dessert**, which are also themed by **nationality** or **category** – such as **Italian**, **Indian**, **Vegetarian** and **Traditional**. Of course, you could always mix and match! So whether you opt for fish cakes or naan bread, risotto or stir-fry, tiramisu or rice pudding, you will be whipping up a feast in no time.

Traditional

Italian

Chinese

Thai

Indian

Vegetarian

Low-fat

Introduction

Food (or eating), like many pursuits, is a voyage of discovery. We start as children before our taste buds have even developed and which in many cases are bombarded with sweetness. For many, this stays with us all our lives, while others are introduced to savoury tastes and this is the start of the great adventure. We would not expect young children to enjoy the delights of caviar, olives or chillies; these sophisticated tastes have to be acquired – and so it is with cooking.

START SIMPLE

We start by learning the simple techniques and playing safe with the food we buy, prepare and cook. However, once we are confident with the early steps, we want to learn more, to experiment and stretch the horizons as far as possible. New skills and techniques need to be learnt, new terminology understood and most probably new equipment invested in. But where to turn for all this information? Look no further – *How to Cook* is the book for you.

WHERE THIS BOOK COMES IN

This invaluable guide and cookbook explains clearly 'how to cook' all those delicious dishes that involve intricate steps and terminology, which up until now you have left to the TV chefs. Here are the answers to all those questions you would like to ask, from how to separate an egg to how to make a sabayon sauce.

Most usefully, *How to Cook* provides the key classic recipes that are invaluable to learn off-by-heart as part of your repertoire, which can then be built on by trying the selection of recipes and meal suggestions in the latter part of the book.

REMEMBER, REMEMBER

Before you start, there are a few guidelines that are important to remember. The most important one is taste. When cooking, the number one rule is 'taste, taste and taste again'. For example, this will help you avoid overdoing it on the salt: if too much salt has been added, it cannot be removed (you can try to disguise it but it will be difficult). However, if not enough salt has been added, that is easily remedied. It is likewise with all the other spices and seasoning as well as the sweeter ingredients.

The guiding and overriding principle is 'food should appeal to all the senses' – first of all, it should smell good, then it should look good and it should taste good – so, no matter whether you are preparing and cooking the simplest of dishes such as scrambled eggs or a highly complicated and elaborate dish such as Boeuf en Croute – both should smell, look and taste superb. That is good cooking. So take your time, do not rush, think about what you are preparing and learn 'how to cook' with us.

Gina Steer

Tools and Equipment

 In this section, I have listed the tools and equipment you will need in order to start cooking, Some of the tools and equipment are absolutely essential and I would recommend that you invest in these first. Other less essential tools and equipment can also be reasonably expensive, so they might be good ideas to suggest as either birthday or Christmas presents.

ESSENTIAL TOOLS

Knives Knives are perhaps the most important tools in the kitchen. It is advisable to have a good selection. First, when buying, make sure that any knife sits comfortably in your hand. You will need a small knife (often called a 'paring' knife) for all the little jobs, such as deseeding a chilli and cutting fruits and vegetables into small pieces. At least a further three to four additional knives would be good: a large chef's knife, which has a long wide blade, is ideal for chopping both meat and fish as well as fresh herbs; a carving knife; a bread knife, with or without a serrated edge; and a medium-sized all-purpose knife for all other jobs. Make sure that the knives are a reputable brand and easy to sharpen – a good knife will last a long while, maybe for ever.

Wooden Spoons I feel you can never have too many wooden spoons! Although they will not last for ever, looked after and washed properly they should last for at least one to two years, depending on what you use them for. I would recommend buying one of the sets that are so readily available. These normally come in different lengths – the shorter one is super for sauces and the other two for stirring food, such as meat that is being sealed in a pan, as well as for mixing cakes and batters. Although they wash perfectly well it is a good idea to keep some spoons for sweet dishes and others for savoury dishes. Then there are the wooden spatulas which are perfect for omelettes or frying meats such as chops as the flat, wider area makes turning food over so much easier.

Kitchen Utensils with Rack These are normally stainless steel and although it is not totally necessary to have the rack fixed to the wall, it is a good idea, especially if close to the cooker. These racks normally contain at least five utensils, all of which play an important part in cooking.

Large Spoons These can be a plain spoon ideal for stirring or dishing out casseroles, stews and vegetables, or a slotted draining spoon – this refers to the gaps in the bowl of the spoon which allow any liquid to drain out, back into the pan, for example when removing meat after sealing it for a stew or casserole.

Measuring Spoons These ensure that the correct amount of an ingredient is used (such as ¼ teaspoon or 1 tablespoon). This is especially useful when either following a specific diet (for example, where oil and butter intake needs to be measured), or for use with a thickening agent such as cornflour/cornstarch, or with spices, where too much could completely ruin the dish.

Vegetable Peeler Using a peeler makes the job easier and will ensure that you get an even look to the peeled fruit or vegetable, such as peeling pears for cooking in wine or peeling potatoes. I prefer the swivel blade peeler as it only removes a very thin layer and this will mean that, since many of the nutrients are just below the skin, they are preserved. However, it is a matter of personal choice, so when buying, try imitating the peeling action and see which fits most comfortably with yourself.

Grater For grating cheese, carrots and other root vegetables, fresh root ginger, chocolate, citrus zest and nutmeg – those last two should be done on the finest side of the grater.

Oven Thermometer Especially useful if you plan to make cakes and desserts. Many ovens vary in temperature, and pastry and baked goods need the correct temperature in order to get good results.

Timer Again, if planning to bake pastries and cakes, time is critical and it is so easy to get distracted, so a timer will ensure that you know when it is time to test to see if the cake or pastry is cooked. Many ovens have timers built in.

Scissors A pair of serrated-edge kitchen scissors is so useful for all the little jobs, such as snipping a few fresh herbs, chopping bacon or dried fruits into small pieces, removing unwanted fat from chicken portions or steaks, cutting out liners for cake tins/pans... the list is endless.

Garlic Press A handy alternative to crushing or mincing garlic with a knife. This removes the need to peel the garlic; a clove is simply placed in the bowl and a small handle is pulled over, then the garlic comes out of the tiny holes. Some can also double up as a cherry stoner.

EXTRA TOOLS

Fish Slice Also known as a 'spatula', this is not the more ornate, usually silver utensil, used when serving fish in front of guests, but the plastic or steel utensil that is superb for turning food over and for removing cooked food from hot baking trays or roasting tins – I like to have at least two. A fish slice may be included in your set of utensils plus rack as discussed earlier.

Ladle Perfect for hot soups, casseroles, stews and any other hot liquids that need transferring or serving.

Potato Masher You would be quite stuck without this if you wanted to make mashed potatoes. It is superb for mashing all manner of vegetables, from potatoes to parsnips, carrots, yams or sweet potatoes.

Kitchen Fork This is perfect for helping to steady large pieces of meat or whole chickens and turkeys when removing from the roasting tin after cooking.

Chopper/Meat Cleaver Good for chopping herbs and vegetables and meat and poultry.

Kebab Sticks and Skewers Either metal or wooden, kebab sticks are for cooking both savoury and sweet kebabs, koftas and satays, and skewering fish or chicken into 'spatchcock' shape – this is where the food is split almost in half, then skewered to keep its shape prior to cooking. Remember that wooden kebab sticks need soaking in cold water for at least 30 minutes and both ends wrapped in kitchen foil to prevent the ends from burning and the cook burning her or his fingers. Skewers are similar to kebab sticks but are always made of metal. They can be used for kebabs but are also

perfect for testing whether cakes are cooked in the middle, or if poultry is completely cooked – especially when cooking turkeys, as the very long skewers will go right through the thickest part straight to the centre cavity.

Pastry Brushes These have a variety of uses, including brushing pans and dishes lightly with oil prior to cooking, brushing the sides of the grater with a clean dry brush to remove any remaining cheese or fruit zest after grating and brushing a glaze or warmed jam over a dessert or cake. You could use them for basting too, but they are not specially designed to cope with the heat of foods you will be basting and the bristles may curl up, so a spoon, special basting brush or baster pipette would be better for that task.

Piping/decorating Bags and Tips

Used mainly for cake decoration, these are for the more adventurous cook. The tips (or 'nozzles') come in two sizes: large, which are referred to as 'potato pipes' (for that is what they are often used for, as well as for meringue dishes such as Pavlovas), and the smaller pipes which are called 'icing pipes'.

Tongs Good for lifting raw and cooked foods when turning over during cooking or placing on plates or dishes.

Zester This is for removing long thin strands of the outer rind ('zest') of lemons, oranges or limes to use for decoration purposes.

Whisks Used for whisking or whipping cream, eggs and sauces in order to create a smooth consistency and incorporate air. They are usually formed from interlocking wires and are available in various types, most commonly the balloon whisk of varying sizes, the mechanically hand operated rotary whisk and a flat whisk. All work well but take longer than one powered by electricity – *see 'Extra Equipment', page 22*.

BASIC EQUIPMENT

Certain pieces of equipment are essential when cooking. There is no need to go out and spend a fortune, as most of the equipment is relatively cheap. However, what I would recommend is that you buy good quality pans, ones that will not buckle in the heat after being used a couple of times. Nonstick pans can also make life a lot easier when it comes to the washing up. Below is a list of equipment that will start the beginner cook on their way and can easily be added to after a little time and some experience is gained.

Chopping Boards Essential for any job that involves cutting. Look for the colour co-ordinated boards, so that you can use a different colour for different types of food (that is, to keep meat, especially chicken, separate from vegetables, for example). That way, there will be no cross-contamination of food. Make sure that you wash them thoroughly after use, washing in the dishwasher if you have one.

Measuring Jugs or Cups Essential for measuring liquids, and solids if you live in the US. These are available in different sizes and again can be bought as glass Pyrex jugs or in plastic. Both do the job well and both have the measurements marked down the side of the jug.

Scales These are essential in British cooking, especially when baking. Although it is possible to buy measuring cups in the UK, ingredients are normally measured in grams or ounces. Most scales,

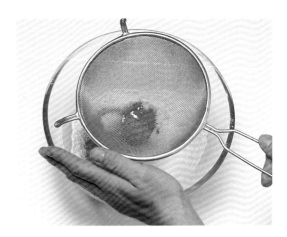

whether digital or conventional, measure in both measurements, and all have a bowl in which to place the ingredients to be measured.

Mixing Bowls Ideally, you will have at least three – in small, medium and large. These can be Pyrex glass or similar and are essential for many jobs in the kitchen, including soaking, storing, creaming butter and sugar for cakes, pastry making, melting chocolate, whipping cream and whisking egg whites.

Pans Perhaps the most expensive investment when first beginning to cook. I would recommend that you buy a set of saucepans, as normally there are three to five of differing sizes and these should be adequate to begin with. It would also be a good idea to have a milk pan for making sauces as well as boiling milk, plus a good frying pan, preferably with a lid to increase its versatility.

Colander and Sieve Used for sifting flours and straining ingredients to remove any lumps, a sieve is usually made of fine mesh wire, while a colander tends to be rather bigger, with bigger holes or slots, and is used for draining cooked pasta and vegetables. The latter come in plastic and metal versions.

Baking Trays Those without edges all round are often referred to as 'sheets'. Baking trays have many varied uses. Dishes such as lasagne can be placed on baking trays so that they are easy to place in the oven as well as remove. They are also good for baking such items as scones, meringues and cookies as well as using to reheat dishes. Other baking equipment can be bought as it is required; to begin with, I would suggest that you keep it to the minimum with one or two baking trays.

EXTRA EQUIPMENT

Food Processor A very versatile piece of equipment and one that I would recommend investing in. It will chop vegetables, fruit, nuts and herbs, and shred vegetables, as well as blend soups, make pastry dough and even cakes. Available at different prices.

Blender or Liquidizer Very similar to a food processor, having a jug rather than a bowl. Blends and chops but does not do all the jobs that a food processor will do. You can also get hand-held blenders.

Food Mixer These can be freestanding and perform many jobs in the kitchen from whipping cream, whisking egg whites, creaming butter and sugar for baking cakes to making dough for bread and rubbing in pastry, or simply placing all the ingredients in the bowl and mixing. Smaller versions are available but these are hand-held whereas the freestanding mixers can be left for a couple of minutes. Either way, some form of food mixer will be greatly appreciated if making cakes – hand whisking and beating can be tiring after a while!

Ice Cream Maker Useful if you love ice cream and very easy to use, producing creamy delicious ice cream straight from the bowl. Be wary, however – such items run the risk of languishing, unused, at the back of a cupboard... The same goes for smoothie machines (see below).

Smoothie Machine Although a blender or liquidizer will make smoothies, they are not as smooth as ones made in a smoothie machine.

Electric Carving Knife A bit of a luxury, but useful for carving small joints that do not stand very well and especially good for a whole turkey, as beautiful thin slices can be achieved.

Trivet A mat, rack or tripod-like structure of some sort, made out of metal, wood, ceramic, fabric, silicone or cork and ideal for placing hot casseroles and saucepans on after cooking – in order to prevent scorching your work surface.

Culinary Terms

Over the years, the language of cooking has developed and now there are many new words and expressions, which perhaps twenty-five years ago no one would have dreamt of using in connection with cooking. Below are some of the words used today, which describe what is required to be done by the cook but in more simple terms.

Au gratin Also known as 'gratinated'. Food is sprinkled with breadcrumbs and/or grated cheese, then baked in the oven until golden. The ovenproof dish is normally a rectangle and is called a gratin dish.

Bain-marie A water bath. Used to cook delicate dishes that may curdle, such as an egg custard. The dish is placed in a roasting tin and the tin half-filled with hot water, then cooked in the oven until set.

Baking Cooking foods in the oven. This normally applies primarily to cakes, breads, pastries and puddings, but can refer to anything cooked in the dry heat of the oven. 'Baking' is often used interchangeably with 'roasting', but a distinction can arguably be drawn by saying that 'roasting' implies greater heat and more pronounced browning. 'Roasting' is also the preferred term for meat, poultry and vegetables, while 'baking' tends to be reserved for fish, seafood and the items mentioned above.

Barding Laying fatty bacon over the top of meat or game in order that the food is basted during cooking.

Basting Brushing or drizzling meat or fish with its own juices, oil or a prepared sauce, while roasting or grilling/broiling, to add flavour and retain moisture.

Beating Using a wooden spoon to mix ingredients together until smooth, such as when making batter for pancakes or Yorkshire pudding.

Beurre manié An uncooked butter and flour paste, usually in equal proportions, used to thicken sauces.

Blanching Pouring boiling water over fresh green vegetables (or immersing them into boiling water for a short time) in order to preserve the colour. They are then typically plunged into cold water to halt the cooking process. This is done when vegetables are either to be frozen or added to a dish towards the end of cooking. It will also speed up their cooking time.

Blanquette A stew or casserole usually made from veal or poultry and with a white sauce enriched with cream and egg.

Brulée French term for 'burnt', normally in relation to sugar – as on the top of crème brûlée.

Bruising
Slightly crushing an ingredient, usually with the flat side of a chef's knife or a rolling pin, in order to release its flavour.

Brut 'Very dry', in reference to the level of sweetness of a wine – usually champagne or sparkling.

Carbonnade Term for a rich stew, normally beef, and which contains beer.

Chaudfoid A cold dish that is coated in a béchamel and aspic sauce.

Clarifying Clearing a sauce or liquid by removing fat or other impurities. For example, butter is melted and the white frothy part is discarded, leaving a clear liquid. And egg shells are used when making jelly/jello.

Creaming Beating butter or margarine with sugar together until lighter in colour and soft and creamy in texture. This applies to cake making.

Crimping Normally used in connection with pastry to give a decorative edge, which helps keep the edges together. Also describes slashing whole fish to allow the heat to penetrate easily.

Coulis A trendy word for a fruit or vegetable sauce that is generally served with the finished dish.

Devilled Food such as chops, kebabs, sausages or seafood that are cooked in a hot spicy sauce or coating.

Deglazing Used when making jus or gravy. After cooking meat, stock or wine is poured into the frying pan or roasting tin, which is then placed on a hot hob. The liquid is brought to the boil, while at the same time, the base of the pan or tin is scraped with a wooden spoon to remove all the little bits of meat that are left after cooking. It is boiled for a few minutes, then strained into a jug and used.

Dressing Preparing food, particularly poultry and seafood, for cooking or serving by cleaning, gutting, plucking, drawing, trussing, etc.

Drizzling Pouring a little sauce or oil over food while taking care not to swamp it.

Dropping consistency This applies in particular to sponges. The finished unbaked mixture should gently fall off the wooden spoon when it is lightly tapped on the edge of the bowl.

Egg wash This applies mainly to pastry and bread. The finished but uncooked dish is lightly brushed with a little beaten egg and this is often repeated halfway through the cooking. It gives a golden colour to the finished dish. It will also help to seal any cracks in a pastry case before filling, to prevent the filling from flowing under the base and sticking. Plus, it will give a crisper pastry base.

En papillote Food wrapped in paper – usually baking parchment – and cooked in the oven. The dish is normally served still in the paper so that, on opening, the eater gets the full aroma from the spices and flavours used.

Espagnole Rich brown sauce – one of the four basic sauces.

Flaking Separating fish into fine flakes.

Flambéing Setting food alight – using brandy or cognac – prior to cooking. Perhaps one of the most famous dishes for this is *crêpes Suzette*.

Folding In This applies to stirring another ingredient into an uncooked mixture such as a meringue or sponge cake mixture. Care must be taken that the mixture is not overmixed, as this will remove the air that has been whisked in, thus preventing a good rise or the required light texture.

Frothing Sprinkling game or poultry (whole birds) with flour towards the end of roasting, to crisp and brown the skin.

Frying Cooking fresh food in, normally, a frying pan or, sometimes, a deep-fat fryer, cooking it to a certain stage or completely. Food is fried in oil or fat until cooked (fats include dripping, lard, margarine, ghee and butter).

Sautéing This simply means frying, and refers mainly to the cooking of meat and vegetables in a frying pan when first starting to cook in order to seal in the meat juices and help preserve their nutrients and flavour.

Glazing Brushing a food with egg, butter or other liquid, sometimes prior to cooking, to give a good colour or to enhance the finished dish.

Grinding The process of crushing hard ingredients to a powder.

Infusing Liquids are heated gently with seasonings or flavours, then left for the flavours to develop in the liquid.

Julienne The style of cut whereby vegetables or zest are cut into very thin strips, often for garnish.

Jus The natural juices from cooking meat, often used as a gravy. The word is also used to mean a slightly more elaborate kind of sauce reduction based on the 'jus'.

Kneading This applies mainly to pastry and bread. The just-made dough is placed on a floured surface. Using the knuckles, the dough is stretched and folded over on itself until smooth. This stretches the dough and makes it more elastic and pliable.

Liaison A thickening agent such as arrowroot or cornflour/cornstarch.

Meunière Used to describe a style of dish that is cooked in butter, with salt and pepper, lemon juice and parsley – these ingredients combine with the pan juices and are poured over the food item (normally fish) to serve.

Panada A thick binding sauce used for croquettes.

Proving Bread dough is left to 'prove' (rise) prior to the last kneading and also before baking.

Quenelles A light stuffing made from fish, meat, poultry or eggs. Shaped either as ovals or balls, lightly poached and used as garnish.

Reduction The process and result of boiling a liquid to both reduce the amount and to make the flavour more intense.

Refreshing Plunging vegetables into cold water to stop the cooking process and to preserve the colour. The vegetables are normally reheated before serving.

Rendering Cooking raw bones or meat trimmings to extract the fat. Can be roasted in a moderate oven or boiled with a minimal amount of water.

Roux A cooked butter and flour paste, normally in equal quantities, used to thicken sauces. Small amounts are added to simmering liquid and whisked in, or the roux is made in a small pan and warm liquid stirred in, then the pan is placed over a gentle heat and cooked, stirring, until thickened.

Scalding Pouring boiling water over something – used to clean jelly cloths before using, or to remove skins from tomatoes, peaches, plums, etc. It also refers to bringing milk to just below boiling point in order to stop the milk going sour.

Scoring Making cuts into pork or gammon rind, both for decorative effect and to help the food cook more quickly.

Searing Cooking meat or other foods very quickly under the grill/broiler or in the oven in order to seal in the juices and to give a golden brown appearance.

Sifting Shaking icing sugar or flour through a sieve, to remove any lumps and to aerate in order to help with the rising of cakes.

Simmering When liquid is brought to the boil, then the heat reduced so that a few bubbles gently break the surface. If the bubbles do not appear, increase the heat slightly.

Sousing Steeping foods, such as fish, in a liquid, such as brine or vinegar, usually to preserve or pickle. Onion or spices may also be added.

Steaming A method of cooking food with steam, rather than directly in the water. Vegetables are especially good if steamed, as most of the nutrients are preserved and not lost into the water as happens when they are boiled. Food is placed in a container that will allow the steam to pass through, which sits on top of a pan with gently simmering water. The steamer is covered with a lid.

Steeping Pouring cold or hot liquid over food in order to tenderize or to extract flavour and colour.

Trussing Tying poultry with string or twine in order to keep its shape during cooking. Done with a trussing needle.

Whipping This is when whipping or double cream is beaten with a whisk until soft peaks are formed in the thickened cream. Can be whipped either by machine or by a hand-held whisk such as a balloon whisk.

Whisking Beating egg whites with a whisk, either in a food mixer or using a hand held whisk, until the egg white is stiff and dry (this means that the bowl of whisked egg whites can be tipped upside down and the egg white does not move).

Zest What is the difference between 'zest' and 'rind'? 'Zest' is the outermost part of the 'rind' of a citrus fruit, as opposed to the white 'pith' underneath, but in a cooking context can refer to the long thin strips of zest made with a 'zester' (which are used for decoration only, as, if eaten, will give a bitter taste) or to grated zest,  which is made by rubbing the unpeeled but washed or scrubbed fruit up and down the fine side of a grater, giving very fine pieces. As these are thinner than zest strips, they can be used to flavour dishes.

LIQUID MEASURES

Metric, Imperial and US Cups/Quarts

2.5 ml	½ tsp	-	-
5 ml	1 tsp	-	-
15 ml	1 tbsp	-	-
25 ml	1 fl oz	⅛ cup	2 tbsp
50 ml	2 fl oz	¼ cup	3–4 tbsp
65 ml	2½ fl oz	⅓ cup	5 tbsp
75–85 ml	3 fl oz	⅓ cup	6 tbsp
100 ml	3½ fl oz	⅓ cup	7 tbsp
120 ml	4 fl oz	½ cup	8 tbsp
135 ml	4½ fl oz	½ cup	9 tbsp
150 ml	5 fl oz	¼ pint	⅔ cup
175 ml	6 fl oz	⅓ pint	scant ¾ cup
200 ml	7 fl oz	⅓ pint	¾ cup
225 ml	8 fl oz	⅜ pint	1 cup
240 ml	8 fl oz	⅜ pint	1 cup
250 ml	8 fl oz	⅜ pint	1 cup

275 ml	9 fl oz	½ pint	1⅛ cups
300 ml	10 fl oz	½ pint	1¼ cups
350 ml	12 fl oz	⅔ pint	1½ cups
400 ml	14 fl oz	⅝ pint	1⅔ cups
450 ml	15 fl oz	¾ pint	1¾ cups
475 ml	16 fl oz	⅞ pint	2 scant cups
500 ml	18 fl oz	⅞ pint	2 cups
600 ml	20 fl oz	1 pint	2½ cups
750 ml	26 fl oz	1¼ pints	3¼ cups
900 ml	-	1½ pints	1 scant quart
1 litre	-	2 pints	1 quart
1.25 litres	-	2¼ pints	1¼ quarts
1.3 litres	-	2⅓ pints	1⅓ quarts
1.5 litres	-	2½ pints	1½ quarts
1.6 litres	-	2¾ pints	1¾ quarts
1.7 litres	-	3 pints	1¾ quarts
1.8 litres	-	3⅜ pints	1⅞ quarts
1.9 litres	-	3⅓ pints	2 quarts
2 litres	-	3½ pints	2 quarts
2.25 litres	-	4 pints	2¼ quarts
2.5 litres	-	4¼ pints	2½ quarts
2.75 litres	-	5 pints	3 quarts

DRY WEIGHTS

Metric/Imperial

10 g	¼ oz	325 g	11½ oz
15 g	½ oz	350 g	12 oz
20 g	¾ oz	375 g	13 oz
25 g	1 oz	400 g	14 oz
40 g	1½ oz	425 g	15 oz
50 g	2 oz	450 g	1 lb
65 g	2½ oz		
75 g	3 oz		
90 g	3½ oz		
100 g	3½ oz		
125 g	4 oz		
150 g	5 oz		
165 g	5½ oz		
175 g	6 oz		
185 g	6½ oz		
200 g	7 oz		
225 g	8 oz		
250 g	9 oz		
275 g	10 oz		
300 g	11 oz		

OVEN TEMPERATURES

Bear in mind that, if using a fan oven, you should reduce the stated temperature by around 20°C/68°F. Check the manufacturer's instructions for guidance.

110°C	225°F	Gas Mark ¼	Very slow oven
120/130°C	250°F	Gas Mark ½	Very slow oven
140°C	275°F	Gas Mark 1	Slow oven
150°C	300°F	Gas Mark 2	Slow oven
160/170°C	325°F	Gas Mark 3	Moderate oven
180°C	350°F	Gas Mark 4	Moderate oven
190°C	375°F	Gas Mark 5	Moderately hot
200°C	400°F	Gas Mark 6	Moderately hot
220°C	425°F	Gas Mark 7	Hot oven
230°C	450°F	Gas Mark 8	Hot oven
240°C	475°F	Gas Mark 9	Very hot oven

TEMPERATURE CONVERSION

−4°F	−20°C	68°F	20°C
5°F	−15°C	77°F	25°C
14°F	−10°C	86°F	30°C
23°F	−5°C	95°F	35°C
32°F	0°C	104°F	40°C
41°F	5°C	113°F	45°C
50°F	10°C	122°F	50°C
59°F	15°C	212°F	100°C

Store Cupboard Essentials

 If you haven't already, the first food shopping trip should be focused on setting up a well-targeted store cupboard. There are lots of ingredients that you can expect to use again and again but which you should not have to buy on a frequent basis – you do not use much at a time and they should keep reasonably well. The store cupboard should also be a source of foods that can make a meal when you have run out of fresh ingredients at the end of the week.

It is worth making a trip to a speciality grocery shop. Our society's growing interest in recent years with travel and food from around the world has led us to seek out alternative ingredients with which to experiment and incorporate into our cooking. Consequently, supermarket chains have had to broaden their product range and often have a specialist range of imported ingredients from around the world.

If the local grocers or supermarket only carries a limited choice of products, do not despair. The internet now offers freedom to food lovers. There are some fantastic food sites (both local and

international) where food can be purchased and delivery arranged online.

When thinking about essentials, think of flavour, something that is going to add to a dish without increasing its fat content. It is worth spending a bit more money on these products to make flavoursome dishes that will help stop the urge to snack on fatty foods.

WHAT TO STOCK IN YOUR STORE CUPBOARD

There are many different types of store cupboard ingredients readily available – including myriad varieties of rice and pasta, which can provide much of the carbohydrate required in our daily diets. Store the ingredients in a cool, dark place and remember to rotate them. The ingredients will be safe to use for six months.

Herbs and spices These are a must, so it is worth taking a look at the section on *pages 73–84* for more information. Often it is preferable to use fresh herbs, but the dried varieties have their merits and dried

Noodles Also very useful and can accompany any Far Eastern dish. They are low fat and also available in the wholemeal/whole-wheat variety. Rice noodles are available for those who have gluten-free diets; like pasta noodles, they provide slow-release energy to the body.

Rice Basmati and Thai fragrant rice are well suited to Thai and Indian curries, as the fine grains absorb the sauce and their delicate creaminess balances the pungency of the spices. Arborio is only one type of risotto rice – many are available, depending on whether the risotto is meant to accompany meat, fish or vegetable dishes. When cooked, rice swells to create a substantial low-fat dish. Easy-cook American rice, both plain and brown, is great for

herbs and spices keep well. Using herbs when cooking at home should reduce the temptation to buy ready-made sauces. Often these types of sauces contain large amounts of sugar and additives.

Pasta It is good to have a mixture of wholemeal and plain pasta as well as a wide variety of flavoured pastas. Whether fresh (it can also be frozen) or dried, pasta is a versatile ingredient with which to provide the body with slow-release energy. It comes in many different sizes and shapes; from the tiny tubettini (which can be added to soups to create a more substantial dish), to penne, fusilli, rigatoni and conchiglie, up to the larger cannelloni and lasagne sheets. *(See also pages 59–64.)*

casseroles and for stuffing meat, fish and vegetables, as it holds its shape and firmness. Pudding rice can be used in a variety of ways to create an irresistible dessert. *(See also pages 54–55.)*

Couscous Now available in instant form, couscous just needs to be covered with boiling water, then forked. Couscous is a precooked wheat semolina. Traditional couscous needs to be steamed and is available from health food stores. This type of couscous contains more nutrients than the instant variety.

Bulgur wheat A cracked wheat that is often used in tabbouleh. Bulgur wheat is a good source of complex carbohydrate.

Pot and pearl barley Pot barley is the complete barley grain, whereas pearl barley has the outer husk removed. A high cereal diet can help to prevent bowel disorders and diseases.

Pulses/beans A vital ingredient for the store cupboard, pulses are easy to store, have a very high nutritional value and are great when added to soups, casseroles, curries and hotpots. Pulses also act as a thickener, whether flavoured or on their own.

They come in two forms: either dried (in which case they generally need to be soaked overnight and then cooked before use – it is important to follow the instructions on the back of the packet), or canned, which is a convenient time-saver because the preparation of dried pulses can take a while. When boiling previously dried pulses, remember that salt should not be added as this will make the skins tough and inedible. If buying canned pulses, try to buy the variety in water with no added salt or sugar. These simply need to be drained and rinsed before being added to a dish.

Kidney, borlotti, cannellini, butter, flageolet and lima beans, and split peas and lentils, all make tasty additions to any dish. Baked beans are a favourite

with everyone and many shops now stock the organic variety, which have no added salt or sugar but are sweetened with fruit juice instead. Puy lentils are a smaller variety. They often have mottled skins and are particularly good for cooking in slow dishes as they hold their shape and firm texture particularly well.

Dried fruit The ready-to-eat variety are particularly good as they are plump, juicy and do not need to be soaked. They are fantastic when puréed into a compote, added to water and heated to make a pie filling and when added to stuffing mixtures. They are also good cooked with meats, rice or couscous.

Flours A useful addition (particularly cornflour/cornstarch, which can be used to thicken sauces). It is worth mentioning that wholemeal/whole-wheat flour should not be stored for too long at room temperature as the fats may turn rancid. While not strictly a flour, cornmeal is a very versatile low-fat ingredient that can be used when making dumplings and gnocchi.

Stock Good-quality stock is a must in low-fat cooking, as it provides a good flavour base for many dishes. Many supermarkets now carry a variety of fresh and organic stocks, which, although need refrigeration, are probably one of the most time- and effort-saving ingredients available. There is also

a fairly large range of dried stock, perhaps the best being bouillon, a high-quality form of stock (available in powder or liquid form) which can be added to any dish whether it be a sauce, casserole, pie or soup.

Sauce ingredients Many people favour meals that can be prepared and cooked in 30–45 minutes, so helpful ingredients that kick-start a sauce are great. A good-quality passata sauce or canned plum tomatoes can act as the foundation for any sauce, as can a good-quality green or red pesto (though pesto can be great to make from scratch). Other handy store cupboard additions include tapenade, mustard and anchovies. These have very distinctive tastes and are particularly flavoursome. Roasted red pepper sauce and sun-dried tomato paste, which tends to be sweeter and more intensely flavoured than regular tomato purée/paste, are also very useful.

Vinegar

This is another worthwhile store cupboard essential and, with so many uses, it is worth splashing out on really good-quality balsamic and wine vinegars. Herbs and spices are a must, so it is worth taking a look at the section on *pages 73–84*. Using herbs when cooking at home should reduce the temptation to buy ready-made sauces. Often these types of sauces contain large amounts of sugar and additives.

Yeast extract This is also a good store cupboard ingredient, which can pep up sauces, soups and casseroles and adds a little substance, particularly to vegetarian dishes.

Other oils and flavours Eastern flavours offer a lot of scope where low-fat cooking is concerned. Flavourings such as fish sauce, soy sauce, red and green curry paste and Chinese rice wine all offer mouthwatering low-fat flavours to any dish. For those who are incredibly short on time, or who rarely shop, it is now possible to purchase a selection of read-prepared freshly minced garlic, ginger and chilli (available in jars which can be kept in the refrigerator).

Hygiene in the Kitchen

 It is well worth remembering that many foods can carry some form of bacteria. In most cases, the worst it will lead to is a bout of food poisoning or gastroenteritis, although for certain groups of people this can be more serious. The risk can be reduced or eliminated by good food hygiene and proper cooking.

CLEANLINESS

Always keep your hands, cooking utensils and food preparation surfaces clean and never allow pets to climb onto any work surfaces.

Dish cloths and dishtowels must be washed and changed regularly. Ideally, use disposable cloths, which should be replaced on a daily basis. More durable cloths should be left to soak in bleach, then washed in the washing machine on a boil wash.Regularly clean, defrost and clear out the refrigerator or freezer.

BUYING FOOD

Do not buy food that is past its sell-by date and do not consume any food that is past its use-by date. When buying food, use the eyes and nose. If the food looks tired, limp or a bad colour or it has a rank, acrid or simply bad smell, do not buy or eat it under any circumstances.

Avoid bulk buying where possible, especially fresh produce such as meat, poultry, fish, fruit and vegetables, unless buying for the freezer – it is worth checking the packaging to see exactly how long each product is safe to freeze. Fresh foods lose their nutritional value rapidly, so buying a little at a time minimizes loss of nutrients. It also eliminates a packed refrigerator, which reduces the effectiveness of the refrigeration process. When buying frozen foods, ensure that they are not heavily iced on the outsideand place them in the freezer as soon as possible after purchase.

FOOD PREPARATION

Make sure that all work surfaces and utensils are clean and dry. Separate chopping boards should be used for raw and cooked meats, fish and vegetables. It is worth washing all fruits and vegetables regardless of whether they are going to be eaten raw or lightly cooked.

All poultry must be thoroughly thawed before cooking. Leave the food in the refrigerator until it is completely thawed. Once defrosted, the chicken should be cooked as soon as possible. The only time food can be refrozen is when the food has been thoroughly thawed, then cooked. Once the food has cooled, it can then be frozen again for one month. Do not reheat food more than once.

All poultry and game (except for duck) must be cooked thoroughly. When cooked, the juices will run clear.

Other meats such as minced meat and pork should be cooked right the way through. Fish should turn opaque, be firm in texture and break easily into large flakes.

STORING, REFRIGERATING AND FREEZING

Meat, poultry, fish, seafood and dairy products should all be refrigerated. The temperature of the refrigerator should be between 1° and 5°C/34° and 41°F, while the freezer temperature should not rise above −18°C/−0.4°F.

When refrigerating cooked food, allow it to cool completely before refrigerating. Hot food will raise the temperature of the refrigerator and possibly affect or spoil other food stored in it.

Food within the refrigerator and freezer should always be covered. Raw and cooked food should be stored in separate parts of the refrigerator. Cooked food should be kept on the top shelves of the refrigerator, while raw meat, poultry and fish should be placed on lower shelves to avoid drips and cross-contamination.

HIGH-RISK FOODS

Certain foods may carry risks to people who are considered vulnerable such as the elderly, the ill, pregnant women, babies and those suffering from a chronic illness. It is advisable to avoid those foods that belong to a higher-risk category.

Eggs

There is a slight chance that some eggs carry the bacterium salmonella. Cook the eggs until both the yolk and the white are firm to eliminate this risk. Sauces including hollandaise, mayonnaise, mousses, soufflés and meringues all use raw or lightly cooked eggs, as do custard-based dishes, ice creams and sorbets. These are all considered high-risk foods to the vulnerable groups mentioned above.

Meat and Poultry

Certain meats and poultry also carry the potential risk of salmonella and so should be cooked thoroughly until the juices run clear and there is no pinkness left.

Unpasteurized Products

Unpasteurized products such as milk, cheese (especially soft cheese), pâté and meat (both raw and cooked) all have the potential risk of the bacterium listeria and should be avoided by those in the at-risk category.

Seafood

When buying seafood, buy from a reputable source. Fish should have bright clear eyes, shiny skin and bright pink or red gills. The fish should feel stiff to the touch, with a slight smell of sea air and iodine. The flesh of fish steaks and fillets should be translucent with no signs of discoloration. Avoid any molluscs (such as mussels) that are open or do not close when tapped lightly. Univalves such as cockles or winkles should withdraw into their shells when lightly prodded. Squid and octopus should have firm flesh and a pleasant sea smell.

Care is required when freezing seafood. It is imperative to check whether the fish has been frozen before. If it has been, it should not be frozen again under any circumstances.

Nutrition

A healthy and well-balanced diet is the body's primary energy source. In children, it constitutes the building blocks for future health as well as providing lots of energy. In adults, it encourages self-healing and regeneration within the body. A well-balanced diet will provide the body with all the essential nutrients it needs. This can be achieved by eating a variety of foods, demonstrated in the pyramid shown here – eat the food groups in proportions roughly equivalent to those shown in the pyramid.

Fats

Fats fall into two categories: saturated and unsaturated. It is very important that a healthy balance is achieved within the

diet. Fats are an essential part of the diet and a source of energy, and provide essential fatty acids and fat-soluble vitamins. The right balance of fats should boost the body's immunity to infection and keep muscles, nerves and arteries in good condition.

Saturated Fats

Saturated fats are of animal origin and are hard when stored at room temperature. They can be found in dairy produce, meat, eggs, margarines and hard white cooking fat (lard), as well as in manufactured products such as pies, cookies and cakes.

A high intake of saturated fat over many years has been proven to increase heart disease and high blood cholesterol levels, and often leads to weight gain.

Fats
milk, yogurt and cheese

Proteins
meat, fish, poultry, eggs, nuts and pulses

Fruits and Vegetables

Starchy Carbohydrates
cereals, potatoes, bread, rice and pasta

The aim of a healthy diet is to keep the fat content low in the foods that we eat. Lowering the amount of saturated fat that we consume is very important, but this does not mean that it is good to consume lots of other types of fat.

Unsaturated Fats

There are two kinds of unsaturated fats: polyunsaturated fats and monounsaturated fats.

Polyunsaturated fats include the following oils: safflower oil, soyabean oil, corn oil and sesame oil. Within the polyunsaturated group are omega oils. The omega-3 oils are of significant interest because they have been found to be particularly beneficial to coronary health and can encourage brain growth and development. Omega-3 oils are mainly derived from oily fish such as salmon, mackerel, herring, pilchards and sardines. It is recommended that we should eat these types of fish at least once a week. However, for those who do not eat fish or who are vegetarians, liver oil supplements are available in most supermarkets and health food shops. It is suggested that these supplements should be taken on a daily basis.

The most popular oils that are high in monounsaturates are olive oil, sunflower oil and groundnut (peanut) oil. The Mediterranean diet, which is based on a diet high in monounsaturated fats, is recommended for heart health. Also, monounsaturated fats are known to help reduce the levels of LDL (the bad) cholesterol.

PROTEINS

Composed of amino acids (proteins' building bricks), proteins perform a wide variety of essential functions for the body, including supplying energy and building and repairing tissues.

Good sources of proteins are eggs, milk, yogurt, cheese, meat, fish, poultry, nuts and pulses. (See the second level of the pyramid.) Some of these foods, however, contain saturated fats. To strike a nutritional balance, eat generous amounts of vegetable protein foods such as beans, lentils, peas and nuts.

FRUITS AND VEGETABLES

Not only are fruits and vegetables the most visually appealing foods, but they are also extremely good for us, providing essential vitamins and minerals essential for growth, repair and protection in the human body. Fruits and vegetables are low in calories and are responsible for regulating the body's metabolic processes and controlling the composition of its fluids and cells.

MINERALS

Calcium Important for healthy bones and teeth, nerve transmission, muscle contraction, blood clotting and hormone function. Calcium promotes a healthy

heart, improves skin, relieves aching muscles and bones, maintains the correct acid–alkaline balance and reduces menstrual cramps. Good sources are dairy products, small bones of small fish, nuts, pulses, fortified white flours, breads and green leafy vegetables.

Chromium Part of the glucose tolerance factor, chromium balances blood sugar levels, helps to normalize hunger and reduce cravings, improves lifespan, helps protect DNA and is essential for heart function. Good sources are brewer's yeast, wholemeal/whole-wheat bread, rye bread, oysters, potatoes, green peppers, butter and parsnips.

Iodine Important for the manufacture of thyroid hormones and for normal development. Good sources of iodine are seafood, seaweed, milk and dairy products.

Iron As a component of haemoglobin, iron carries oxygen around the body. It is vital for normal growth and development. Good sources are liver, corned beef, red meat, fortified breakfast cereals, pulses, green leafy vegetables, egg yolks and cocoa and cocoa products.

Magnesium Important for efficient functioning of metabolic enzymes and development of the skeleton. Magnesium promotes healthy muscles by helping them to relax and is therefore good for PMS. It is also important for heart muscles and the nervous system. Good sources are nuts, green vegetables, meat, cereals, milk and yogurt.

Phosphorus Forms and maintains bones and teeth, builds muscle tissue, helps to maintain the body's pH and aids metabolism and energy production. Phosphorus is present in almost all foods.

Potassium Enables nutrients to move into cells, while waste products move out; promotes healthy nerves and muscles; maintains fluid balance in the body; helps secretion of insulin for blood sugar control to produce constant energy; relaxes muscles; maintains heart functioning and stimulates gut movement to encourage proper elimination. Good sources are fruit, vegetables, milk and bread.

Selenium
Antioxidant properties help to protect against free radicals and carcinogens. Selenium reduces inflammation,  stimulates the immune system to fight infections, promotes a healthy heart and helps vitamin E's action. It is also required for the male reproductive system and is needed for metabolism. Good sources are tuna, liver, kidney, meat, eggs, cereals, nuts and dairy products.

Sodium Important in helping to control body fluid and balance, preventing dehydration. Sodium is involved in muscle and nerve function, and helps to move nutrients into cells. All foods are good sources, but processed, pickled and salted foods are richest in sodium.

Zinc Important for metabolism and the healing of wounds. It also aids ability to cope with stress, promotes a healthy nervous system and brain, especially in the growing foetus, aids bone and tooth formation and is essential for constant energy. Good sources are liver, meat, pulses, wholegrain cereals, nuts and oysters.

VITAMINS

Vitamin A Important for cell growth and development, and for the formation of visual pigments in the eye. Vitamin A comes in two forms: retinol and beta-carotenes. Retinol is found in liver, meat and meat products and whole milk and its products. Beta-carotene is a powerful antioxidant and is found in red and yellow fruits and vegetables such as carrots, mangoes and apricots.

Vitamin B1 Important in releasing energy from carbohydrate-containing foods. Good sources are yeast and yeast products, bread, fortified breakfast cereals and potatoes.

Vitamin B2 Important for metabolism of proteins, fats and carbohydrates to produce energy. Good sources are meat, yeast extracts, fortified breakfast cereals and milk and its products.

Vitamin B3 Required for the metabolism of food into energy production. Good sources are milk and milk products, fortified breakfast cereals, pulses, meat, poultry and eggs.

Vitamin B5 Important for the metabolism of food and energy production. All foods are good sources, but especially fortified breakfast cereals, wholegrain bread and dairy products.

Vitamin B6 Important for metabolism of protein and fat. Vitamin B6 may also be involved in the regulation of sex hormones. Good sources are liver, fish, pork, soya beans and peanuts.

Vitamin B12 Important for the production of red blood cells and DNA. It is vital for growth and the nervous system. Good sources are meat, fish, eggs, poultry and milk.

Biotin Important for metabolism of fatty acids. Good sources of biotin are liver, kidney, eggs and nuts. Micro-organisms also manufacture this vitamin in the gut.

Vitamin C Important for healing wounds and the formation of collagen, which keeps skin and bones strong. It is an important antioxidant. Good sources are fruit, particularly soft summer fruits, and vegetables.

Vitamin D Important for absorption and handling of calcium to help build bone strength. Good sources are oily fish, eggs, whole milk and milk products, margarine and of course sufficient exposure to sunlight, as vitamin D is made in the skin.

Vitamin E Important as an antioxidant vitamin helping to protect cell membranes from damage. Good sources are vegetable oils, margarines, seeds, nuts and green vegetables.

Folic acid Critical during pregnancy for the development of the brain and nerves. It is always essential for brain and nerve function, and is needed for utilizing protein and red blood cell formation. Good sources are wholegrain cereals, fortified breakfast cereals, green leafy vegetables, oranges and liver.

Vitamin K Important for controlling blood clotting. Good sources are cauliflower, Brussels sprouts, lettuce, cabbage, beans, broccoli, peas, asparagus, potatoes, corn oil, tomatoes and milk.

CARBOHYDRATES

Carbohydrates are an energy source and come in two forms: starch and sugar carbohydrates. Starch carbohydrates are also known as complex carbohydrates and they include all cereals, potatoes, breads, rice and pasta. (See the fourth level of the pyramid *on page 40*). Eating wholegrain varieties of these foods also provides fibre. Diets high in fibre are believed to be beneficial in helping to prevent bowel cancer and can also keep cholesterol down. High-fibre diets are also good for those concerned about weight gain. Fibre is bulky, so fills the stomach, therefore reducing hunger pangs.

Sugar carbohydrates, which are also known as fast-release carbohydrates (because of the quick fix of energy they give to the body), include sugar and sugar-sweetened products such as jams and syrups. Milk provides lactose, which is a milk sugar, and fruits provide fructose, which is a fruit sugar.

Eggs

No other food is as important in cooking as the egg – it is used in many diverse ways and is an essential ingredient for all good cooks. Eggs are used to thicken, enrich and flavour sauces and soups; to bind croquettes, burgers, patties, meat loaves and stuffings; to coat fish, meat and vegetables before rolling in flour, breadcrumbs or batter; and to make delicious meringues *(see page 170)*. **The shell and white are used for clarifying jellies and consommés. Then of course they are eaten in their own right as part of a healthy diet. This section gives a wide range of ways to cook the humble egg.**

Boiled Eggs

Eggs should be boiled in gently simmering water. Remove the egg from the refrigerator at least 30 minutes before cooking.

1. Bring a pan of water to the boil, then, once boiling, lower the heat to a simmer.

2. Gently lower the egg into the water and cook for 3 minutes for lightly set, or 4 minutes for a slightly firmer set.

3. Remove and lightly tap to stop the egg continuing to cook.

4. Serve lightly boiled eggs with toast or buttered bread cut into fingers to use as dippers.

Hard-boiled eggs should be cooked for 10 minutes, then plunged into cold water and left until cold before shelling.

Coddled Eggs

These are very lightly set eggs. Do not forget to remove the eggs from the refrigerator 30 minutes before cooking.

1. Carefully place the eggs in boiling water and cover with a lid.

2. Remove from the hob and leave for 8–10 minutes.

3. Drain and shell. Ideal to use for a Caesar Salad when a lightly cooked egg is preferred to an almost raw egg.

Fried Eggs

1. Put a little sunflower oil or butter in a frying pan and heat.

2. Break an egg into a cup or small jug. Carefully slip into the pan.

3. Cook, spooning the hot oil or fat over the egg, for 3–4 minutes until set to personal preference.

4. Remove with a palette knife or fish slice.

5. Serve with freshly grilled/broiled bacon or sausages or on toast with baked beans and tomatoes.

Poached Eggs

1. Half-fill a frying pan with water. Bring to a gentle boil, then reduce the heat to a simmer.

2. Add either a little salt or a few drops of vinegar or lemon juice – this will help the egg to retain its shape.

3. Break the egg into a cup or small jug and carefully slip into the simmering water. Lightly oiled round, plain pastry cutters can be used to contain the eggs, if preferred.

4. Cover the pan with a lid and cook for 3–4 minutes until set to personal preference.

5. Once cooked, remove by draining with a fish slice or flat spatula.

6. Serve either on hot buttered toast or on top of sliced ham or freshly cooked spinach.

Alternatively, special poaching pans are available, if preferred. With these, half-fill the pan with water and place the tray with the egg containers on top. Place a little butter in the cups and bring to the boil. Swirl the melted butter around and carefully slip in the eggs. Cover with the lid and cook for 3–4 minutes.

Scrambled Eggs

For sufficient scrambled eggs, allow two eggs per person.

1. Melt 1 tablespoon butter in a small pan.

2. Break the eggs into a small bowl and add 1 tablespoon milk and seasoning to taste. Whisk

with a fork until blended, then pour into the melted butter.

3. Cook over a gentle heat, stirring with a wooden spoon, until set and creamy.

4. Serve on hot buttered toast with smoked salmon, if liked, or stir in some freshly snipped chives or chopped tomatoes.

OMELETTES

For a basic omelette, allow two eggs per person.

1. Break the eggs into a small bowl, add seasoning to taste and 1 tablespoon milk. Whisk with a fork until frothy.

2. Heat 2 teaspoons olive oil in a frying pan and, when hot, pour in the egg mixture.

3. Cook gently, using a wooden spoon to bring the mixture from the edges of the pan to the centre and let the uncooked egg mixture to flow to the edges.

4. When the egg has set, cook without moving for an extra minute before folding the omelette into three and gently turning out onto a warmed serving plate. Take care not to overcook.

Cheese Omelette

Proceed as before, then sprinkle 25–40 g/1–1½ oz/¼–⅓ cup grated mature Cheddar cheese on top of the lightly set omelette. Cook for a further 2 minutes, or until the cheese starts to melt. If liked, place under a preheated grill/broiler for 2–3 minutes until golden. Fold and serve.

Tomato Omelette

Proceed as for a plain omelette. After 2 minutes of cooking time, add 1 chopped tomato on top of the omelette. Cook as above until set.

Fine Herbes Omelette

Stir in 1 tablespoon finely chopped, fresh mixed herbs into the beaten eggs before cooking. Proceed as for a plain omelette.

Mushroom Omelette

Wipe and slice 50 g/2 oz/½ cup button mushrooms. Heat 1 tablespoon butter in a small pan and cook the mushrooms for 2–3 minutes. Drain and reserve. Cook the omelette as above, adding the mushrooms once set.

OEUFS EN COCOTTES

These are eggs cooked in ramekins to create individual portions. There are all sorts of variations, but here we use classic cream. A few lightly sautéed sliced mushrooms, a little chopped ham or some chopped tomatoes could be placed in the base of each dish or even some wilted spinach (remember to squeeze out any excess liquid).

1. Preheat the oven to 160°C/325°F/Gas Mark 3 and lightly butter small ramekin dishes.

2. Carefully break 1 or 2 eggs into each ramekin. Season to taste with freshly ground black pepper and salt, if preferred.

3. Cover the egg with 1–2 tablespoons warm cream. Place the ramekins in a tin and pour in enough boiling water to come halfway up the sides of the dishes. Cook in the preheated oven for 5–8 minutes until lightly set.

Tip It is not strictly necessary to use the *bain-marie* method, but greater care would be required to ensure that the oven temperature and cooking time are correct so as not to overcook the eggs.

QUAIL EGGS

Quail eggs make an attractive starter for both formal and informal occasions.

1. Ensure that the eggs are at room temperature, then carefully slip into lightly boiling water and cook for 4–5 minutes.

2. Remove and plunge into cold water for 2–3 minutes.

3. Drain the eggs lightly, then carefully shell.

SEPARATING EGGS

Separate eggs (that is, separate the white from the yolk) as follows:

1. Crack an egg in half lightly and cleanly over a bowl, being careful not to break the yolk and keeping the yolk in the shell.

2. Tip the yolk backwards and forwards between the two shell halves, allowing as much of the white as possible to spill out into the bowl.

Keep or discard the yolk and/or the white as needed. Make sure that you do not get any yolk in your whites, as this will prevent successful whisking of the whites. It takes practice!

SOUFFLÉS

One of the best examples of using eggs is in the making of soufflés. There are two types of soufflé: a baked soufflé and a cold soufflé set with gelatine. Many regard making a soufflé as difficult, but in fact, as long as you follow the recipe, they are perfectly simple and look spectacular when brought to the table.

Cheese Soufflé

This is the basic, classic baked soufflé that first comes to mind when asked to think of a soufflé.

25 g/1 oz/2 tbsp unsalted butter
3 heaped tbsp plain white/all-purpose flour
150 ml/¼ pint/⅔ cup milk, warmed
4 medium/large eggs, separated
½–1 tsp mustard powder
50 g/2 oz/1 scant cup mature Cheddar or
    Gruyère cheese, finely grated

1. Lightly butter 4 small soufflé dishes and preheat the oven to 180°C/350°F/Gas Mark 4, 10 minutes before baking. Place a baking tray in the oven to heat 5 minutes before cooking the soufflé – this will start the soufflé cooking from the base and ensure a good rise.

2. Melt the butter in a saucepan, then stir in the flour. Cook, stirring, for 2 minutes.

3. Draw off the heat and gradually stir in the warm milk. Return to the heat and cook, stirring, until the mixture thickens and is smooth.

4. Stir the egg yolks into the white sauce, one at a time, stirring thoroughly. When all the egg yolks have been added, stir in the mustard powder, to

taste, along with all but one tablespoon of the cheese. Spoon into a large bowl.

5. Whisk the reserved egg whites until stiff and soft peaks are formed, then fold 1 tablespoon into the cheese mixture. Repeat twice more, then carefully fold in all the remaining egg whites. Spoon into the prepared dish and sprinkle the top with the remaining cheese.

6. Place on the hot baking tray and cook in the preheated oven for 30 minutes, or until well risen and golden brown. Serve immediately.

Tip Try adding 75 g/3 oz skinned and finely chopped smoked haddock or mushrooms.

Lemon Soufflé
Here is a recipe for a classic cold lemon soufflé.

4 tbsp boiling water
11 g/$\frac{1}{4}$ oz sachet/envelope (or leaf) gelatine
2–3 unwaxed or organic lemons
4 medium/large eggs, separated
125 g/4 oz/$\frac{2}{3}$ cup caster/superfine sugar
300 ml/$\frac{1}{2}$ pint/1$\frac{1}{4}$ cups double/heavy cream
fresh raspberries and cream, or 50 g/2 oz dark/
    bittersweet chocolate, or 50 g/2 oz/$\frac{2}{3}$ cup nuts,
    to decorate (optional)

1. Prepare 4 small soufflé dishes by taking four double strips of greaseproof/waxed paper long enough to wrap round each dish and to stand at least 5 cm/2 inches above the rims. Secure firmly with string or an elastic band under the rims. Reserve.

2. Pour the boiling water into a glass bowl or small measuring jug. Sprinkle the gelatine over the top, then stir with a teaspoon until completely dissolved. If the gelatine does not completely dissolve (the liquid should be clear with no granules), then stand the bowl or jug in a saucepan of boiling water and stir until clear. Always add sachet gelatine to the liquid; never pour liquid onto the gelatine. (If using leaf gelatine, place into a shallow dish and cover with cold water. Leave until softened, then squeeze out any excess liquid. Place in a bowl over a pan of boiling water and stir until dissolved.) Reserve the gelatine.

3. Finely grate the zest from the lemons and place in a bowl with the egg yolks and caster/superfine sugar.

4. Place over a pan of gently simmering water and whisk until pale, thick and creamy. To test if the mixture is creamy enough, drag the whisk across the surface; if a trail is left, it is ready. Remove from the heat and continue to whisk until the mixture is cool.

5. Squeeze the lemons and strain the juice – you will need 75 ml/3 fl oz/⅓ cup – then gently stir into the mixture.

6. Stir the gelatine to ensure it is thoroughly dissolved and not starting to set. If it starts to set, place over a pan of simmering water until clear. Pour the gelatine in a thin steady stream into the mixture at a height of approximately 15 cm/6 inches from the bowl. Stir in using a large spoon in a figure of eight movement. Take care not to pour it in too quickly, otherwise you could end up with lumps of gelatine in the mixture.

7. Whip the double/heavy cream until soft peaks form, then stir into the mixture.

8. Whisk the egg whites until stiff (so that you can turn the bowl upside down and the egg whites do not move). Stir into the mixture a little at a time, ensuring that it is thoroughly incorporated.

9. Spoon the mixture into the prepared soufflé dish and level the top. Leave to set in the refrigerator for at least 6 hours, or overnight if time permits. When ready to serve, carefully remove the collar from around the dish. Serve with raspberries and cream or finely grate the dark chocolate or chop the nuts and press into the sides. Serve.

ROULADES

Though the word 'roulade' can refer to cakes and meat rolled round a filling, it can also be used to describe a soufflé-type mixture that is baked in a flat pan and rolled around a filling.

Spinach Roulade

350 g/12 oz/12 cups fresh spinach
40 g/1½ oz/⅓ cup Gruyère cheese, finely grated
salt and freshly ground black pepper

pinch freshly grated nutmeg
4 large/extra-large eggs, separated
225 g/8 oz/1 3/4 cups prawns/shrimp,
    thawed and peeled
5–6 tbsp mayonnaise
salad leaves, to garnish

1. Preheat the oven to 190°C/375°F/Gas Mark 5, 10
   minutes before baking. Lightly oil and line a
   Swiss-roll tin/jelly-roll pan, or baking tray, with
   baking paper. Reserve.

2. Lightly rinse the spinach, then place in a saucepan
   and cook just with the water left on the leaves for
   2–4 minutes. Drain, then chop and squeeze out
   any excess water. Return to the saucepan and
   place over a gentle heat until all the moisture
   has evaporated.

3. Remove and stir in the cheese with seasoning and
   a little freshly grated nutmeg to taste.

4. Beat the egg yolks one at a time into the spinach
   mixture. When all the yolks have been added,
   whisk the egg whites until stiff and gradually stir
   into the spinach mixture. Spoon into the prepared
   tin and lightly smooth the surface. Bake in the
   preheated oven for 7–10 minutes until set and just
   beginning to shrink away from the sides of the tin.

5. Reserve a few prawns/shrimp and mix the rest
   with the mayonnaise. Carefully invert the baked
   mixture onto a large sheet of baking paper and
   spread with the prawn mixture. Carefully roll up
   and place on a serving dish. Garnish with whole
   prawns and salad leaves and serve.

Other fillings can be used, if liked, with the
mayonnaise or in a prepared white or cheese sauce.
Try smoked salmon and cream cheese, chopped ham
with sweetcorn, roasted vegetables with feta cheese
or chopped chicken breast with seedless grapes.

Rice

Rice is the staple food of many countries throughout the world. Every country and culture has its own repertoire of rice recipes – India, for example, has the aromatic biryani, Spain has the saffron-scented paella, and Italy has the creamy risotto. Rice is grown on marshy, flooded land where other cereals cannot thrive, and because it is grown in so many different areas, there is a huge range of rice types.

VARIETIES

Long-grain white rice Probably the most widely used type of rice. Long-grain white rice has been milled so that the husk, bran and germ are removed. Easy-cook long-grain white rice has been steamed under pressure before milling. Precooked rice, also known as par-boiled or converted rice, is polished white rice that is half-cooked after milling, then dried again. It is quick to cook but has a bland flavour.

Long-grain brown rice Where the outer husk is removed, leaving the bran and germ behind. This retains more of the fibre, vitamins and minerals. It has a nutty flavour and slightly chewy texture and takes longer to cook than white rice.

Basmati rice This slender long-grain rice, which may be white or brown, is grown in the foothills of the Himalayas. After harvesting, it is allowed to mature for a year, giving it a unique aromatic flavour, hence its name, which means fragrant.

Risotto rice Grown in the north of Italy, this is the only rice that is suitable for making risotto. The grains are plump and stubby and have the

Jasmine rice   Also known as Thai fragrant rice, this long-grain rice has a delicate, almost perfumed aroma and flavour and has a soft, sticky texture.

Japanese sushi rice   This is a fairly glutinous rice in that it has a sticky texture. When mixed with rice vinegar, it is easy to roll up with a filling inside to make sushi.

Pudding rice   This rounded, short-grain rice is ideal for rice desserts. The grains swell and absorb large quantities of milk during cooking, giving puddings a rich, creamy consistency.

ability to absorb large quantities of liquid without becoming too soft, cooking to a creamy texture with a slight bite. There are two grades of risotto rice: superfino and fino. Arborio rice is the most widely sold variety of the former, but you may also find carnaroli, Roma and baldo in Italian delicatessens. Fino rice such as vialone nano has a slightly shorter grain, but the flavour is still excellent.

Valencia rice   Traditionally used for Spanish paella, Valencia rice is soft and tender when ready. The medium-sized grains break down easily, so should be left unstirred during cooking to absorb the flavour of the stock and other ingredients.

Wild rice This is an aquatic grass grown in North America rather than a true variety of rice. The black grains are long and slender and after harvesting and cleaning, they are toasted to remove the chaff and intensify the nutty flavour and slight chewiness. It is often sold as a mixture with long-grain rice.

Rice flour Raw rice can be finely ground to make rice flour, which may be used to thicken sauces (1 tbsp will thicken 300 ml/½ pint/1¼ cups liquid) or in Asian desserts. It is also used to make rice noodles.

HEALTH AND NUTRITION

Rice is low in fat and high in complex carbohydrates, which are absorbed slowly and help to maintain blood sugar levels. It is also a reasonable source of protein and provides many B vitamins and the minerals potassium and phosphorus. It is a gluten-free cereal, making it suitable for coeliacs. Brown rice is richer in nutrients and fibre than refined white rice.

BUYING AND STORING RICE

Rice will keep for several years if kept in sealed packets. However, it is at its best when fresh. To ensure freshness, always buy rice from reputable shops with a good turnover and buy in small quantities.

Once opened, store the rice in an airtight container in a cool, dry place to keep out moisture. Most rice (but not risotto) benefits from washing before cooking – tip into a sieve and rinse under cold running water until the water runs clear. This removes any starch still clinging to the grains.

Cooked rice will keep for up to 2 days if cooled and stored in a covered bowl in the refrigerator. If eating rice cold, serve within 24 hours – after this time, it should be thoroughly reheated.

HOW TO COOK RICE

There are countless ways to cook rice, but much depends on the variety of rice being used, the dish being prepared and the desired results. Each variety of rice has its own characteristics. Some types of rice cook to light, separate grains, some to a rich, creamy consistency and some to a consistency where the grains stick together. Different types of rice have different powers of absorption. Long-grain rice will absorb three times its weight in water, whereas 25 g/1 oz/⅛ cup short-grain pudding rice can soak up a massive 300 ml/½ pint/1¼ cups liquid.

Cooking Long-grain Rice

The simplest method of cooking long-grain rice is to add it to plenty of boiling, salted water in a large saucepan. Allow 50 g/2 oz/¼ cup rice per person when cooking as an accompaniment.

1. Rinse under cold running water until clear, then tip into rapidly boiling water.

2. Stir once, then, when the water returns to the boil, reduce the heat and simmer uncovered.

3. Allow 10–12 minutes for white rice and 30–40 minutes for brown – check the packet for specific timings.

4. The easiest way to test if rice is cooked is to bite a couple of grains – they should be tender but still firm.

5. Drain immediately, then return to the pan with a little butter and herbs, if liked. Fluff up with a fork and serve.

To keep the rice warm, put it in a bowl and place over a pan of barely simmering water. Cover the top of the bowl with a dishtowel until ready to serve.

Absorption Method

Cooking rice using the absorption method is also simple. This method is good for cooking jasmine and Valencia rice. Weigh out the quantity, then measure it by volume in a measuring jug – you will need 150 ml/¼ pint/⅔ cup for two people.

1. Rinse the rice, then tip into a large saucepan. If liked, cook the rice in a little butter or oil for 1 minute.

2. Pour in 2 parts water or stock to 1 part rice, season with salt and bring to the boil.

3. Cover, then simmer gently until the liquid is absorbed and the rice is tender. White rice will take 15 minutes to cook, whereas brown rice will take 35 minutes. If there is still a little liquid left

when the rice is tender, uncover and cook for 1 minute until evaporated.

4. Remove from the heat and leave covered for 4–5 minutes, then fluff up before serving.

Oven-baked Method

The oven-baked method works by absorption too, but takes longer than cooking on the hob/stove top. For oven-baked rice for two:

1. Fry a chopped onion in 1 tablespoon olive oil in a 1.2 litre/2 pint/1¼ quart flameproof casserole dish until soft and golden.

2. Add 75 g/3 oz/⅓ cup long-grain rice and cook for 1 minute.

3. Stir in 300 ml/½ pint/1¼ stock cups – add a finely pared strip of lemon zest or a bay leaf if liked.

4. Cover and bake in a preheated oven at 180°C/350°F/Gas Mark 4 for 40 minutes, or until the rice is tender and all the stock has been absorbed. Fluff up before serving.

Cooking in the Microwave

1. Place the rinsed long-grain rice in a large heatproof bowl.

2. Add boiling water or stock, allowing 300 ml/½ pint/1¼ cups for 125 g/4 oz/½ cup rice and 500 ml/18 fl oz/2 cups for 225 g/8 oz/1 cup rice. Add a pinch of salt and a knob of butter, if desired.

3. Cover with pierced plastic wrap and cook on high for 3 minutes.

4. Stir, re-cover and cook on medium for 12 minutes for white rice and 25 minutes for brown.

5. Leave covered for 5 minutes before fluffing up and serving.

Cooking in a Pressure Cooker

Follow the quantities given for the absorption method and bring to the boil in the pressure cooker. Stir, cover and bring to a high 6.8 kg/15 lb pressure. Lower the heat and cook for 5 minutes if white rice or 8 minutes for brown.

Cooking in a Rice Cooker

Follow the quantities given for the absorption method. Put the rice, salt and boiling water or stock in the cooker, return to the boil and cover. When all the liquid has been absorbed, the cooker will turn off automatically.

Pasta

We all eat a lot of pasta and so are familiar with the many varieties of dried and fresh pasta available to buy. However, it can be very rewarding to have a go at making your own...

HOW TO MAKE PASTA

Home-made pasta has a light, almost silky texture and is different from the fresh pasta that you can buy vacuum-packed in supermarkets. It is also easy to make and little equipment is needed, just a rolling pin and a sharp knife. If you make pasta regularly, it is perhaps worth investing in a pasta machine.

Basic Egg Pasta Dough

225 g/8 oz/2 cups type '00' pasta flour, plus
    extra for dusting
1 tsp salt
2 eggs, plus 1 egg yolk
1 tbsp olive oil
1–3 tsp cold water

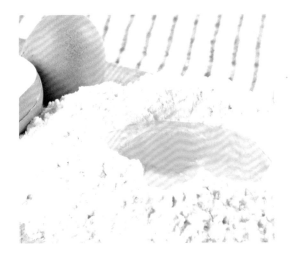

1. Sift the flour and salt into a mound on a work surface and make a well in the middle, keeping the sides high so that the egg mixture will not trickle out when added.

2. Beat the eggs, yolk, oil and 1 teaspoon water together. Add to the well.

3. Gradually work in the flour, adding extra water if needed, to make a soft but not sticky dough.

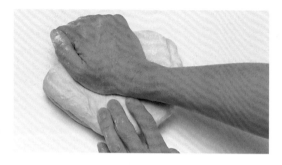

4. Knead on a lightly floured surface for 5 minutes, or until the dough is smooth and elastic. Wrap in plastic wrap and leave for 20 minutes at room temperature.

Using a Food Processor

Sift the flour and salt into a food processor fitted with a metal blade. Add the eggs, yolk, oil and water and pulse-blend until mixed and the dough begins to come together, adding extra water if needed. Knead for 1–2 minutes, then wrap and rest as before.

Rolling Pasta by Hand

1. Unwrap the pasta dough and cut in half. Work with just half at a time and keep the other half wrapped in plastic wrap.

2. Place the dough on a lightly floured work surface, then flatten and roll out. Always roll away from

you. Start from the centre, giving the dough a quarter turn after each rolling. Sprinkle a little more flour over the dough if it starts to get sticky.

3. Continue rolling and turning until the dough is as thin as possible, ideally 3 mm/⅛ inch thick.

Rolling Pasta by Machine

Always refer to the manufacturer's instructions before using.

1. Clamp the machine securely and attach the handle. Set the rollers at their widest setting and sprinkle with flour.

2. Cut the pasta dough into four pieces. Wrap three of them in plastic wrap and reserve.

3. Flatten the unwrapped dough slightly, then feed it through the rollers.

4. Fold the strip of dough in three, rotate and feed through the rollers a second time.

5. Continue to roll the dough, narrowing the roller setting by one notch every second time and flouring the rollers if the dough starts to get sticky. Only fold the dough the first time it goes through each roller width. If it is hard to handle, cut the strip in half and work with one piece at a time.

6. Fresh pasta should be dried before cutting. Drape over a wooden pole for 5 minutes or place on a dishtowel sprinkled with a little flour for 10 minutes.

Shaping Up

For shaping freshly made pasta, have several lightly floured dishtowels ready.

Farfalle Use a fluted pasta wheel to cut the pasta sheets into rectangles 2.5 x 5 cm/1 x 2 inches. Pinch the long sides of each rectangle in the middle to make a bow. Spread on a floured dishtowel. Leave for 15 minutes.

Lasagne Trim the pasta sheets until neat and cut into lengths. Spread the sheets on a dishtowel sprinkled with flour.

Noodles If using a pasta machine, use the cutter attachment to produce tagliatelle or use a narrower one for spaghetti. To make by hand, sprinkle the rolled-out pasta with flour, then roll up like a Swiss roll and cut into thin slices. Unravel immediately after cutting. Leave over a wooden pole for 5 minutes to dry.

Ravioli Cut the rolled-out sheet of dough in half widthways. Cover one half. Brush the other sheet of dough with beaten egg. Place 1 teaspoon filling in even rows, at 4 cm/1½ inch intervals. Remove the plastic wrap from the reserved pasta sheet and, using a rolling pin, lift over the dough with the filling. Press down between the pockets to push out any air. Cut into squares. Leave on a floured dishtowel for 45 minutes before cooking.

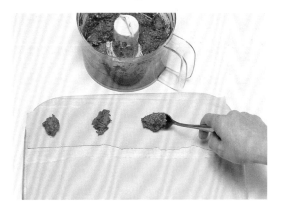

Variations

Flavoured pastas are simple and there are many ways to change the flavour and colour of pasta.

Chilli Add 2 teaspoons crushed dried red chillies to the egg mixture.

Herb Stir 3 tablespoons chopped fresh herbs into the flour.

Olive Blend 2 tablespoons black olive paste with the egg mixture and omit the water.

Porcini Soak 15 g/½ oz/⅓ cup dried porcini mushrooms in boiling water for 20 minutes. Drain and squeeze out as much water as possible, then chop finely. Add to the egg mixture.

Spinach Finely chop 75 g/3 oz/½ cup cooked fresh spinach. Add to the egg mixture.

PASTA VARIETIES

There are two types of dried pasta: 'secca' is factory-made from wheat and water and 'pasta all'uovo' is made with eggs. Egg pasta can be bought 'fresh', but should be used within 3 days of opening, so dried tends to be a more useful store cupboard ingredient.

Buckwheat A gluten-free pasta made from buckwheat flour.

Coloured and flavoured pasta Varieties are endless, the most popular being spinach and tomato. Others include beetroot/beet, herb, garlic, chilli, mushroom and black ink.

Durum wheat pasta Most readily available and may be made with or without eggs. Look for 'durum wheat' or 'pasta di semola di grano duro' on the packet, as pastas made from soft wheat tend to become soggy when cooked.

Wholemeal/whole-wheat pasta Made with wholemeal flour, this has a higher fibre content than ordinary pasta. Wholemeal pasta takes longer to cook than the refined version.

PASTA SHAPES

There are numerous different shapes and some of the most popular ones are listed below.

Long Pasta

Spaghetti Probably the best-known type of pasta, spaghetti derives its name from the word 'spago' meaning string, which describes its round, thin shape perfectly.

Tagliatelle Most common type of ribbon noodle pasta. It is traditionally from Bologna, where it accompanies bolognese sauce (rather than spaghetti). **Fettuccine** is the Roman version of tagliatelle and is cut slightly thinner.

Short Pasta

Conchiglie Pasta shapes resembling conch shells. Sizes vary from tiny to large. They may be smooth or ridged ('conchiglie rigate').

Eliche and fusilli These are twisted into the shape of a screw.

Farfalle Bow or butterfly shaped, often with crinkled edges.

Macaroni Known as elbow macaroni or maccheroni in Italy. A thin, quick-cook variety is also available.

Penne Slightly larger than macaroni, the ends of these tubes are cut and pointed like quills.

Pipe Curved, hollow pasta and often sold ridged as 'pipe rigate'.

Rigatoni Substantial, chunky, tubular pasta, often used for baking.

Rotelle Thin, wheel-shaped pasta, often sold in packets of two or three colours.

Stuffed Pasta

Tortellini The most common variety, consisting of tiny, stuffed pieces of pasta. Larger ones are called tortelloni.

Cappelletti, **ravioli** and **agnalotti** These are sometimes sold dried, but are more often available fresh.

HOW TO COOK PERFECT PASTA

As an approximate guide, allow 75–125 g/3–4 oz/
$^3/_4$ –1 cup uncooked pasta per person. The amount will depend on whether the pasta is being served for a light or main meal and the type of sauce that it is being served with. Follow a few simple rules to ensure that your pasta is cooked to perfection every time:

1. Choose a large saucepan – there needs to be plenty of room for the pasta to move around so it does not stick together.

2. Cook the pasta in a large quantity of fast-boiling, well-salted water, ideally 4 litres/7 pints/4 quarts water and 1½–2 tablespoons salt for every 350–450 g/12 oz–1 lb/3½–4½ cups pasta.

3. Tip in the pasta all at once, stir and cover. Return to a rolling boil, then remove the lid. Once it is boiling, lower the heat to medium-high and cook the pasta for the required time. It should be *al dente*, or tender but still firm to the bite.

4. Drain, reserving a little of the cooking water to stir into the drained pasta. This helps to thin the sauce, if necessary, and helps prevent the pasta sticking together as it cools.

Potatoes

 The humble potato is generally taken for granted and the versatility and huge number of varieties of this delicious vegetable are often forgotten. Worldwide, there are thousands of different types of potatoes and for about two-thirds of the world, they are the staple food.

GENERAL GUIDANCE

Nutritionally, potatoes are high in complex carbohydrates, providing sustained energy. They are also an excellent source of vitamins B and C and minerals such as iron and potassium. They contain almost no fat and are high in dietary fibre.

Types

Potatoes are classified according to how early in the season they are ready for harvesting and are named as follows: first early, second early and maincrop. The first earlies (such as the Maris Bard variety) are the first new potatoes on the market; they are very fresh and young and the skins can simply be rubbed off. The second earlies (such as Anya) are still new potatoes, but their skins will have begun to set.

These potatoes will be difficult to scrape and are better cooked in their skins. Maincrop potatoes (such as Maris Piper, King Edward, Charlotte, Désirée) are available all year round and may have been stored for several months.

Choosing

When buying potatoes, always choose ones with smooth, firm skins. When purchasing new potatoes, check that they are really young and fresh by scraping the skin – it should peel away very easily. Only buy the quantity you need and use within a couple of days.

Check maincrop potatoes to make sure that they are firm and not sprouting or showing any signs of mould. Avoid buying and discard any potatoes with greenish patches or carefully cut them out. These parts of the potato are toxic and a sign that they have been stored in light.

Storing

Potatoes should be stored in a cool, dark place but not in the refrigerator as the dampness will make them sweat, causing mould to grow. If the potatoes come in plastic bags, take them out and store in a paper bag or on a vegetable rack. If you prefer to buy in bulk, keep the potatoes in a cold, dark, dry place such as a larder or garage, making sure that they do not freeze in cold weather.

Sweet potatoes should be stored in a cool, dry place but, unlike ordinary potatoes, do not need to be kept in the dark.

Which Potato for Which Method?

Generally, new potato varieties have a firm and waxy texture that do not break up during cooking, so are ideal for boiling, steaming and salads. Maincrop potatoes, on the other hand, have a more floury texture and lend themselves to mashing and roasting – both types are suitable for chips. Individual potato varieties have their own characteristics. Some maincrop varieties are better for boiling than baking and vice versa, so choose the most appropriate type of potato for the dish being prepared (check the label or ask your retailer).

Whichever way you choose to serve potatoes, allow 175–225 g/6–8 oz per person (about 4–6 new potatoes or 1–2 medium potatoes). (One whole smallish potato – 4.5–6 cm/1¾ –2½ inches in diameter – weighs around 175 g/6 oz; one whole medium potato – 5.5–8 cm/2¼–3¼ inches – weighs around 210 g/7½ oz; and one whole large potato – 7.5–11 cm/3–4¼ inches – weighs around 375 g/13 oz.)

BOILING

New Potatoes

Most of the new potatoes available nowadays are fairly clean – especially those sold in supermarkets – and simply need a light scrub before cooking in their skins.

1. If the potatoes are very dirty, use a small scrubbing brush or scourer to remove both the skins and dirt (or leave the skins on if they are second earlies, and peel when cooked, if liked).

2. Add them to a pan of cold, salted water and bring to the boil. Cover the pan with a lid and simmer

for 12–15 minutes until tender. Very firm new potatoes can be simmered for 8 minutes, then left to stand in the hot water for a further 10 minutes until cooked through.

3. Add a couple of sprigs of fresh herbs to the pan if you like – fresh mint is traditionally used to flavour potatoes.

4. Drain the potatoes thoroughly and, if you want to peel them now, hold the hot potatoes with a fork to make this easier. Serve hot, tossed in a little melted butter or, for a change, a tablespoon of pesto.

'Old' (Maincrop) Potatoes

1. Choose a maincrop potato suitable for boiling, then peel thinly and cut into even-sized pieces. Alternatively, you can cook the potatoes in their skins and peel them after cooking.

2. Add to a saucepan of cold, salted water and bring to the boil. Cover the pan with a lid and simmer for 20 minutes, or until tender. Drain. (It is particularly important to cook floury potatoes gently or the outsides may start to fall apart before they are tender in the centre. Drain the potatoes in a colander, then return them to the pan to dry out over a very low heat for 1–2 minutes.)

Mashed Potatoes

1. Boil your maincrop potatoes as described and, once cooked, roughly mash and add a knob of butter and 2 tablespoons of milk per person.

Mash until smooth, with a hand masher,] grater or a potato ricer.

2. Season to taste with salt, freshly ground black pepper and a little freshly grated nutmeg if liked, then beat for a few seconds with a wooden spoon until fluffy.

As an alternative to butter, use a good-quality olive oil or crème fraîche. Finely chopped red and green chillies, crispy-cooked crumbled bacon, fresh herbs or grated Parmesan cheese can also be stirred in for additional flavour.

STEAMING POTATOES

All potatoes are suitable for steaming. Floury potatoes, however, are ideal for this method of cooking, as they fall apart easily when boiled.

1. New and small potatoes can be steamed whole, but larger ones should be cut into even-sized pieces.

2. Place the potatoes in a steamer, colander or sieve over boiling water and cover. Steam for 10 minutes if the potatoes are very small or, if they are cut into large chunks, cook for 20–25 minutes.

FRYING POTATOES

Chipped Potatoes

Slightly finer chips/fries are known as pommes frites (or 'French fries'), even finer ones as pommes allumettes and the finest of all as pommes pailles (straw chips). Paper-thin slices of peeled potatoes, cut with a sharp knife or using a mandoline or food processor, can be deep-fried a few at a time to make crisps or game chips. To make standard chipped potatoes, however, proceed as follows:

1. Wash, peel and cut the potatoes into 1.5 cm/⅝ inch slices. Cut the slices into long strips about 1.5 cm/⅝ inch wide.

2. Place the strips in a bowl of cold water and leave for 20 minutes, then drain and dry well on paper towels – moisture will make the fat spit.

3. Pour some oil into a deep heavy-based saucepan or deep-fat fryer, making sure that the oil does not go any further than halfway up the sides of the pan. Heat the oil to 190°C/375°F, or until a chip dropped into the fat rises to the surface straight away and is surrounded by bubbles.

4. Put the chips into a wire basket, lower into the oil and cook for 7–8 minutes until golden.

5. Remove and increase the heat of the oil to 200°C/400°F. Lower the chips into the oil again and cook for 2–3 minutes until they are crisp and golden brown. Drain on paper towels before serving.

Healthy Chips

To make lower-fat chips, preheat the oven to 200°C/400°F/Gas Mark 6 and place a nonstick baking tray in the oven to heat up.

1. Cut the potatoes into chips as above or into chunky wedges, if preferred. Put the chips or wedges in a pan of cold water and quickly bring to the boil.

2. Simmer for 2 minutes, then drain in a colander. Leave for a few minutes to dry.

3. Drizzle over 1½–2 tablespoons of olive or sunflower/corn oil and toss to coat.

4. Tip on to the heated baking tray and cook in the preheated oven for 20–25 minutes, turning occasionally, until golden brown and crisp.

Sautéed Potatoes

1. Cut peeled potatoes into rounds about 0.5 cm/¼ inch thick and pat dry.

2. Heat 25 g/1 oz/2 tbsp unsalted butter and 2 tablespoons oil in a large heavy-based frying pan until hot.

3. Add the potatoes in a single layer and cook for 4–5 minutes until the undersides are golden. Turn with a large fish slice/spatula and cook the other side until golden and tender.

4. Drain on paper towels and sprinkle with a little salt before serving.

BAKING POTATOES

Allow a large (300–375 g/11–13 oz) potato per person and choose a variety such as Maris Piper, Cara, King Edward, Russet Burbank or Russet Arcadia.

1. Wash and dry the potatoes, prick the skins lightly, then rub each one with a little oil and sprinkle with salt.

2. Bake at 200˚C/400˚F/Gas Mark 6 for 1–1½ hours until the skins are crisp and the centres are very soft. To speed up the cooking time, thread onto metal skewers, as this conducts heat to the middle of the potatoes.

ROASTING POTATOES

For crisp and brown outsides and fluffy centres, choose potatoes suitable for baking.

1. Thinly peel the potatoes and cut into even-sized pieces.

2. Drop into a pan of boiling, salted water and simmer for 5 minutes.

3. Turn off the heat and leave for a further 3–4 minutes.

4. Drain well and return the potatoes to the pan over a low heat for a minute to dry them and to roughen the edges.

5. Carefully transfer them to a roasting tin containing hot oil or dripping. Baste well, then bake at 220˚C/425˚F/Gas Mark 7 for 20 minutes.

6. Turn them and cook for a further 20–30 minutes, turning and basting at least one more time. Serve as soon as the potatoes are ready.

POTATO CROQUETTES

1. Mash dry, boiled potatoes with just a little butter or olive oil.

2. Stir in 1 egg yolk mixed with 1–2 tablespoons milk or crème fraîche/sour cream to make a firm mixture.

3. Shape the mashed potatoes into small cylinders about 5 cm/2 inches long and roll them in flour.

4. Dip in beaten egg and then in fresh white breadcrumbs, then chill the croquettes in the refrigerator for 30 minutes.

5. Place a little unsalted butter and oil in a heavy-based frying pan and slowly heat until the butter has melted.

6. Shallow fry the croquettes, turning occasionally until they are golden brown and crisp.

ROSTI

These small rostis can be elaborated on by adding other ingredients, such as smoked fish or ham, and herbs and spices, and making one big rosti.

1. Parboil peeled, waxy potatoes in boiling, salted water for 8 minutes, then drain and leave to cool.

2. Coarsely grate the potatoes into a bowl. Season well with salt and freshly ground black pepper and freshly chopped herbs, if liked.

3. Heat a mixture of unsalted butter and oil in a heavy-based frying pan until bubbling.

4. Add tablespoonfuls of the grated potato into the pan and flatten with the back of a fish slice. Cook over a medium heat for about 7 minutes, or until crisp and golden. Turn and cook the other side.

COOKING POTATOES IN A CLAY POT

Terracotta potato pots can cook up to 450 g/1 lb whole potatoes (2–3 medium potatoes) at a time.

1. Soak the clay pot for at least 20 minutes before use, then add even-sized, preferably smallish potatoes.

71

2. Drizzle over a little olive oil and season generously with salt and freshly ground black pepper.

3. Cover the pot with the lid and put in a cold oven, setting the temperature to 200°C/400°F/ Gas Mark 6. The potatoes will take about 45 minutes to cook.

MICROWAVING POTATOES

The microwave can be used to boil new potatoes or peeled chunks of potato as follows:

1. To cook new potatoes in the microwave, prick the skins with a skewer to prevent them from bursting.

2. Place in a bowl with 3 tablespoons boiling water.

3. Cover with plastic wrap which has been pierced two or three times and cook on High for 12–15 minutes until tender.

You can also 'bake' potatoes in the microwave, providing you do not want the skins to be crispy:

1. Place each potato on a circle of paper towels. Make several cuts in each to ensure that the skins do not burst.

2. Transfer to the microwave plate and cook on High for 4–6 minutes per potato, allowing an extra 3–4 minutes for every additional potato. Turn the potatoes at least once during cooking.

3. Leave to stand for 5 minutes before serving.

Herbs and Spices

 In a culture where fast food, ready-made meals and processed foods are popular, home-made food can sometimes taste bland by comparison, due to the fact that the palate can quickly become accustomed to additives and flavour enhancers. The use of herbs and spices, however, can make all the difference in helping to make delicious home-made dishes.

Traditionally, most of the countries throughout the world have used different herbs and spices in their dishes and this is perhaps one of the main reasons

for the differing flavours throughout Europe and the rest of the world. For example, India and East/Southeast Asia use coriander, sweet basil, cardamom, chilli, lemon grass and galangal, amongst many other flavours, while in Europe, others are more common. Italy uses basil, sage and rosemary, France uses tarragon, garlic, thyme and bay, while Greece enjoys marjoram and oregano. Scandinavian countries rely on dill and Britain and America use parsley, mint, sage and thyme.

As the world gets smaller thanks to increased travel and air freight transporting exotic herbs and spices to our supermarket shelves, today's cooks are combining the many different ingredients now so readily available with herbs and spices more traditional to their cuisine, thus providing a fusion of flavours to delight our taste buds.

NATURAL REMEDIES AND GATHERING HERBS

Herbs and spices are used not only for culinary purposes but also for their natural medicinal properties. Many people like to gather their herbs in woods and forests to make the remedies. However, a word of caution is needed here, for many of the herbs that are used for medicinal purposes can be poisonous if used to excess or incorrectly, so great care must be taken when gathering any wild herbs unless you are confident in your identification and use.

This luckily does not apply to cultivated herbs which can be bought in our supermarkets or farm shops, or grown at home.

DRIED HERBS

If choosing between fresh or dried herbs, I would always advocate fresh, but dried herbs can work well too. As long as these guidelines are followed, dried herbs offer a viable alternative when fresh are unavailable.

Buying and Storing

As dried herbs quickly lose their flavour and colour, they need to be bought in very small quantities and used quickly. Store them in a cool, dark place, never in small glass bottles on the work surface in direct light or, even worse, sunlight – they quickly lose any flavour and there is little point in using them.

Using

- As a guide to quantities, generally use one third of dried herbs to fresh. So if a recipe calls for 1 tablespoon fresh herb, use 1 teaspoon dried herb.

- Generally add at the beginning of cooking rather than at the end as would happen with fresh herbs. This allows longer for the flavour to be released.

- Ensure that they are used with a liquid, such as stock, as this again helps the flavour.

- Strong herbs, such as rosemary, mixed herbs, sage, thyme and oregano, retain their flavour better than the more delicate flavours of basil, dill and chervil.

FRESH HERBS

Fresh herbs are delightfully aromatic and flavoursome. Buy easily or grow your own.

Growing

Planting a few herbs is worth the effort – they are easy to grow, as they do not require much attention or nurturing, and do not necessarily need a garden, as they can easily thrive on a small patio, window box or even on a windowsill. The reward will be a range of fresh herbs available whenever needed and fresh flavours that cannot be beaten – not to mention the money you will save and the pleasure of picking your own produce. Once picked, wash thoroughly, ensuring that there are no tiny bugs and shake or pat dry on paper towels.

Drying

It is quite simple to dry herbs yourself and, with a good crop of home-grown herbs, it is a good option, providing that you use them quickly and the herbs are stored correctly once dried. Avoid drying the delicate herbs such as basil, dill or chervil – these are better frozen *(see page 76)*.

1. Lightly wash the herb sprigs and pat dry, then tie into small bundles.

2. Hang in a well-ventilated room, out of the glare of direct sunlight and in a dry atmosphere. The herbs will not dry in a damp place, and excessive heat will evaporate the essential oils, thus removing the flavour.

3. They will vary in the length of time they need to dry, but are ready when the leaves feel brittle. Strip the leaves from the stalks and store in airtight containers or screw-top jars. Small leaves and flower heads can be rubbed through the fingers to crumple.

Herbs can also be dried in a microwave. This method helps to preserve their colour.

1. Simply scatter the herbs in a single layer over doubled paper towels.

2. Place in the microwave and heat on High for 2 minutes.

3. Remove and allow to cool, then store as dried herbs.

Freezing

Frozen herbs can sometimes be found in specialist shops or in some supermarkets' freezer cabinets, but they are very easy to prepare yourself. If gathered early in the season, many herbs are prolific growers and will provide quite a few more harvests which can be frozen to avoid wastage.

1. First, pick your herbs, choosing ones that are fully grown but not bolted (that is, avoid ones that have flowered or produced seeds prematurely). Do not choose sprigs that are very delicate and have not reached maturity, as these should be left for a later picking.

2. Wash thoroughly, ensuring that there are no tiny bugs, dry on paper towels, then chop.

3. Spread out on paper towels placed on a baking tray and allow to dry naturally. Open freeze on the baking tray for about 1 hour.

4. Carefully gather into heaps and place in a small freezable container. Label clearly and remember to date. Freeze for up to 1–2 months.

To use, simply take out as much as you require and add to your dish. This method is good for adding flavour rather than using for a garnish, where fresh is best.

Which Herbs to Use

With fresh herbs, in order to get the maximum benefit from their use, it is imperative first of all that you know what the herb tastes like. For example, the use of strongly flavoured herbs such as thyme or sage with the delicate flavour of sole will completely overpower the fish. Remember that strongly flavoured herbs need robust sauces and ingredients – rosemary goes with lamb, and sage with pork, while dill works with sole. If unsure, first chew a little of the herb raw. This will give an excellent indication of the finished dish.

It is good to remember that the flavour and aroma will be modified by cooking, so use the herb sparingly at first – once you are familiar with the taste and aroma of each herb, you will quickly know how much or little to use.

Which Part to Use

With most herbs, the parts used are the leaves and small sprigs. The leaves or sprigs are stripped off the stems and then chopped. If to be used whole, place in the dish before cooking and then remove at the end of cooking.

With fresh coriander/cilantro, the whole of the herb can be used. The root can be washed and chopped, as can the stem, for maximum flavour. The leaves are rinsed and added at the end for a good flavour and colour burst. The use of the root and stem of coriander is often overlooked by many.

When to Use

Fresh herbs should be used very soon after picking or buying. If to be chopped, chop at the last possible moment – once chopped, all the flavour is immediately released and herbs should be added to the dish at once so that none of the flavour is lost.

How to Chop

All of these methods work well, so it is up to you.

Mezzaluna herb chopper Also known as a 'hachoir', this half-moon shaped stainless steel chopper, with a wooden or stainless steel handle, is designed to be used either on a chopping board or in its own wooden bowl.

Electric mini chopper This works in a similar manner to a mini food processor and chops herbs in seconds. It can also be used for grinding spices.

Bistro herb chopper This has seven double-edged stainless steel rotary blades placed in a small bowl with a lid. It maximizes the chopping, making it very fast.

Herb and nut mill This works on the same principle as a pepper mill.

By hand Rinse the herbs and pat dry, then strip the leaves from the stem and place on a chopping board. Hold a large cook's knife at the tip with one hand, then, taking the knife handle in the other hand, chop in a half-circular movement, keeping the tip of the knife in the same position. Chop to the required fineness. Alternatively, place in a small jug or mug, and chop using a pair of kitchen scissors. This will give a rougher chop, as it cannot be controlled so well.

Bouquets Garnis

Bouquets garnis are an excellent way of using herbs and are easily made. Take 2 small clean celery pieces and place a small bunch of mixed herbs in between the celery, then tie together securely.

For example, for a lamb stew or casserole, use 1 fresh rosemary sprig, 2 bay leaves, 1 fresh thyme sprig and 3 flat-leaf/Italian or curly parsley sprigs between the celery. This can be added at the beginning of cooking and, when tasting, if you feel that the dish has plenty of flavour, it can easily be removed.

Herbs as Garnish

Fresh herbs are also used extensively as a garnish in order to add to the visual appeal of the finished dish. The herb is used either as sprigs, leaves or finely chopped. Sprigs tend to be used when there is very little colour on the dish, to fill a gap after it has been arranged on the plate or to disguise something (a small bunch is often placed in the rear – parson's nose – of a cooked turkey or chicken, for example). Leaves, again, are used to lift the colour of a cooked dish or are added to be eaten with the food, such as fresh basil with a tomato and mozzarella salad, or a

few tiny mint leaves with an ice cream sundae. Chopped herbs function in the same way as sprigs and leaves but are also used to provide extra flavour or to emphasise the flavour.

Fresh Herb as the Main Ingredient

Quite often, herbs are the main ingredient in a recipe. Pesto is a good example – here, basil is combined with garlic, pine nuts, olive oil and Parmesan cheese to make the classic Italian sauce that is now used throughout the world. Other sauces that rely on herbs are salsa verde – a green herb sauce using parsley, basil and mint – and, of course, mint sauce, among many others. Here is how to make a **basic pesto**:

50 g/2 oz/2 cups fresh basil leaves
1 garlic clove, peeled
3 tbsp pine nuts, toasted
6 tbsp extra virgin olive oil
salt and freshly ground black pepper
2 tbsp Parmesan cheese, finely grated
dash lemon juice (optional)

1. Tear the basil leaves and pound in a pestle and mortar with the garlic clove and toasted pine nuts.

2. Gradually work in the olive oil, then add seasoning to taste.

3. Spoon into a small bowl and stir in the Parmesan cheese. Add a little lemon juice, if liked, check the seasoning and use as required. Store in the refrigerator for up to 1 week in a small screw-top jar.

SPICES

As with herbs, so it is with spices – their main function in food is to enhance the dish and to impart flavour (even though, originally, their main function was to help in the preservation of food). Often, both spice and herb are used in conjunction with one another, each complementing the other. Again, as it is with herbs, spices vary widely both in taste and aroma and should be used sparingly until you are sure of what you like.

Storage

It is imperative that spices are used and stored correctly. Over time, they lose their taste and aroma and can become musty and stale – especially ground spices. Buy in small quantities from a reputable store that has a good turnover. It is worth travelling to an area with appropriate ethnic populations if wishing to buy spices relevant to their traditional cuisine. Here you can be sure that the store has a good turnover and the spices will be fresh.

If possible, do not buy ready-ground spices; buy the seeds and pods, as these will keep for longer if stored in airtight containers in a cool, dark place. Also, if the spice is freshly roasted and ground before use, it gives a greater pungency, taste and aroma.

Roasting

There are various ways to 'roast' your unground spices – and not necessarily in the oven.

Dry frying Place the spices in a heavy-based frying pan and cook over a medium heat. Stir frequently, taking care not to allow the spices to burn, for 5–10 minutes until they darken. Remove and cool before grinding.

Oven roasting Place no more than 250 g/9 oz of your spice on a baking tray and cook in a preheated oven at 230°C/450°F/Gas Mark 8 for 10–25 minutes until the spices look toasted. Stir occasionally. Remove and cool, then use as required.

In a microwave Place 2–4 tablespoons of spice on a microwaveable plate or dish. Cook, uncovered, on full power for 2–4 minutes. Stir once during cooking. Cool before grinding.

Grinding Spices

Spices can be ground or crushed using a couple of methods. The most usual, but labour intensive, is to use a pestle and mortar.

Pestle and mortar Place the spices in the mortar and grind or crush with the pestle to the required fineness – create a paste, if liked, by adding a little oil towards the end of grinding.

Coffee grinder or mini chopper If using either of these, do ensure that the bowl of the grinder is completely clean. Fill the bowl approximately one-third full and grind in short bursts. When ground to the required fineness, place in a bowl or on a plate and continue with the remaining seeds.

Using in Cooking

When using spices that have not been roasted, it is important that they are cooked first, before other ingredients are added. If not, the spices will taste raw and no amount of cooking will change this.

When recipes call for whole spices as well as ground, the whole spices need to be fried first. Heat a heavy-based frying pan and pour in a thin layer of sunflower oil. Heat until hot (this can be tested by adding a couple of the spice seeds or pods – if they sizzle, then the oil is ready), add the whole spices and cook for 1–2 minutes until the spices darken and the pods (if applicable) puff up. Watch them closely to ensure that they do not burn and have a lid to hand, as some seeds, such as mustard seeds, jump when added to hot oil. Add the spices to the pan in the order that they are listed in the recipe.

KEY HERBS AND SPICES

A variety of herbs and spices and their uses are listed below.

Allspice The dark allspice berries come whole or ground and have a flavour similar to that of cinnamon, cloves and nutmeg. Although not the same as mixed spices, allspice can be used with

pickles, relishes, cakes and milk puddings, or whole in meat and fish dishes.

Aniseed Comes in whole seeds or ground. It has a strong aroma and flavour and should be used sparingly in baking and salad dressings.

Basil Best fresh but also available in dried form, basil can be used raw or cooked and works well in many dishes, but is particularly well suited to tomato-based dishes and sauces, salads and Mediterranean dishes.

Bay leaves Available in fresh or dried form as well as ground. They make up part of a bouquet garni and are particularly delicious when added to meat and poultry dishes, soups, stews, vegetable dishes and stuffing. They also impart a spicy flavour to milk puddings and egg custards.

Caraway seeds These have a warm, sweet taste and are often used in breads and cakes, but are also delicious with cabbage dishes and pickles.

Cayenne The powdered form of a red chilli pepper said to be native to Cayenne. It is similar in appearance to paprika and can be used sparingly to add a fiery kick to many dishes.

Cardamom Has a distinctive sweet, rich taste. Can be bought whole in the pod, in seed form or ground. This sweet aromatic spice is delicious in curries, rice, cakes and cookies and is great served with rice pudding and fruit.

Chervil Reminiscent of parsley and available either in fresh or dried form, chervil has a faintly sweet, spicy flavour and is particularly good in soups, cheese dishes, stews and with eggs.

Chilli Available whole, fresh, dried and in powdered form. Red chillies tend to be sweeter in taste than their green counterparts. They are particularly associated with Spanish and Mexican-style cooking and curries, but are also delicious with pickles, dips, sauces and in pizza toppings.

Chives Best used when fresh, but also available in dried form, this member of the onion family is ideal for use when a delicate onion flavour is required. Chives are good with eggs, cheese, fish and vegetable dishes. They also work well as a garnish for soups, meat and vegetable dishes.

Cinnamon Comes in the form of reddish-brown sticks of bark from an evergreen tree and has a sweet, pungent aroma. Either whole or ground, cinnamon is delicious in cakes and milk puddings, particularly with apple, and is used in mulled wine and for preserving.

Cloves Mainly used whole, although available ground, cloves have a very warm, sweet, pungent aroma and can be used to stud roast ham and pork,

in mulled wine and punch and when pickling fruit. When ground, they can be used in mincemeat and in Christmas puddings and cookies.

Coriander/cilantro Coriander seeds have an orangey flavour and are available whole or ground. Coriander is particularly delicious (whole or roughly ground) in curries, casseroles and as a pickling spice. Coriander/cilantro leaves are used both to flavour spicy aromatic dishes and as a garnish.

Cumin Also available ground or as whole seeds, cumin has a strong, slightly bitter flavour. It is one of the main ingredients in curry powder and complements many fish, meat and rice dishes.

Dill These leaves are available fresh or dried and have a mild flavour, while the seeds are slightly bitter. Dill is particularly good with salmon, new potatoes and in sauces. The seeds are good in pickles and vegetable dishes.

Fennel As whole seeds or ground, fennel has a fragrant, sweet aniseed flavour and is sometimes known as the fish herb because it complements fish dishes so well.

Ginger Comes in many forms, but primarily as a fresh root and in dried, ground form, which can be used in baking, curries, pickles, sauces and Chinese cooking.

Lemon grass Available fresh and dried, with a subtle, aromatic, lemony flavour, lemon grass is essential to Thai cooking. It is also delicious when added to soups, poultry and fish dishes.

Mace The outer husk of nutmeg has a milder nutmeg flavour and can be used in pickles, cheese dishes, stewed fruits, sauces and hot punch.

Marjoram Often dried, marjoram has a sweet, slightly spicy flavour, which tastes fantastic when added to stuffing, meat or tomato-based dishes.

Mint Available fresh or dried, mint has a strong, sweet aroma that is delicious in a sauce or jelly to serve with lamb. It is great with fresh peas and new potatoes and an essential part of Pimm's.

Nutmeg The large whole seeds have a warm, sweet taste and complement custards, milk puddings, cheese dishes, parsnips and creamy soups.

Oregano These strongly flavoured dried leaves are similar to marjoram and are used extensively in Italian and Greek cooking.

Paprika Often comes in two varieties. One is quite sweet and mild and the other has a slight bite to it. Paprika is made from the fruit of the sweet pepper and is good in meat and poultry dishes, and as a garnish. The rule of buying herbs and spices little and often applies particularly to paprika, as unfortunately it does not keep very well.

Parsley The stems as well as the leaves of parsley can be used to complement most savoury dishes, as they contain a lot of flavour. They can also be used as a garnish.

Poppy seeds These small, grey-black-coloured seeds impart a sweet, nutty flavour when added to cookies, vegetable dishes, dressings and cheese dishes.

Rosemary Delicious fresh or dried, these small, needle-like leaves have a sweet aroma that is particularly good with lamb, stuffing and vegetable dishes. Also delicious when added to charcoal on the barbecue to give a piquant flavour to both meat and corn on the cob.

Saffron Deep orange in colour, saffron is traditionally used in paella, rice and cakes, but is also delicious with poultry. Saffron is the most expensive of all spices.

Sage These fresh or dried leaves have a pungent, slightly bitter taste that is delicious with pork and poultry, sausages, stuffing and with stuffed pasta when tossed in a little butter.

Sesame Sesame seeds have a nutty taste, especially when toasted, and are delicious in baking, on salads or with Far Eastern cooking.

Tarragon The fresh or dried leaves of tarragon have a sweet aromatic taste that is particularly good with poultry, seafood, fish, creamy sauces and stuffing.

Thyme Available fresh or dried, thyme has a pungent flavour and is included in bouquet garni. It complements many meat and poultry dishes and stuffing.

Turmeric Obtained from the root of a lily from Southeast Asia. This root is ground and has a brilliant yellow colour. It has a bitter, peppery flavour and is often used in curry powder and mustard. Also delicious in pickles, relishes and dressings.

Meat

 Meat plays an important part in most people's diet, offering an excellent source of protein, B vitamins and iron. However, it also contains saturated fatty acids which are linked to raised blood cholesterol levels and increased risk of coronary heart disease. For this reason, it is now recommended that red meat is only eaten 2–3 times per week. Both home-grown and imported meat is readily available from supermarkets, butchers, farm shops and markets.

GENERAL GUIDANCE

Home-grown meat is normally more expensive than imported meat, often brought into the country frozen. Meat also varies in price depending on the cut: the more expensive and tender meats are usually those cuts that exercised less. They need a minimal amount of cooking and are suitable for roasting, grilling/broiling, griddling, frying and stir-frying. The cheaper cuts need longer, slower cooking and are used in casseroles and for stewing.

Quality, and thus cost, is also linked to the quality of life the animal led – the flavour and texture of the meat depends on how the animal was reared. Livestock raised on lush rich pastures with the freedom to roam will taste far better than those that are kept in cramped conditions. Stress can also play a large part in the quality of meat. So animals that have a good quality existence right up to slaughter will produce the best results.

Choosing

When choosing meat, it is important to buy from a reputable source (bearing the above in mind) and to choose the correct cut for the cooking method. Look for meat that is lean without an excess of fat, is a

good colour and has no unpleasant odour. If in doubt about the suitability of a cut, ask the butcher, who should be happy to advise.

Frozen Meat

If buying frozen meat, allow to thaw before using. This is especially important for both pork and poultry. It is better to thaw meat slowly, lightly covered on the bottom shelf of the refrigerator. Use within 2–3 days of thawing, providing it has been kept in the refrigerator. If buying meat to freeze, do not freeze large joints in a home freezer, as it will not be frozen quickly enough.

Storing

Store thawed or fresh meat out of the supermarket wrappings, on a plate, lightly covered with greaseproof or baking paper and then wrap with plastic wrap, if liked. Do not secure the paper tightly round the meat, as it needs to breathe. Ensure that the raw meat juices do not drip onto cooked foods. The refrigerator needs to be at a temperature of 5°C/40°F. Fresh meat such as joints, chops and steaks can be stored for up to 3 days. Minced/ground meats, sausages and offal/variety meats should be stored for only 1 day.

Different cultures and religions affect the way the meat has been killed and the carcass cut. The following is a description of different cuts of meat. They may be called by different names, depending on where you live.

BEEF

When choosing beef, look for meat that is a good vibrant, uniform colour, with creamy yellow fat. There should be small flecks of fat (marbling) throughout, as this helps the meat to be tender. Avoid meat with excess gristle. Bright red beef means that the animal has been butchered recently, whereas meat that has been hung in a traditional manner should be a deep, dark ruby red, almost purple. The darker the colour, especially with roasting joints, the more tender and succulent the beef will be.

Rib or fore rib (1) Suitable for roasting. Sold either on or off the bone. Look for meat that is marbled for tenderness and succulence.

Topside/Round (2) Suitable for pot roasting, roasting or braising. A lean, tender cut from the hindquarters.

Sirloin/Shortloin, Tenderloin, Top/Bottom Sirloin Suitable for roasting, grilling/broiling, frying or barbecuing. Sold either on or off the bone. A lean and tender cut from the back.

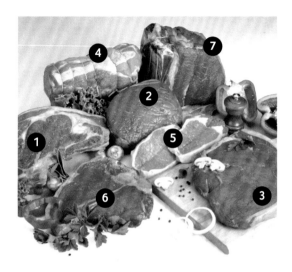

Rump/Shortloin, **Tenderloin**, **Top/Bottom Sirloin (3)** Suitable for grilling/broiling, frying, griddling or barbecuing. Not as tender as fillet or sirloin, but reputed to have more flavour.

Silverside/Round (4) Suitable for boiling and pot roasts. Used to be sold ready-salted, but is now normally sold unsalted.

Flash-fry steaks (5) Suitable for grilling/broiling, griddling or frying. Cut from the silverside, thick flank or topside.

Braising steak (6) Chuck, blade or thick rib, ideal for all braising or stews. Sold either in pieces or ready diced.

Flank/Bottom Sirloin (7) Suitable for braising or stewing. A boneless cut from the mid- to hindquarters.

Minute steaks Suitable for grilling/broiling or griddling. A thin steak cut from the flank and beaten to flatten.

Skirt Suitable for stewing or making into mince. A boneless, rather gristly cut.

Brisket/Plate Suitable for slow or pot roasting. Sold boned and rolled and can be found salted.

T-bone steak Suitable for grilling/broiling, griddling, barbecuing or roasting. A tender, succulent cut from the fillet end of the sirloin.

Top rib Suitable for pot roasting or braising. Sold on or off the bone.

Fillet steak Suitable for grilling/broiling, frying, barbecuing or griddling. A whole fillet is used to make Châteaubriand, some say the best of all cuts. The most tender and succulent cut with virtually no fat. Comes from the centre of the sirloin.

Minced/ground beef Suitable for meat sauces such as bolognese and also burgers, shepherd's pie and moussaka. Normally cut from clod, skirt, neck, thin rib or flank. Can be quite fatty. Steaks can also be minced to give a leaner result, if it is preferred.

Ox kidney Suitable for using in casseroles and stews. Strong flavour with hard central core that is discarded.

Oxtail Suitable for casseroles or braising. Normally sold cut into small pieces.

HOW TO COOK BEEF

A beautifully tender piece of beef can be ruined if not cooked properly; there are a few guidelines which, if followed, will give a truly delicious result.

Griddle, Fry or Grill/broil

First of all, choose the right method of cooking for the cut of meat *(see earlier lists, pages 86–88)* – all steaks should be cooked quickly, and are ideal to be grilled/broiled, griddled or fried. Look for meat that is lightly rippled with thin streaks of fat and wherever possible choose meat that is not bright red but that is turning slightly purple, for maximum flavour.

1. Prepare the meat first by either marinating for at least 30 minutes in a mixture of herbs or spices with oil, wine and a little juice or vinegar, or simply 'bash' the meat with a meat mallet or rolling pin and coat in a dry rub (a mixture of crushed spices and herbs) and leave for up to 30 minutes. *(See Marinades and Butters, pages 148–50.)*

2. Heat the pan or grill/broiler until it is very hot (and a few drops of water sprinkled over the pan sizzle and evaporate immediately).

3. Drain the meat, if a wet marinade has been used, then place in the pan and press down with a spatula for 1 minute to seal the juices in, thus preserving the flavour.

4. For rare, cook for a further 1–2 minutes on that side, before turning over and cooking the other side for the same length of time. For a medium-cooked steak, cook on each side for 3–4 minutes, and for a well done steak, cook for 5–6 minutes on each side. This method applies for all steaks when cooked in either a frying pan or griddle pan.

Grill/broil the steak on the same principle, but it may take 2–3 minutes longer, as the steak is not in direct contact with the heat. Grilling produces a lot of smoke, so the meat needs to be a little way away from the hot grill bars. Flash-fry steaks are normally very thin and may only take 1–2 minutes on each side to cook.

Beef in Sauce (Beef Stroganoff)

It is also possible to cook all of the above steaks, except for flash-fry steak and minute steak, in a sauce on the hob/stove top, such as the classic beef stroganoff recipe provided here. Here, the steak is normally cut into long thin strips and combined with onions, mushrooms and wine and cooked for about 20–30 minutes.

2 large onions
65 g/2½ oz/5 tbsp unsalted butter
675 g/1½ lb rump or fillet steak
3 tbsp plain/all-purpose flour
1 tsp mustard powder
1 tbsp tomato purée/paste
300 ml/½ pint/1¼ cups beef stock
salt and freshly ground black pepper
¼–½ tsp freshly grated nutmeg
75 g/3 oz/1 cup button mushrooms, wiped and sliced
4 tbsp sour cream
freshly chopped parsley, to garnish
freshly cooked rice, to serve

1. Peel and thinly slice the onions, then melt 50 g/ 2 oz/¼ cup (4 tbsp) of the butter in a saucepan, add the onions and cook for 12 minutes, or until softened and golden. Remove from the pan with a slotted draining spoon and reserve.

2. Trim the beef, discarding any fat or gristle, and cut into thin strips. Add to the saucepan and cook, stirring, for 5 minutes, or until sealed. Sprinkle in the plain/all-purpose flour and mustard powder and cook for 2 minutes, stirring frequently.

3. Draw the pan off the heat and stir in the reserved onions together with the tomato purée/paste blended with the stock. Add salt, pepper and

nutmeg to taste. Bring to the boil, reduce the heat to a simmer and cover with a lid. Cook for 15 minutes, stirring occasionally.

4. Meanwhile, melt the remaining butter and fry the mushrooms for 3 minutes. Stir into the beef. Continue to cook, stirring occasionally, for a further 10 minutes, or until the beef is tender.

5. Stir in the sour cream, adjust the seasoning then sprinkle with a little chopped parsley and serve with freshly cooked rice.

Roasting

Again, it is vital that the correct cut is used for this, otherwise the result will be tough to eat *(see earlier lists, pages 86–88)*. Beef can be roasted slowly or quickly, with or without the bone where applicable (all the ribs can be either on or off the bone). Roast beef slowly as follows:

1. Preheat the oven to 190°C/375°F/Gas Mark 5. Trim the joint, discarding any excess fat. (There needs to be a little fat on the joint to ensure the meat is moist.) Tie firmly with string to ensure the joint keeps its shape during roasting.

2. Weigh the joint and calculate the cooking time, allowing 27 minutes per 450 g/1 lb, plus 27 minutes

if on the bone, and 33 minutes per 450 g/1 lb, plus 33 minutes if boned (off the bone) and rolled.

3. Wipe the meat and place in a roasting tin/pan, fat-side uppermost, and season lightly.

4. Cook in the preheated oven for the calculated time.

5. Allow to rest for at least 10 minutes before carving. Remove the cooked joint from the tin, cover with kitchen foil and a clean dishtowel and leave in a warm place. This allows the meat to relax and it will carve more easily.

Cooking the beef quickly will produce a rarer meat:

1. Preheat the oven to 220°C/425°F/Gas Mark 7. Weigh the joint and calculate the cooking time. Allow 20 minutes per 450 g/1 lb, plus 20 minutes if on the bone, for rare; 25 minutes plus 25 minutes for medium; and 30 minutes plus 30 minutes for well done. (If the meat is boned and rolled, allow 25 minutes per 450 g/1 lb for rare, 30 minutes plus 30 for medium, 35 minutes plus 35 for well done.)

2. If the meat is on the bone, place in the roasting tin fat-side uppermost and season lightly. If there is not much fat, drizzle lightly with a little oil before cooking.

3. Cook and rest as before.

Gravy After cooking, while the meat is resting, is when the gravy is made. After removing the meat from the roasting tin/pan, place the tin on the hob/stove top on a low heat. With a wooden spoon, stir the base of the tin, dislodging any of the tiny pieces of meat and stirring into the meat juices. Add either some good-quality wine or stock, or a mixture of both, and bring to the boil, stirring. Add a little redcurrant jelly, if liked, then strain into a jug and serve. (If liked, a little of the vegetable cooking water can be used – strain first before using.)

Braising, Casseroles and Slow Cooking

These methods are for the slightly tougher cuts of beef such as flank *(see earlier lists, page 86–88)*. Top side/round is sometimes also used for casseroles. The meat is sold either cut into cubes or as a whole piece. Casseroles, stews and many other similar dishes can be said to be forms of braising, since it simply means cooking the meat in liquid. However, 'braising' is generally distinct in that it usually refers to whole pieces of meat cooked in less liquid, such as with pot roasts.

Casseroles With casseroles, the meat is always sealed in a pan first so that the flavour is retained. It is then cooked in the oven with plenty of liquid,

usually at a medium heat between 160˚C/325˚F/Gas Mark 3 and 180˚C/350˚F/Gas Mark 4, for at least 1½–2 hours.

Stews This is for the cheaper cuts such as skirt and is cooked on the hob for a much longer time than a casserole.

Pot roasts (Boiled Beef & Dumplings) Again, pot roasts are cooked on the hob and demand long slow cooking, normally with root vegetables. Silverside and brisket are the cuts most normally used. Silverside is often bought salted and is the cut used for the classic recipe of Boiled Beef & Dumplings as provided below, which serves 8–10 people.

1.5 kg/3 lb 5 oz piece fresh silverside/round
  or brisket/plate joint
2 tbsp salt per 450 g/1 lb meat
1 bouquet garni *(see page 78)*
6 small onions, peeled
4–6 small carrots, peeled
2 leeks, washed thoroughly, trimmed and sliced

For the dumplings:
300 g/11 oz/2⅓ cups self-raising flour
150 g/5 oz/1¼ cups shredded suet
2 tbsp mixed fresh herbs, chopped

1. Weigh the beef and calculate the cooking time, allowing 30 minutes per 450 g/1 lb, plus 30 minutes. Rinse lightly and place in a large saucepan with the salt. Bring to the boil and discard any scum that rises to the surface.

2. Add the bouquet garni to the pan. Reduce the heat to a simmer, cover with a lid and cook for the calculated time.

3. Forty-five minutes before the end of the cooking time, add all the prepared vegetables. Return to the boil, then reduce to a simmer and cook until the meat is tender.

4. To make the dumplings, place the flour, suet and chopped herbs in a bowl. Add 6–8 tbsp cold water, a little at a time, and mix to form a soft but not sticky dough. Shape into small balls.

5. Add the dumplings to the beef 15 minutes before the end of the cooking time. Simmer for about 15 minutes until the dumplings rise to the surface. Serve the meat with the cooked vegetables, dumplings and broth.

Slow cooking The use of slow cookers is gaining in popularity and is the perfect cooking method for families with busy life styles. The dish can be prepared in the morning (or even the night before and left in the refrigerator), then placed in the slow cooker and either set to automatic or switched on so that it is cooking very slowly during the day and is ready for the evening meal. When preparing, do remember that any root vegetable must be covered completely with liquid during cooking.

LAMB

Lamb is probably at its best in the spring, when the youngest lamb is available. It is tender to eat, with a delicate flavour, and its flesh is a paler pink than the older lamb, where the flesh is more red. The colour of the fat is also a good indication of age: young lamb fat is a very light, creamy colour. As the lamb matures, the fat becomes whiter and firmer. Imported lamb also has firmer, whiter fat. Lamb is naturally a fattier meat than beef, so take care when choosing. It used to be possible to buy mutton (lamb that is at least one year old), but this now tends to be available only in specialist outlets. It has a far stronger, almost gamey flavour and the joints tend to be larger.

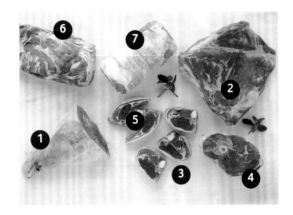

Leg (1) Suitable for roasting. Often sold as half legs and steaks cut from the fillet end. These can be grilled/broiled, griddled or barbecued. Steaks are very lean and need a little additional oil to prevent the meat from drying out. Can be used for casseroles if liked, and diced leg can be pan fried.

Shank Suitable for braising. A cut off the leg.

Shoulder (2) Suitable for roasting. Can be sold boned, stuffed and rolled. Is fattier than the leg and has more flavour. Can also be used for casseroles

but, as it will give a fattier result, it would be best if cooked the day before so that the fat can be skimmed off the surface

Loin (3) Suitable for roasting or slow pot roasting. Sold on or off the bone. Can be stuffed and rolled. Can also be cut into chops, often as double loin chops – suitable for grilling/broiling, griddling and barbecuing. Diced loin can also be pan fried.

Noisette Suitable for grilling/broiling, griddling or barbecuing. A small boneless chop cut from the centre of the loin.

Valentine steak Suitable for grilling/broiling, griddling or barbecuing. Cut from a loin chop.

Chump chop (4) Suitable for grilling/broiling, griddling or barbecuing. Larger than loin chops and can be sold boneless.

Best end of neck (5) Suitable for roasting, grilling/broiling or griddling. Sold as a joint or cutlets, but can be boned and rolled and stuffed.

Neck fillet Suitable for griddling, grilling/broiling or pan frying. Sold whole or diced. Can also be used for casseroles.

Middle and scrag end (6) Suitable for pot roasting, braising or stewing. A cheaper cut with a high ratio of fat and bone.

Breast (7) Suitable for pot roast if boned, stuffed and rolled. Can be marinated and grilled/broiled.

Mince Suitable for burgers, pies, meatballs and for stuffing vegetables such as peppers. From various cuts and is often fatty.

Liver Suitable for pan frying or grilling/broiling. Milder than ox or pig liver and cheaper than calves' liver.

Kidney Suitable for grilling/broiling, pan frying or casseroles. Milder than ox or pig kidney and normally sold encased in suet, which is discarded.

HOW TO COOK LAMB

When cooking lamb, the same principles apply as to beef. Different cuts of meat demand different methods of cooking. When using, wipe lightly with a clean damp cloth and, if grilling/broiling, it is advisable to marinate first.

Griddle or Grill/broil
Choose a cut that is suitable for this method of cooking *(see earlier list, pages 93–94)*.

1. Heat the pan or grill/broiler as described in the beef section and, when hot, drain the meat to be cooked and place in the hot pan.

2. Press down with the spatula to seal, then continue to cook until cooked to personal preference.

Equally, to grill, follow as with beef. Lamb can be eaten slightly pink, if liked, although many people prefer lamb well cooked. To test if cooked, pierce in the centre with a small sharp knife – the juices should run out either slightly pink or clear. Allow to rest for 2–3 minutes before eating.

Pan Frying with Other Ingredients
Diced lamb *(see earlier list, pages 93–94)* can be cooked on the hob/stove top in a frying pan and

make a welcome speedy change from grilling/ broiling, roasting or casserole.

1. Cut the meat into small pieces, then brown in a hot frying pan in a little oil with some onion and garlic.

2. Cook until sealed, then stir in 1–2 tablespoons flour and cook for 2 minutes. Draw the pan off the heat and gradually stir in some wine, if liked, and some stock.

3. Add other ingredients such as mushrooms and chopped pepper, with seasoning to taste, and a little redcurrant jelly. Cover with a lid and cook for about 20 minutes, stirring occasionally. Check seasoning and serve.

Roasting

Choose a cut that is suitable for this method of cooking (see earlier list, pages 93–94).

1. Prepare the lamb as required, then weigh and calculate the cooking time, allowing 20 minutes per 450 g/1 lb, plus 20 minutes if on the bone, or 25 minutes per 450 g/1 lb, plus 25 minutes if boned and rolled.

2. If roasting a leg or shoulder, pierce the skin with a small knife and insert tiny slivers of garlic and tiny

sprigs of fresh rosemary. The joint could be spread with mustard instead of using garlic, if liked.

3. Cook for the calculated time, then remove, cover and allow to stand for at least 10 minutes before carving.

Casseroles and Slow Cooking

Choose a cut that is suitable for this method of cooking (see earlier list, pages 93–94) – if possible, boneless meat.

1. Prepare the meat by discarding any excess fat and cutting into cubes if off the bone. If still on the bone, chop into smaller pieces if necessary. Rinse to remove any bone splinters.

2. Seal the meat in a hot pan with a little oil, then remove from the pan and reserve while preparing the rest of the ingredients.

3. Add the meat and other ingredients to a casserole dish. Cook in a preheated oven between 160°C/325°F/Gas Mark 3 and 180°C/350°F/Gas Mark 4, and cook for 2–3 hours. Allow to cool, then skim off the fat. Reheat before serving.

PORK

Pork should be pale pink in colour and slightly marbled with small flecks of fat. There should be a layer of firm white fat with a thin elastic skin (rind), which can be scored before roasting to provide crackling. All cuts of pork are tender, as the pigs are slaughtered at an early age and are reared to be lean rather than fatty. Pork used to be well cooked, if not overcooked, due to the danger of the parasite trichina. This no longer applies, however, and it is now recommended that the meat is cooked less to keep it moist and tender.

Leg (1) Suitable for roasting. Sold either on the bone or boned. Can be cut into chunks and braised or casseroled.

Steaks (2) Suitable for grilling/broiling, frying,

griddling or barbecuing. A lean cut from the leg or the shoulder. Very tender but can be dry.

Fillet Sometimes called tenderloin and suitable for roasting, pan frying, griddling, grilling or barbecuing. A tender cut, often sold already marinated. Also good for slow-cooker cooking.

Loin (3) Suitable for roasting as a joint or cut into chops for griddling, frying or grilling. Often sold with the kidney intact.

Shoulder (4) Suitable for roasting. This includes

the 'spare rib' (not to be confused with the classic spare ribs from the belly), shoulder blade and the 'hand and spring' (lower shoulder). It is sold cubed for casseroles and stews or boned and rolled. A fatty cut.

Spare ribs From the belly. Suitable for grilling, barbecuing, casseroles and roasting. Sold either as 'Chinese', where thin ribs are marinated then cooked, or 'American Style' ribs, which are larger.

Escalope/cutlet Suitable for grilling/broiling, frying, griddling or barbecuing. Thin and very lean and tender, so requires very little cooking.

Minced/ground pork Suitable for burgers, meatballs or similar recipes. Often from the cheaper cuts and can be fatty.

Belly (5) Suitable for grilling/broiling or roasting. Can be salted before cooking. Is generally used to provide streaky bacon and is perhaps the fattiest cut of all. Also good for slow-cooker cooking.

Knuckle, hock and trotters These cuts are ideal to be cooked in a slow cooker.

Liver Suitable for casseroles or frying. Stronger than lamb or calves' liver.

Kidney Suitable for casseroles or frying. Often sold as part of a loin chop. Stronger than lambs' kidneys.

Bacon, Gammon and Ham

Bacon and gammon are cured pork produced by injections of brine as well as immersion in brine or salt. The meat becomes a much paler pink with creamy white fat and rind. For smoked bacon, the meat is smoked after it is cured, which produces the darker brown rind and meat. Another name for unsmoked bacon is 'green' bacon, although this term is not used as much these days. Before cooking, it is often soaked in cold water in order to remove some of the salt. Cuts of bacon vary according to regions and in some areas, bacon is called ham.

Back bacon Sold as rashers, small joints or chops and comes from the back. The rashers and chops can be grilled/broiled, griddled or fried.

Streaky/fatty bacon This is far fattier than back bacon and is often used to flavour dishes. When grilled/broiled, it will become very crisp and makes a perfect topping to add instant flavour to stews, casseroles or soups. It is often used to add fat where the food being cooked has little of its own – laid across a turkey breast, for example.

Middle cut bacon This is both back and streaky rasher and is excellent value for money. It can also be bought as a joint, which is perfect for boiling.

Collar bacon Bought either as thick rashers or boiling joints, this is an inexpensive cut.

Ham Many people think that gammon, bacon and ham are all the same. But not so. Strictly speaking, ham is the leg only, which is cut straight from the carcass and cured separately. Each region has their own recipe for curing hams and many have become well known over the years.

Gammon Sold either as gammon steaks, which many people would instantly recognize if served with a slice

of pineapple or a fried egg on top – these are grilled/broiled, griddled or fried – or as a joint, which can be boiled first and finished in the oven, completely boiled or completely cooked in the oven.

HOW TO COOK PORK

The same principles apply to pork as with beef and lamb, but the cooking times may differ slightly. Pork can be cooked by grilling/broiling, griddling, frying, roasting (which includes pot roasting), stewing, braising and slow cooking. Unlike beef and lamb, pork should be completely cooked through. It should not be eaten slightly pink; if it is, it may cause stomach problems.

Griddle, Fry or Grill/broil

Choose a cut that is suitable for this method of cooking *(see earlier list, pages 96–98)*. Cook by sealing first, then either continue to cook without a sauce, taking care that the meat does not dry, or add a sauce with vegetables and continue until completely cooked through. American-style spare ribs need cooking either on the barbecue or in the oven.

Roasting

Choose a cut that is suitable for this method of cooking (see earlier list).

1. If on the bone, preheat the oven to 220°C/425°F/Gas Mark 7; if boned and rolled, preheat to 190°C/375°F/Gas Mark 5.

2. Calculate the cooking time. Allow 25 minutes per 450 g/1 lb, plus 25 minutes, if still on the bone. If boned and rolled, allow 30–35 minutes per 450 g/1 lb, plus 30 minutes.

3. If a good crackling is required, score the rind into small diamonds with a very sharp knife, taking

care when doing this, rub the rind with a little good-quality oil and sprinkle with a little rock or table salt.

4. Place the joint on a trivet or rack so that it is not sitting directly in the roasting tin/pan. Place in the preheated oven and cook for the calculated time.

5. Twenty minutes before the end of the cooking time, sprinkle the top with a little extra rock or table salt.

Gammon Joints

You can cook the joint by boiling for half the cooking time and then roasting for the remaining time. Alternatively, cook by either boiling or roasting alone. Allow 20–25 minutes per 450 g/ 1 lb, plus 25 minutes for joints under 4.5 kg/10 lb and for joints over this weight, allow 15–20 minutes per 450 g/1 lb.

1. If you wish to soak the joint, do this for no more than 8 hours. Alternatively, you can use heat to speed the process along: place the joint in a large saucepan, cover with cold water, bring to the boil and skim off the scum that rises to the surface.

2. Remove from the heat and carefully discard the water; rinse both pan and joint, then return the

joint to the pan and cover again with more water. Return to the boil.

3. Add 1 peeled onion and carrot, a chopped celery stalk, a few parsley sprigs, whole cloves and some black peppercorns. Reduce the heat to a simmer, cover with a lid and either cook completely or for half the cooking time.

4. If completing the cooking in the oven, remove the joint from the pan, allow to cool for 5–10 minutes, then carefully strip off the rind and score the fat. Stud with whole cloves, if liked.

5. Wrap in kitchen foil and place in a preheated oven at 180°C/350°F/Gas Mark 4 to continue to cook for the rest of the calculated cooking time.

6. Remove the foil for the last 30 minutes of cooking time and increase the oven temperature to 220°C/425°F/Gas Mark 7. If liked, add a topping of demerara/turbinado sugar and orange zest to the joint, pressed into the fat, and continue to cook.

7. Baste occasionally with the juices. Remove from the oven once cooked and, if serving hot, allow to stand in a warm place for 10 minutes before carving.

OFFAL

These days of plenty have seen a decline in the eating of various cuts of offal (the edible internal parts of an animal) – sometimes also known as 'variety meats' – which is a shame, as it contains many nutrients. The most popular cuts are liver, kidney and oxtail, while sweetbreads (derived from certain glands), brain, tripe and heart in many cases are not eaten at all, or in very limited amounts (though sweetbreads have enjoyed a renewed popularity).

Calves' Liver

The best liver there is. Cut either in paper thin slices and lightly fried in butter on both sides to seal and eaten still slightly pink, or it can be cut slightly thicker and cooked in the same manner as lambs liver.

Lambs' Liver

This has a more pronounced flavour than calves' liver and care must be taken to remove all the tubes and gristle before cooking.

1. Rinse the liver and pat dry, then roll in seasoned flour.

2. Heat a pan with oil and/or butter and seal the liver on both sides.

3. Add onions and bacon and cook for a further 5 minutes, then either continue cooking for 5–8 minutes or add stock and continue to cook. The liver should feel tender when pierced with a sharp knife. It also can be eaten slightly pink. Take care not to overcook, as it will then be tough and chewy.

Pigs' Liver

This can be cooked in the same manner as lambs' liver or can be cooked in a casserole. It has a stronger, more pronounced flavour.

1. If wishing to casserole the liver, it should be cut into strips, sealed and added to vegetables such as onion, carrot and peppers with stock.
2. Cook in a preheated moderate oven at 180°C/350°F/Gas Mark 4 for about 40 minutes.

3. Add a little redcurrant jelly towards the end of the cooking time. Sprinkle with parsley to serve.

Ox Liver

The strongest tasting of all the livers, this is best casseroled. Take care to remove the tubes and gristle.

Heart

It is possible to buy lambs' hearts, but ox and calves' heart, which used to be very popular in the 1940s–50s, is rarely seen. The lamb heart has a milder flavour than the others and can be stuffed and cooked in a casserole or roasted whole.

Kidney

Ox, pigs' and lambs' kidney are the three types that are available, with lambs' kidneys being the most popular. They are used in casseroles – often with beef to make the classic steak and kidney pie or pudding – but can be cooked by themselves either to serve in a full English breakfast or in such classic dishes as rognons turbigo.

Poultry and Game

'Poultry' relates to turkey, chicken, poussin/game hen, duck and goose. Poultry and game are low in saturated fat and provide a good source of protein as well as selenium, an antioxidant mineral. Remove the skin from poultry before eating if following a low-fat diet.

GENERAL GUIDANCE

Most is sold plucked, drawn and trussed. Due to intensive farming used since the war, chicken in particular offers a good source of cheap meat. However, there is a growing movement to return to the more traditional methods of farming, for better quality and better animal welfare. Free-range and organically grown chickens offer a far more succulent bird with excellent flavour, although they tend to be more expensive.

Buying

Both home-grown and imported poultry, fresh and frozen are available. When buying fresh poultry, look for plump birds with a flexible breast bone, and no unpleasant odour or green tinge. Frozen poultry should be rock hard with no ice crystals, as this could mean that the bird has thawed and been re-frozen. Avoid any produce where the packaging is damaged.

Thawing and Storing

When thawing, place in the refrigerator on a large plate and ensure that none of the juices drip onto other foods. Once thawed, remove all packaging, remove the giblets, if any, and reserve separately. Place on a plate and cover lightly. Use within 2 days. Treat fresh poultry the same way.

Cooking

Ensure that poultry is thoroughly cooked and the juices run clear. Rest for 10 minutes before carving. Use within 2 days of cooking.

POULTRY

Turkey Whole birds are suitable for roasting and traditionally served at Christmas and Thanksgiving. Various turkey cuts are eaten throughout the year, ranging from breast steaks, diced thigh, escalopes/cutlets, small whole breast fillets, drumsticks, wings and minced/ground turkey. Specific cuts include:

- **Crown** The whole bird with the legs removed.
- **Saddle** Two turkey breast fillets, boned, with the wings inserted.
- **Butterfly** The two breast fillets.
- **Breast roll** Boned breast meat, rolled and tied or contained in a net.

Chicken Suitable for all cooking: roasting, grilling/broiling, griddling, stewing, braising, frying and barbecuing. Also available in many different

breeds and varieties, offering a good choice to the consumer. There are many cuts of chicken readily available: breast, wing and leg quarters, which are still on the bone, drumsticks, thighs, breast fillets, escalopes (boneless, skinless portions), diced and stir-fry strips, as well as minced/ground chicken.

Capon Suitable for roasting. These are young castrated cockerels and are normally bred for their excellent flavour.

Broilers These are chickens industrially reared quickly for their meat, which can be grilled/broiled, roasted or fried. Normally about 1.6 kg/3½ lb.

Poussin/game hen Suitable for roasting, grilling/broiling or casseroles. These are very young or spring chickens. Technically, in Commonwealth countries, in order to qualify as a 'poussin', they must have a carcass weight not exceeding 750 g/1 lb 10 oz or not be more than 28 days old at slaughter. In the US, birds that are sometimes referred to as 'poussins' are also known as 'Rock Cornish game

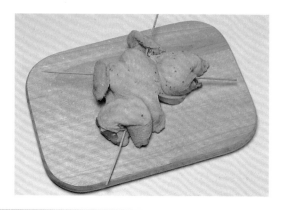

hens'. These are also young chickens (not game), but tend to be older – usually 5 to 6 weeks – and weigh no more than 900 g/2 lb. Poussins can be bought whole or spatchcocked – this is where the bird has had the backbone removed, and has then been then opened up and flattened, with skewers inserted diagonally through the legs and wings. One bird normally serves one person if small (450 g/1 lb), or two people if larger (900 g/2 lb).

Guinea fowl Suitable for roasting or casseroles. Available all year round, with a slightly gamey flavour. Most are sold ready for the table. When roasting, use plenty of fat or bacon as they can be dry.

Goose Suitable for roasting and often served as an alternative to turkey. Once dressed for the table, a goose will weigh around 4.5 kg/10 lb, but there is not much meat and this will serve around 6–8 people. It is very fatty, so pierce the skin well and roast on a trivet so the fat can be discarded or used for other cooking. Has a rich flavour, slightly gamey and a little like duck. Goose liver is highly prized and is used for foie gras.

Duck Suitable for roasting, grilling/broiling, griddling and casseroles. Ducklings between 6 weeks and 3 months old are normally used for the table;

adult ducks are not normally eaten. Duck has an excellent flavour, but it is a fatty bird, so cook on a trivet as for goose. Available fresh or frozen and, on average, weighs 1.75–2.75 kg/4–6 lb. Also available in cuts, as boneless breast fillets, ideal for grilling or griddling, and leg portions, suitable for casseroles. The meat is also used to make pâté. There are quite a few varieties available, with perhaps the best-known being the Aylesbury. Long Island/Pekin and Barbary are also popular varieties.

GAME

'Game' traditionally describes birds or animals that are hunted, not farmed, although some, such as pheasant, quails and rabbits, are now being farmed. Game is not as popular as most meat or poultry, as its stronger flavour is an acquired taste; some is even at its best when 'high' and smelling quite strong.

Game is not as readily available as other meats; this is partly because some game is protected by law and can only be hunted at certain times of the year, and there are not many game farms which produce all year round. It can be bought from either farm shops or butchers that have a game licence. Supermarkets also sell some, but the choice is limited. Normally sold oven-ready, it is advisable to buy from a

reputable source who can guarantee the quality. Most game needs hanging before eating and the longer it is hung, the more tender the meat. It is always hung by the retailer, so if you know that you would like some, it is a good idea to order beforehand. When buying game, it is important to know its age, as this dictates the method of cooking.

Pigeon Suitable for casseroles or stews, although the breast from young pigeons can be fried or grilled/broiled. Sometimes classified as poultry. Not widely available, mainly from licensed game sources.

Pheasant Suitable for roasting or casseroles. Breast, which can be grilled/broiled, is also available. Pheasant needs to be hung well to give the best flavour.

Rabbit Suitable for casseroles and stews and can be roasted or, if young, fried. Also makes excellent pies and fricassée. Sold whole or in portions, both with and without the bone, and available both fresh and frozen. Frozen rabbit often comes from China. If a milder flavour is preferred, soak in cold salted water for 2 hours before using. Generally regarded as country food and not served as haute cuisine.

Hare Suitable for casseroles. The best-known recipe is Jugged Hare, where the blood is used to thicken the dish. Has a strong, gamey flavour. If a milder flavour is preferred, soak in cold water for up to 24 hours. Available from reputable game dealers.

Venison Suitable for roasting, grilling/broiling, casseroles or making into sausages. The saddle, haunch and shoulder are best for roasting, although the loin and fillet can also be used. All cuts benefit from marinating to help tenderize.

Other game Less widely available are partridge, grouse, quail, snipe and boar.

COOKING GAME

When starting to cook game, it is advisable to follow a recipe to begin with. However, a general rule when cooking game is to 'keep it simple'.

Game Birds

Older birds are better cooked slowly in a casserole, while for young birds, the best way is to roast:

1. Once the bird has been plucked, drawn and trussed, lightly rinse inside and out and, if liked, place some herbs and a knob of butter in the body cavity. Cover the breast and legs with fatty bacon, as most game has little natural fat.

2. Roast in an oven preheated to 230°C/450°F/Gas Mark 8, for 15 minutes.

3. Reduce the oven to 190°C/375°F/Gas Mark 5 and cook for a further 30–40 minutes until tender. Sprinkle the breast with a little flour in order to crisp and brown the bird. (This is for a medium-sized bird such as pheasant; smaller birds will take a little less time.)

Game Meat

- Venison joints, steaks and chops are best if either roasted or casseroled. They also benefit from leaving overnight in a marinade.

- If a strong flavour is not required when cooking hare, soak in lightly salted cold water for at least 6 hours, changing the water occasionally.

Fish and Seafood

 Requiring only minimal cooking, all fish is an excellent choice for speedy and nutritious meals. There are two categories of fish: white and oily *(see pages 107–09)*. The remaining types of seafood can be divided into three categories: shellfish, crustaceans and molluscs *(see pages 111–13)*.

BUYING AND STORING SEAFOOD

Both types of fish are sold fresh or frozen as small whole fish, fillets or cutlets. Store as soon as possible in the refrigerator. Remove from the wrappings, place on a plate, cover lightly and store towards the top. Use within one day of purchase. If using frozen, thaw slowly in the refrigerator and use within one day of thawing.

Seafood should be eaten as fresh as possible. Live seafood gives the best flavour, as long as it is consumed on the day of purchase. If live is not available, buy from a reputable source and eat on the day of purchase, refrigerating until required.

TYPES OF FISH AND SEAFOOD

White Fish

White fish such as cod, haddock, plaice or coley are an excellent source of protein and have a low fat content. They also contain vitamin B12 and niacin, plus important minerals such as phosphorous, iodine, selenium and potassium.

Bass Sea fish. Suitable for grilling/broiling or frying. Large bass can be poached whole. Has very white flesh. At its best from May to August.

Sea bream/porgy Sea fish. Suitable for grilling/broiling, poaching and frying, can also be stuffed and baked or poached. Has white, firm flesh with a delicate flavour. At its best from June to December in the UK, or June to October in the USA.

Brill   Sea fish. Suitable for grilling/broiling, baking or poaching and serving cold. Has firm flesh with a slight yellow tinge. At its best from April to August, but available all year in the UK. Not fished in the USA.

Cod   Sea fish. Also available smoked. Suitable for all types of cooking. Perhaps the most popular and versatile of all fish, with white flesh and a very delicate flavour. At its best from October to May, but available all year round.

Coley/pollock   Sea fish. Suitable for all types of cooking. One of the cheaper varieties of fish. Has a greyish-coloured flesh which turns slightly white on cooking. Available all year round in the UK, and in the USA, depending on the variety.

Haddock   Sea fish. Also available smoked. Suitable for all types of cooking. Has a firm, white flesh with a slightly stronger flavour than cod. At its best from September to February, but available all year round, in the UK. Available from June to October in the USA.

Hake   Sea fish. Suitable for all methods of cooking. Has a firm, close-textured, white flesh and is considered to have a better flavour than cod. At its best from June to January, but available all year round.

Halibut   Sea fish. Suitable for all methods of cooking except deep frying. A large flat fish with excellent flavour. At its best from August to April, but available all year round in the UK. Available from March to November in the USA, depending on the variety.

John Dory   Sea fish. Suitable for poaching or baking whole, or fillets can be cooked as for sole. Has a firm, white flesh with good flavour. Can be difficult to find. At its best from October to December in the UK. Not fished in the USA.

Monkfish   Sea fish. Suitable for all methods of cooking, including roasting. A firm, white fish with 'meaty' texture. A good substitute for lobster. Only the tail is eaten – the central bone is normally discarded and the two fillets are used. Available all year round.

Plaice/flounder   Sea fish. The whole fish is suitable for grilling/broiling and pan frying, whilst fillets can be steamed, stuffed and rolled or used as goujons. A flat fish with distinctive dark grey/black skin with red spots. Has soft, white flesh with a very delicate flavour. Available all year round.

are soft and gelatinous. A white fish with a delicate flavour. At its best from September to April.

Sole Sea fish. Suitable for frying or grilling/broiling. Has a firm yet delicate white skin with a delicious flavour. Available all year round. Dover sole is recognized by its dark grey/black skin and is thought by many to be the finest of the sole varieties. Lemon sole is more pointed, and Witch and Torbay soles have the same qualities but the flavour is not as good.

Turbot Sea fish. Suitable for grilling/broiling or baking. Normally sold in cutlets, it has a creamy, white flesh with a delicious flavour which is reputed to be the best of all flat fish. At its best from March to August in the UK. Not fished in the USA.

Whiting Sea fish. Suitable for all methods of cooking. Cooked whole or in fillets, it has a white, delicately flavoured flesh. Available all year round, depending on the variety.

Oily Fish

Oily fish such as sardines, mackerel, salmon and herring have a higher fat content than white fish, but are an excellent source of Omega-3 polyunsaturated fatty acids, important in fighting heart disease, cancers and arthritis. Oily fish also contain niacin, B6, B12 and D vitamins, and the minerals selenium, iodine,

Red mullet Sea fish. Suitable for grilling/broiling, frying or baking. Has a firm, white flesh and red skin. At its best from May to September.

Skate Sea fish. Suitable for grilling/broiling, frying or poaching. Only the wings are eaten and the bones

potassium and phosphorous. The taste is stronger and more robust, enabling stronger flavours such as chilli and garlic to be used. It is recommended that at least one portion of oily fish should be eaten each week.

Herring   Sea fish. Suitable for frying, grilling/broiling or preserving in vinegar to make rollmops. A small fish with creamy-coloured flesh and fairly strong flavour, herring contains many bones. At its best in spring and summer.

Mackerel   Sea fish. Suitable for grilling/broiling and frying, whilst whole fish can be stuffed or baked. Has a distinctive bluish-coloured skin with blue/black lines and a creamy underside. At its best from late spring to early summer in the UK, or September to November in the USA.

Pilchard   Sea fish. Normally sold canned, but fresh pilchards are sometimes available. Similar to herring but smaller. Caught off the Cornish coast all year round, as well as in South America.

Salmon   Freshwater fish. The whole fish is suitable for poaching or baking to serve hot or cold. Fillets or cutlets can be fried, grilled/broiled, baked, steamed or barbecued. Farmed salmon has a milder flavour than wild, and the deep pink flesh is not as firm as that of wild salmon. The smaller wild salmon is much

paler in colour, with a far superior flavour and texture. Nowadays, farmed salmon is available all year round – wild salmon is at its best from February to August.

Sardine   Sea fish. Suitable for grilling/broiling or frying. Sardines are young pilchards, sprats or herrings. Available all year round.

Sprat   Sea fish. Suitable for frying or grilling/broiling. A small fish similar to herring and at its best from November to March. Not fished in the USA.

Brown trout Freshwater fish. Suitable for grilling/broiling or frying. The darker pink/red flesh is thought to be better than that of rainbow trout. At its best from March to September. Not fished in the USA.

Rainbow trout Freshwater fish. Suitable for grilling/broiling, frying, poaching and baking. Can be cooked whole or in fillets. Has a delicate pale pink flesh. Available all year round.

Salmon trout Freshwater fish. Suitable for poaching or baking whole. Cutlets or fillets can be fried, grilled/broiled or griddled. At its best from March to August. Treat as for salmon. Has a pinker flesh than salmon and the flavour is not as good.

Tuna Sea fish (mostly). Suitable for all methods of cooking. Does not count as an oily fish when canned. Available all year round. Due to overfishing concerns and danger to dophins, it is advisable to avoid bluefin and ideally yellowfin too, sticking to skipjack, preferably pole-and-line caught.

Other Kinds of Seafood

Shellfish include crustaceans, such as lobsters, which have hard shells that they shed and replace during their lifetime, and molluscs, which are animals that have hinged shells, such as scallops, or single shells, such as whelks. Other seafood includes cephalopods, such as squid, cuttlefish and octopus.

Clams Available all year round, but best in September. Usually eaten raw like oysters, or cook as for mussels.

Cockles Available all year round, but best in September. Normally eaten cooked. Eat plain with vinegar or use in recipes such as paella.

Crab Best from May to August, but also available canned and frozen. Normally sold ready-cooked either whole or as dressed crab.

Crayfish/crawfish Available from September to May. Resemble mini-lobsters and have a delicate flavour.

Mussels Best from September to March, but available most of the year due to farming. Normally sold live and eaten cooked.

Oysters Available from September to April. Usually eaten raw on day of purchase, but can be cooked. Must be eaten absolutely fresh.

Dublin Bay prawns Small prawn-like lobster. Also known as langoustines and scampi (not to be confused with the fried prawns known as scampi). Available all year round. Sold live or cooked. Other large prawns are often confused with them.

Tiger or king/jumbo prawns Available all year round, raw or cooked. Just some of many varieties of large prawns that are available. They are grey when raw and turn pink once cooked. Use within one day of purchasing if live or thawed.

Prawns/shrimp Available all year round, fresh or frozen. Shrimp are the smaller of the two and are not used as much in everyday cooking. Shrimp are brown in colour prior to cooking and prawns are grey, both turning pink once cooked.

Scallops Best from October to March, but available frozen all year. Usually sold live on the shell, but can be bought off the shell, often frozen. Scallops have a bright orange core which is edible. Serve cooked.

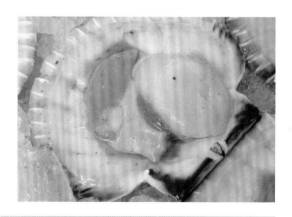

Squid or octopus Available all year round, sold fresh and frozen. Their black ink is often used in sauces and is also used to make black pasta.

Whelks Best from September to February. Usually sold cooked and shelled and served with vinegar.

Winkles/periwinkles Best from October to May in the UK, and May to November in the USA. Can be sold cooked or raw. Served cooked and with vinegar.

CLEANING SEAFOOD

Clean all seafood thoroughly.

Mussels and Clams
Discard any that do not close when tapped lightly before cooking. After cooking, discard any that have not opened.

Whole Fish
First, remove the scales. Using a round-bladed knife, gently scrape the knife along the fish, starting from the tail, towards the head. Rinse frequently.

Round fish Make a slit along the abdomen from the gills to the tail using a small, sharp knife and scrape out the innards. Rinse thoroughly.

Flat fish Open the cavity under the gills and remove the innards. Rinse. Remove the gills and fins and, if preferred, the tail and head. Rinse thoroughly in cold water and pat dry. Cutlets and fillets simply need lightly rinsing in cold water and patting dry.

SKINNING FISH
Flat Fish

1. Clean and remove the fins as before.

2. Make a small cut on the dark side of the fish across the tail and slip your thumb between the skin and flesh. Loosen the skin along the side.

3. Holding the fish firmly with one hand, rip the skin off with the other. The white skin can be removed in the same way.

Round Fish

These are normally cooked with the skin on, but if you do wish to skin them, do so as follows:

1. Start from the head and cut a narrow strip of skin along the backbone.

2. Cut below the head and loosen the skin with the point of the knife.

3. Dip your fingers in salt for a better grip and gently pull the skin down towards the tail. Take care not to break the flesh.

FILLETING FISH

Flat Fish

1. Use a sharp knife and make a cut along the line of bones.

2. Insert the knife under the flesh and carefully cut it with long sweeping strokes.

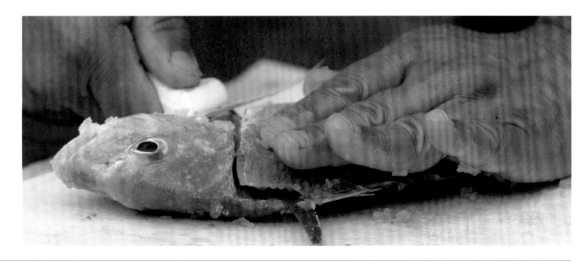

3. Cut the first fillet from the left-hand side, working from head to tail. Turn the fish round and repeat, this time cutting from tail to head.

4. Turn the fish over and repeat on this side.

Round Fish
This is suitable for larger fish such as salmon.

1. Cut along the centre of the back to the bone and then cut along the abdomen.

2. Cleanly remove the flesh with short, sharp strokes from the head downwards, pressing the knife against the bones.

3. Turn the fish over and repeat.

Herring and Mackerel
1. Discard the head, tail and fins and clean, reserving any roe if applicable.

2. Place on a chopping board and gently press along the backbone to open fully and loosen the bone.

3. Turn the fish over, ease the backbone up and remove, taking as many of the small bones as possible at the same time.

BASIC COOKING METHODS FOR FISH

Poached Fish
This method is suitable for fillets and small whole fish.

1. Clean the fish, remove scales if necessary and rinse thoroughly.

2. Place in a large frying pan with 1 small peeled and sliced onion and carrot, 1 bay leaf, 5 peppercorns and a few parsley stalks.

3. Pour over sufficient cold water to barely cover, then bring to the boil over a medium heat.

4. Reduce the heat to a simmer, cover and cook gently for 8–10 minutes for fillets and 10–15 minutes for whole fish.

5. When the fish is cooked, the flesh should yield easily when pierced with a round-bladed knife, and the fish should look opaque.

Grilled/broiled Fish

This method is suitable for fresh fish fillets (not smoked), sardines and other small whole fish. Make three slashes across whole fish before grilling.

1. Line a grill/broiler rack with kitchen foil and preheat the grill to medium-high just before grilling.

2. Lightly rinse the fish, pat it dry and place on the foil-lined grill rack. Season with salt and pepper and brush lightly with a little oil.

3. Cook under the grill for 8–10 minutes until cooked, turning the heat down if the fish is cooking too quickly.

4. Sprinkle with herbs or pour over a little melted butter or herb-flavoured olive oil to serve.

Griddled Fish

1. Rinse the fish fillet, pat dry and, if desired, marinate in a marinade of your choice for 30 minutes.

2. Heat a griddle pan until smoking and add the fish, skin-side down. Cook for 5 minutes, pressing the fish down with a fish slice.

3. Turn the fish over and continue to cook for a further 4–5 minutes until cooked to personal preference.

Vegetables and Salads

Vegetables add colour, texture, flavour and valuable nutrients to a meal. They play an important role in the diet, providing necessary vitamins, minerals and fibre. Vegetables are versatile: they can be served as an accompaniment to other dishes – they go well with meat, poultry and fish – or they can be used as the basis for the whole meal.

TYPES OF VEGETABLES

Vegetables are classified into different groups: leaf vegetables; roots and tubers; beans, pods and shoots; bulb vegetables; fruit vegetables; brassicas; cucumbers and squashes; sea vegetables; and mushrooms.

Leaf Vegetables

This includes lettuce and other salad leaves, such as oakleaf, frisée, radicchio, lamb's lettuce and lollo rosso as well as rocket/arugula, spinach, Swiss chard and watercress. These are available all year round, as most are now grown under glass. Many leaf vegetables, such as watercress and spinach, are delicious cooked and made into soups.

Roots and Tubers

This group includes beetroot/beet, carrots, celeriac, daikon, Jerusalem artichokes, parsnips, potatoes, radishes, salsify, sweet potatoes, swede/rutabaga, turnips and yams. Most are available all year round.

Beans, Pods and Shoots

This category includes all the beans, such as broad/fava beans, French/green beans, mangetout/snow peas and runner/string beans, as well as peas and sweetcorn, baby corn and okra. Shoots include asparagus, bamboo shoots, celery, chicory, fennel, globe artichokes and palm hearts. The majority are available all year round.

Bulb Vegetables

This is the onion family and includes all the different types of onion, from the common brown-skinned globe onion, Italian red onion and Spanish onion to shallots, pickling onions, pearl onions and spring onions/scallions. This category also includes leeks, chives and garlic. All are available throughout the year.

Brassicas

This is the cabbage family and includes all the different types of cabbage, broccoli, Brussels sprouts,

and other squashes. There are two types of squash – summer squashes, which include courgettes/zucchini, marrows and pattypan/white squashes, and winter squashes such as pumpkins and butternut, acorn, gem and spaghetti squashes. Courgettes and cucumbers are available all through the year, but pumpkins and other winter squashes and marrow are seasonal.

Sea Vegetables

The vegetables from this group may be quite difficult to find in supermarkets. The most readily available are seaweed (normally available dried) and sea kale.

Mushrooms and Fungi

This category includes all the different types of mushroom: the cultivated button mushrooms,

cauliflower, curly kale, Chinese cabbage, pak choi/bok choy and purple sprouting broccoli. Some of the cabbages are only seasonal, such as the winter cabbages Savoy cabbage and red cabbage, while there are also summer cabbages.

Fruit Vegetables

This group originates from hot climates, such as the Mediterranean, and includes aubergines/eggplants, avocados *(see page 129)*, chilli peppers, sweet peppers and tomatoes. These are available all year round, but are more plentiful in the summer.

Cucumbers and Squashes

These vegetables are members of the gourd family and include cucumbers, gherkins/pickles, pumpkins

chestnut mushrooms, large portobello or flat mushrooms, oyster and shiitake mushrooms, as well as wild mushrooms such as porcini (or ceps), morels, chanterelles and truffles. Cultivated mushrooms are available throughout the year, but wild ones are only around from late summer. If you collect your own wild mushrooms, make sure you correctly identify them before picking, as some are very poisonous and can be fatal if eaten. Dried mushrooms are also available, including porcini/ceps, morels and oyster mushrooms. They add a good flavour to a dish, but need to be reconstituted (soaked) before use.

HEALTH AND NUTRITION

Vegetables contain many essential nutrients and are especially high in vitamins A, B and C. They contain important minerals, in particular iron and calcium, and are also low in fat, high in fibre and have low cholesterol value. Red and orange vegetables, such as peppers and carrots, and dark green vegetables, such as broccoli, contain excellent anti-cancer properties as well as helping to prevent heart disease. Current healthy eating guidelines suggest that at least five portions of fruit and vegetables should be eaten per day, with vegetables being the more essential.

AVAILABILITY

There is a huge range of fresh vegetables on sale today in supermarkets, greengrocers and local markets. Also available is an ever-growing selection of fresh organic produce, plus a wide variety of seasonal pick-your-own vegetables from specialist farms. For enthusiastic gardeners, a vast range of vegetable seeds are available. In addition, the increase of ethnic markets has introduced an extensive choice of exotic vegetables, such as chayote and breadfruit.

With improved refrigeration and transport networks, vegetables are now flown around the world, resulting in year-round availability. Of course, you may want to do your best to stick to locally grown and seasonal food to avoid the higher environmental impact of imported and out-of-season vegetables.

BUYING

When buying fresh vegetables, always look for ones that are bright and feel firm to the touch, and avoid any that are damaged or bruised. Choose onions and garlic that are hard and not sprouting; avoid ones that are soft, as they may be damaged. Salad leaves and other leaf vegetables should be fresh, bright and crisp – do not buy any that are wilted, look limp or have yellow leaves.

STORING

Many vegetables can be kept in a cool, dry, dark place, but some should be refrigerated.

Root vegetables, tubers and winter squashes These should be kept in a cool, dry, dark place that is free of frost, such as a larder or garage. Winter squashes can be kept for several months if stored correctly.

Green vegetables, fruit vegetables and salad leaves These should be kept in the salad drawer of the refrigerator.

Vegetables such as peas and beans These do not keep for very long, so try to eat them as soon as possible after buying or picking.

PREPARING

Always clean vegetables thoroughly before using. Brush or scrape off any dirt and wash well in cold water. Prepare the vegetables just before cooking, as once peeled, they lose nutrients. Do not leave them in water, as valuable water-soluble vitamins will be lost.

Lettuce and other salad Wash leaves gently under cold running water and pull off and discard any tough stalks or outer leaves. Tear rather than cut the leaves. Dry thoroughly in a salad spinner or on paper towels before use, otherwise the leaves tend to wilt.

Spinach This should be washed thoroughly to remove all traces of dirt. Cut off and discard any tough stalks and damaged leaves.

Leeks These need to be thoroughly cleaned before use to remove any grit and dirt. After trimming the root and tough ends, make one cut lengthways (but not all the way along if you are intending to cook whole), and rinse under running water, getting right between the leaves.

Mushrooms Since mushrooms have a high water content, it is generally advised not to wash them, in order to avoid them absorbing even more water. Therefore, most mushrooms can just be wiped with paper towels or a damp cloth.

COOKING TECHNIQUES

Vegetables can be cooked in a variety of different ways, such as baking, barbecuing, blanching, boiling, braising, deep-frying, grilling/broiling, roasting, sautéing, steaming and stir-frying.

Boiling

Always cook vegetables in a minimum amount of water and do not overcook, or valuable nutrients will be lost. It is best to cut vegetables into even-sized pieces and cook them briefly.

Blanching and parboiling

These mean lightly cooking raw vegetables for a brief period of time, whether parboiling potatoes before roasting *(see page 70)*, cooking cabbage before braising or cooking leaf vegetables such as spinach. Spinach should be cooked in only the water clinging to its leaves for 2–3 minutes until wilted.

Blanching is also used to remove skins easily from tomatoes. Cut a small cross in the top of the tomato

and place in a heatproof bowl. Cover with boiling water and leave for a few seconds, then drain and peel off the skin.

Braising

This method is a slow way of cooking certain vegetables, notably red or white cabbage. The vegetable is simmered for a long period of time in a small amount of stock or water.

Steaming

This is a great way to cook vegetables such as broccoli, cauliflower, beans, carrots, parsnips and peas.

1. Cut the vegetables into even-sized pieces. Fill a large saucepan with about 5 cm/2 inches water, bring to the boil, then reduce to a simmer.

2. Place the vegetables in a metal steamer basket or colander and lower into the saucepan, then cover and steam until tender. Alternatively, use a plate standing on a trivet in the pan. Asparagus is traditionally cooked in an asparagus steamer. Do not let the water boil – it should just simmer.

3. Once tender, serve – there is no need to drain!

Microwaving

Vegetables can be cooked very successfully in the microwave and retain all their flavour and nutrients as well as their colour.

1. Prepare the vegetables, cutting into even-sized pieces. Place in a microwaveable bowl or arrange in a shallow dish.

2. For firm vegetables such as root vegetables, add 1–3 tablespoons water and cover with microwaveable wrap. Pierce in a couple of places. Cook on high for 2–4 minutes, depending on how many vegetables and which variety are being cooked. The more delicate vegetables will require less cooking time and less water. Refer to manufactuer's guidelines to be sure of times.

3. Remove from the oven and leave to stand for 1–2 minutes before serving. Do not season until after cooking, especially with salt, as this will toughen the vegetables.

Grilling/broiling (to remove skins)

For peppers, aubergines/eggplants and tomatoes, brush them with a little oil first, as they quickly dry out. To remove the skins from peppers:

1. Cut in half lengthways and deseed. Place skin-side up on the grill/broiler rack under a preheated hot grill and cook until the skins are blackened.

for stir-frying are: peppers, courgettes/zucchini, sugar snaps, beans, baby corn, carrots, pak choi/bok choy, spinach, tiny broccoli florets, spring onions/scallions, and mushrooms, as well as sprouting seed and shoots. To stir-fry:

1. Prepare all the vegetables before starting to cook. Peel, trim then cut any large pieces of vegetables into thin strips.

2. Heat a wok for 1 minute or until very hot, then add 1–2 tablespoons oil and carefully swirl the wok with the hot oil.

3. Add spices and flavours such as grated root ginger, chopped chilli and lemon grass and cook for 1 minute, then add the prepared vegetables, starting with the firmest, such as carrot.

2. Remove with tongs and place in a polythene/plastic bag, which will retain moisture. Seal and leave for 8–10 minutes, until the peppers are cool enough to handle.

3. Once cool, remove from the bag and carefully peel away the blackened skin.

Deep-frying

This method is suitable for most vegetables except leafy ones. The vegetables can be cut into small pieces, coated in batter, then deep-fried briefly in hot oil.

Stir-frying

Stir-frying is an excellent way of serving all manner of vegetables. This way, all the nutrients are retained due to the short cooking time. Vegetables suitable

4. Using a large spatula or spoon, stir-fry over a high heat, adding soy or other sauce as required. Cook for about 3–4 minutes, ensuring that the vegetables are still crisp.

Sweating

This method cooks vegetables such as onions in their own juices with or without a little oil. The vegetables should not be browned by this method and will retain masses of flavour and nutrients.

1. Prepare cleaned vegetables, cutting into small or medium-sized pieces.

2. Place in a frying pan or large saucepan and place over a low heat, with a little oil, if liked.

3. Cover with a lid and cook very gently in the steam that is generated. Stir occasionally. Use either in a casserole or as the basis for a soup or sauce.

Caramelizing Onions

This is very simple to do but requires patience.

1. Peel the onions – and garlic, if using – and slice very thinly.

2. Melt a little unsalted butter in a heavy-based saucepan; you will need about 50 g/2 oz/¼ cup (4 tbsp) butter to 450 g/1 lb/4 cups sliced onions.

3. Once the butter has melted, add the onions and garlic and cook very gently, stirring, until all the onions are coated in the butter. Continue to cook over a low heat, stirring occasionally with a wooden spoon.

4. If liked, 1 teaspoon sugar can be added, which will speed up the caramelizing process. The onion will slowly soften and then begin to change colour and finally will caramelize. It will take anything from 15–30 minutes.

Some cooks advocate cooking for up to 1 hour. This gives an intense flavour, but great care must be taken that the onions do not disintegrate or burn. Use as the basis of a brown sauce or casserole.

Roasting

Suitable for vegetables such as fennel, courgettes/zucchini, pumpkin, squash, peppers, garlic, aubergines/eggplants and tomatoes. Cut the vegetables into even-sized chunks. Heat some oil in a roasting tin/pan in a preheated oven at 200°C/400°F/Gas Mark 6. Put the vegetables in the hot oil, baste and roast in the oven for 30 minutes. Garlic can be split into different cloves or whole heads can be roasted. It is best not to peel them until cooked.

Fruit

 Fruits, like salad ingredients, require looking after so that they do not deteriorate more quickly than they should. Fruit comes in different categories, which includes berries, stoned fruit, citrus fruit, exotic fruit, currants and seeds.

BERRIES

These include strawberries, raspberries, blueberries, blackberries, tayberries, loganberries and gooseberries. Once they are ripe enough to eat, they need using quickly as they will not last for long – for this reason, ideally use either home-grown or locally grown produce. Do not prepare soft fruits until required and, if possible, store in a cool place and not the refrigerator. If this cannot be avoided, then remove and allow to come to room temperature for at least 30 minutes before using, or longer if time permits.

If there is a glut of a particular berry, freeze by rinsing lightly, then spreading out on a tray lined with a clean cloth or baking paper and 'open freeze' for 1–2 hours. Pack into polythene/freezer bags and label. They will keep for up to 2 months and are ideal for preserves, pies, summer pudding or crumbles/ crisps, sponges and fruit sauces.

Gooseberries

Gooseberries do not sit that comfortably with the other softer berries. There are two varieties: the cooking gooseberry and the dessert gooseberry. The cooking variety are small and hard when picked, and very tart. They need a reasonable amount of sugar. After picking, they need topping and tailing. They can be stored for up to a week in a cool place, but need using before they start to wrinkle. They are normally better if lightly cooked first, before using in crumbles and pies. Dessert gooseberries are far larger and are a golden yellow colour. Once completely ripe, they are delicious if eaten raw, but can be cooked as well. Store as for cooking gooseberries.

STONE FRUITS

These include all the Prunus (plum) fruits: common plums, cherries, apricots, peaches, nectarines, greengages and damsons. Plums can be home-grown or bought from farm shops, farmers' markets or supermarkets. Normally picked and sold slightly under-ripe (and thus hopefully avoiding wasp damage), they will ripen quickly if left in a warm sunny position. Otherwise, store uncooked stone fruit in a cool place, not in direct sunlight. The raw fruit does not freeze well.

Poaching Stone Fruit

Stone fruit can be gently poached.

1. Make a **sugar syrup** by dissolving 1–2 tbsp sugar in 150 ml/¼ pint/⅔ cup water.

2. Rinse the fruit and, if ripe enough, cut in half and remove the stone. Place in the syrup and cook for 8–10 minutes until tender. Leave to cool, then spoon into a serving dish or bowl and use as required.

Roasting Stone Fruits

Stone fruit can also be lightly roasted.

1. Rinse the fruit and either leave whole or cut in half.

2. Place in a roasting tin/pan, drizzle with a little clear honey and pour over about 150 ml/¼ pint/⅔ cup juice, wine or water.

3. Cook in a preheated oven at 180°C/350°F/ Gas Mark 4 for 15 minutes, or until the fruit is beginning to caramelize. Serve warm with ice cream.

CITRUS FRUITS

These include oranges, clementines, mandarins, kumquats, lemons, limes, grapefruits and pomelos and, unless you live in a sunny and humid part of the world, are likely to be imported. It is possible to grow lemons and oranges in cooler climates, but these trees are usually ornamental.

Citrus fruit play an important part in food and are often used to flavour both sweet and savoury dishes by the use of their zest and/or juice. The fruits themselves are normally eaten raw, and will keep for up to 2–3 weeks if stored in the salad compartment in the refrigerator. When wishing to eat or use in cooking, allow to come to room temperature for 30 minutes first. They do not freeze well.

APPLES AND PEARS

Store apples and pears in a cool, dark, dry place, if not to be used immediately. If keeping under-ripe home- or farm-picked apples and pears, wrap in newspaper or similar and store on racks so they do not touch each other. Check occasionally to ensure they are not going rotten.

Cooking v. Eating Apples

There are many varieties of apple, which include both cooking (or 'baking') as well as eating varieties. Bramley cooking apples are the best for cooking and the most widely available in the UK. American cooking apples include Gravenstein and Rome. Cooking apples cook extremely well due to the malic acid that they contain (they are of course rather tart, so more sugar is needed than if using eating apples). When gently poached or baked whole, they retain both flavour and shape, and they are excellent for making purées. Eating apples can be cooked too, but they may have a rubbery or chewy texture. Apples can be used in pies, baked and steamed hot puddings, crumbles/crisps, sponges and sauces.

Apple Purée

To make a purée for sponges and sauces:

1. Cut the apple into quarters, peel and core, then chop roughly.

2. Place in a saucepan with sugar to taste and a little water. Cook over a gentle heat for 10–15 minutes, stirring occasionally. Add a stick of cinnamon, if liked.

3. When the apple has collapsed, remove from the heat and either beat with a wooden spoon to the desired consistency or whizz in a food processor.

Pear Varieties

There are quite a few varieties of pears available, such as Comice, Conference, Williams and Beurre Hardy. Normally they crop well. Pears should be picked before they are thoroughly ripe and allowed to ripen in a cool place out of direct sunlight. They can be eaten both raw and cooked – often poached, or used in baked sponges such as upside-down pudding or in a compote.

Poaching Pears

If cooking pears, choose those that are slightly under-ripe.

1. Peel, halve and core, then place in a sugar or wine syrup *(see page 126)*. Gently poach for 10–15 minutes until tender.

2. If eating cold, allow to cool in the syrup. Using a slotted draining spoon, place the pear halves in a dish.

3. Boil the syrup vigorously for a few minutes to reduce, allow to cool, then pour over the pears and chill.

GRAPES

These are grown in many countries, mainly to produce wine, but also to be dried to produce raisins, sultanas/golden raisins and currants. However, they are also popular eaten fresh and whole. For eating purposes, the Thompson table grape comes in three different colours: white, black or flame (red), both with and without pips.

Store grapes in the refrigerator for up to 1 week and remember to rinse lightly before eating. If kept in a fruit bowl, they will not keep for long. Grapes can be used both in savoury and sweet dishes, but mainly sweet.

CURRANTS

There are three varieties of currants: white, red and black, with blackcurrants being the most popular and readily available when in season. White currants are rarely on sale, although they can sometimes be found in pick-your-own outlets. Redcurrants are used mainly commercially for making redcurrant jelly, although when in season, they are on sale in supermarkets and farm shops.

Storing

Use currants as soon as possible after picking. Leave in the refrigerator for no longer than 2 days. If you need to keep them for longer, pick over the currants, discarding the stems and any leaves, rinse lightly, then spread out on paper towels until dry. Line a baking tray with either baking paper or kitchen foil and spread the fruit in a single layer. Open freeze for at least 1 hour, then carefully place in a polythene bag, label and freeze for up to 2–3 months. They can be used from frozen.

To Use

If still attached to the stems, hold a stem of currants and strip off the fruit with the prongs of a fork, rinse and use as required. Currants can be gently cooked in a sugar syrup and used in pies or crumbles/crisps, with the addition of some more sugar, as currants can be quite tart, unless very ripe. The fruit is excellent for making jelly or combined with other soft fruits to make summer pudding *(see page 338)*, as well as pies, sponges, sweet sauces and jam. They also make an attractive garnish for both sweet and savoury dishes.

EXOTIC FRUITS

This category covers many different types of fruit, most of which are readily available in our supermarkets thanks to air freight. These fruits include pineapples, melons, mangos, papayas, bananas, figs, dates, cape gooseberries, lychees, pomegranates, passion fruits, granadillas and persimmons (Sharon fruit).

In most cases, the fruits are eaten raw and should be kept in a cool, dark place until ripe enough to eat. It is inadvisable to keep fruit, with the exception of berries, in the refrigerator, as chilling slows up the ripening process and the flavour will be affected if eaten chilled. If wishing to cook any of these exotic fruits, gently poach in a sugar syrup. However, most of them are better eaten raw.

AVOCADOS

Avocados are technically fruit (in fact, they are a large 'berry'), but in culinary terms you might be forgiven for calling them vegetables, since they are normally served in savoury dishes. They have a smooth, creamy texture with pale cream flesh with a bright green flesh between the skin and the cream flesh. If slightly under-ripe, leave in a warm place for 1–2 days and, once ripe, store in a cool, dark place (but not the refrigerator) and use quickly.

Using Avocados

Perhaps the dish that avocados are best-known for is guacamole, a South American salsa, but they can also be used in salads, prawn cocktails or on a mixed hors d'oeuvre platter. Avocados are generally served cold, but can be stuffed and baked. If baking, do ensure that the avocado is firm, but for most other uses, it should be ripe. This is tested by gently squeezing. If it yields easily, it is ready to use. Cut round the centre from top to bottom, then gently twist. Discard the stone in the centre, peel and use as required. Discard any black or very soft flesh.

RHUBARB

Rhubarb is technically a vegetable, but is generally served as a dessert and so is often thought of as a fruit. It could easily be good in a savoury dish too, though. There are two types of rhubarb: 'garden' (or 'ordinary'), which has a thick greenish stalk flecked with red, and a 'champagne' variety, which has pale pink, very thin tender stems and is normally grown under glass. Once

picked, store the champagne variety in a cool, dark place and use within 2 days. Home-grown varieties can last up to 4 days, again stored in a cool, dark place.

Using Rhubarb

The leaves must never be eaten on either as they are poisonous. Rhubarb is always cooked – either from raw, in crumbles *(see page 211)* or pies, or first on its own, as below. It is also used in pickles and preserves.

1. Discard the leaves, if applicable, then trim the base of the stem and wash. Cut into small lengths and place in a pan.

2. Add sugar to taste – about 50–75 g/2–3 oz/ ¼–⅓ cup per 450 g/1 lb/3½ cups diced rhubarb, depending on how sweet you like your food (bearing in mind that rhubarb is quite tart).

3. Add some ground ginger or chopped root ginger or ginger wine, as this will also help moderate the tartness.

4. Add 4–6 tablespoons water (the rhubarb will produce juice on cooking). Cook for 5–10 minutes.

Rhubarb can also be cooked in the microwave – prepare as above and cook on high for 3–5 minutes in a microwaveable bowl lightly covered with plastic wrap.

Key Recipes: Sauces

 Sauces are an integral part of a meal, used both to enhance and complement food. Some are quick and easy to make, while others are more involved and take time, but all are well worth the effort.

WHITE POURING SAUCE

This is the basic white sauce from which all manner of other sauces diverge.

Makes 300 ml/½ pint/1¼ cups

15 g/½ oz/1 tbsp butter or margarine
2 tbsp plain/all-purpose white flour
300 ml/½ pint/1¼ cups milk
salt and freshly ground black pepper

1. Melt the butter or margarine in a small saucepan and stir in the flour. Cook, stirring, over a gentle heat for 2 minutes.

2. Draw the pan off the heat and gradually stir in the milk.

2. Return the pan to the heat and cook, stirring with a wooden spoon, until the sauce thickens and coats the back of the spoon. Add seasoning to taste and use as required.

3. For a coating sauce, use 25 g/1 oz/2 tbsp butter or margarine and 3 tablespoons flour to 300 ml/½ pint/1¼ cups liquid. Proceed as above.

4. For a binding sauce, use 50 g/2 oz/¼ cup (4 tbsp) butter or margarine and 50 g/2 oz/½ cup flour to 300 ml/½ pint/1¼ cups liquid and proceed as above.

Herb Sauce

Make a white sauce as before, then stir in 1 tbsp freshly chopped herbs, such as parsley, basil, oregano or a mixture of fresh herbs.

Cheese Sauce

Proceed as before, to your desired consistency, stirring in 1 tsp dried mustard powder with the flour. When the sauce has thickened, remove from the heat

and stir in 50 g/2 oz mature Cheddar cheese, grated, or any other cheese of choice. Stir until melted.

Mushroom Sauce

Make as before and lightly sauté 50 g/2 oz/1½ cups sliced mushrooms in 15 g/½ oz/1 tbsp butter for 3 minutes, or until tender. Drain and stir into the prepared white sauce.

BECHAMEL SAUCE

This is the classic white sauce used for many classic dishes, such as lasagne.

Makes 300 ml/½ pint/1¼ cups

1. Peel 1 small onion and place in a small saucepan together with a small piece of peeled carrot, a small celery stalk, 3 whole cloves and a few black peppercorns. Add 300 ml/½ pint/1¼ cups milk and bring slowly to just below boiling point.

2. Remove from the heat, cover with a lid and leave to infuse for at least 30 minutes.

3. When ready to use, strain off the milk and use to make a white sauce as before. If liked, 1–2 tablespoons single/light cream can be stirred in at the end of cooking.

SOUBISE SAUCE

Ideal to serve with beef, pork or lamb.

Makes about 350 ml/12 fl oz

2 medium onions
25 g/1 oz/2 tbsp unsalted butter
1 tbsp water
300 ml/1/2 pint/1¼ cups prepared béchamel
 sauce *(see opposite page)*
salt and freshly ground black pepper

1. Peel and finely chop the onions. Melt the
 butter in a heavy-based saucepan, add the
 onions and water and cook over a gentle heat
 for 10–15 minutes until soft. Stir frequently
 during cooking.

2. When soft, pass the onions through a blender or
 food processor to form a purée. Stir into the
 prepared béchamel sauce, add seasoning to taste
 and reheat before serving.

AURORE SAUCE

Ideal to serve with fish, egg and chicken dishes.
If wishing to use with cold dishes such as prawn

cocktail, replace the béchamel sauce with freshly
prepared mayonnaise and replace the butter with
2 tablespoons single/light cream.

Makes 300–325 ml/11–11½ fl oz/1¼–1⅓ cups

300 ml/½ pint/1¼ cups prepared béchamel
 sauce *(see opposite page)*
1 tbsp tomato purée/paste
25 g/1 oz/2 tbsp unsalted butter
salt and freshly ground black pepper

Heat the béchamel sauce, if cold, then stir in the tomato purée/paste and butter. Stir over a gentle heat until blended, then add seasoning to taste. Use with hot dishes.

BREAD SAUCE

Normally served with poultry, especially roast turkey.

Makes about 600 ml/1 pint/2½ cups

600 ml/1 pt/2½ cups milk
1 small onion, peeled
3–4 whole cloves
1–2 bay leaves, preferably fresh
few black peppercorns
1 blade mace
125 g/4 oz/2¾ cups fresh white breadcrumbs
25 g/1 oz/2 tbsp butter
salt and freshly ground black pepper
¼ tsp, or to taste, freshly grated nutmeg
1 tsp freshly chopped parsley (optional)

1. Pour the milk into a heavy-based saucepan. Stud the onion with the whole cloves and add to the milk together with the bay leaves, peppercorns and mace.

2. Bring slowly to the boil, then remove from the heat and cover with the lid. Leave to infuse for at least 30 minutes.

3. When ready to make, strain the milk, then return to the rinsed pan. Add the breadcrumbs and cook for 5–10 minutes, stirring frequently, until thickened.

4. Add the butter with seasoning and the nutmeg to taste. Heat until the butter has melted, stir well and spoon into a warm serving dish. Sprinkle with the parsley or nutmeg and serve.

If a stronger flavour is preferred, leave the onion studded with the cloves in the sauce until serving. For a creamier sauce, replace 2–3 tablespoons of the milk with single/light cream, but add the cream at the end of cooking.

GRAVY

Make your meat gravy at the same time as your roast dinner, using the remnants of the meat and its juices.

Makes 300 ml/½ pint/1¼ cups

1. Once the meat is cooked, remove from the roasting tin/pan, cover and keep warm.

If no meat juices are available, heat 2 tablespoons oil and stir in 1–2 tablespoons flour. Cook for 2 minutes, then draw off the heat and stir in 300 ml/½ pint/1¼ cups stock of your choice. Return to the heat and cook, stirring, until thickened. Add seasoning, flavourings and gravy browning according to personal preference.

ESPAGNOLE SAUCE

Ideal with most meat dishes requiring a sauce, and is the basis of many other meat sauces.

Makes about 300 ml/½ pint/1¼ cups

1 streaky/fatty bacon rasher,
   de-rinded and chopped
25 g/1 oz/2 tbsp unsalted butter
1 shallot, peeled and chopped
few mushroom stalks, wiped and chopped
1 small carrot, peeled and chopped
3 tbsp plain white/all-purpose flour
300 ml/½ pint/1¼ cups
   good-quality beef stock
1 bouquet garni *(see page 78)*
2 tsp tomato purée/paste
salt and freshly ground black pepper
1 tbsp sherry (optional)

2. Pour off all but 2–3 tablespoons of the meat juices and heat the remainder on the hob/stove top.

3. Stir in 2 tablespoons plain white/all-purpose flour and cook for 2 minutes, stirring the sediment that is left in the tin/pan into the gravy.

4. Draw off the heat and gradually stir in 300 ml/½ pint/1¼ cups stock, according to the flavour of the meat. Return to the heat and cook, stirring, until the gravy comes to the boil and thickens.

5. Add seasoning to taste and, if liked, a little port, wine or redcurrant jelly. Gravy browning can be added to give a darker colour.

135

5. Add the bouquet garni and tomato purée/paste with seasoning, then reduce the heat to very low. Cook for 1 hour, stirring occasionally to prevent the sauce sticking to the base of the pan. If the sauce is becoming too thick, reduce the heat a little more and add a little extra stock.

6. Allow to cool, then skim off any fat that may have risen to the surface. Reheat when wishing to use, adding seasoning to taste and the sherry, if using.

DEMI-GLAZE (OR DEMI-GLACE)

Ideal to serve with beef recipes.

Makes 450 ml/¾ pint/1¾ cups

150 ml/¼ pint/⅔ cup beef gravy or
jellied beef stock
300 ml/½ pint/1¼ cups Espagnole sauce
(see pages 135–36)

Stir the gravy or stock into the Espagnole sauce and boil until a smooth and glossy sauce is achieved and the sauce is thick enough to coat the back of a wooden spoon. This is the easy version of the classic sauce and gives an excellent result.

1. Place the bacon in a heavy-based medium saucepan and cook for 2–3 minutes until the fat begins to run.

2. Add the butter and, when melted, add the shallot, mushroom stalks and chopped carrot. Cook for 3–4 minutes until the shallot has softened.

3. Sprinkle in the flour and cook for 5–6 minutes until the flour has browned. Take care not to burn the flour.

4. Draw the pan off the heat and gradually stir in the stock, then return to the heat and cook, stirring, until thickened.

BARBECUE SAUCE

Ideal to serve with all barbecued foods. For the more delicately flavoured foods, reduce the spices a little so as not to overpower the food.

Makes about 350 ml/12 fl oz/1 1/2 cups

2 tbsp olive or sunflower/corn oil
2 medium onions, peeled and chopped
1–2 garlic cloves, peeled and crushed
1 tbsp tomato purée/paste
1 tbsp vinegar
1–2 tsp prepared wholegrain mustard
1 tbsp, or to taste, Worcestershire sauce

1–2 tbsp, or to taste, demerara/turbinado sugar
300 ml/1/2 pint/1 1/4 cups vegetable or beef stock

1. Heat the oil in a heavy-based saucepan and fry the onions for 3 minutes. Add the garlic and cook for a further 2 minutes.

2. Stir the remaining ingredients together, then add to the onion and garlic mixture and bring to the boil. Reduce the heat to a simmer and cook for 15 minutes, stirring occasionally. Use as required.

RED WINE SAUCE

Ideal to serve with all red meats and game.

Makes about 200 ml/7 fl oz/3/4 cup

150 ml/1/4 pint/2/3 cup Espagnole sauce
   (see page 135–36) or gravy
1–2 tsp redcurrant jelly
50 ml/2 fl oz/scant 1/4 cup red wine

Place all the ingredients into a heavy-based saucepan and bring to the boil, stirring occasionally, until blended. When boiling, reduce the heat to a gentle simmer and cook for 5–10 minutes until clear and syrupy. Serve.

HOLLANDAISE SAUCE

Ideal with poached eggs, asparagus, other vegetables and fish.

Makes 150–200 ml/ 5–7 fl oz/⅔–¾ cup

2 tbsp wine or
    tarragon vinegar
1 tbsp water
2 medium/large egg yolks
75–125 g/3–4 oz/⅓ cup (6 tbsp)–½ cup (8 tbsp)
    unsalted butter
salt and freshly ground black pepper

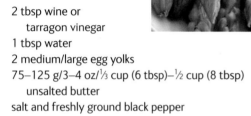

1. Pour the vinegar and water into a small saucepan. Bring to the boil and boil for 1–2 minutes or until reduced by half. Leave to cool for a few minutes.

2. Beat the egg yolks, then whisk in the cooled vinegar. Place the bowl over a pan of gently simmering water and whisk in the butter a little at a time, whisking well after each addition.

3. When all the butter has been added and the sauce has thickened, add seasoning to taste. Serve warm.

BÉARNAISE SAUCE

Ideal to serve with fish, steak, vegetables and poached eggs.

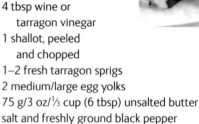

Makes about 150 m/¼ pint/⅔ cup

4 tbsp wine or
    tarragon vinegar
1 shallot, peeled
    and chopped
1–2 fresh tarragon sprigs
2 medium/large egg yolks
75 g/3 oz/⅓ cup (6 tbsp) unsalted butter
salt and freshly ground black pepper

1. Pour the vinegar into a small saucepan and add the chopped shallot and fresh tarragon. Bring to the boil and boil for 2–3 minutes until reduced by half. Strain and leave to cool for a few minutes.

2. Whisk the egg yolks, then beat in the cooled vinegar. Place the bowl over a pan of gently simmering water.

3. Whisk in the butter a little at a time, whisking well

after each addition. When all the butter has been added and the sauce is thickened, add seasoning to taste and serve warm. If a thinner sauce is required, stir in a little extra vinegar or lemon juice.

TOMATO SAUCE

Ideal with pasta.

Makes 450 ml/¾ pint/1¼ cups

1 tbsp olive or sunflower/corn oil
1 small onion, peeled and finely chopped
1–2 garlic cloves, peeled and crushed
50 g/2 oz streaky bacon, chopped (optional)
4 ripe tomatoes, peeled if preferred, chopped
    or 400 g/14 oz can chopped tomatoes
1–2 tbsp tomato purée/paste
150 ml/¼ pint/⅔ cup vegetable stock
salt and freshly ground black pepper
1 tbsp freshly chopped oregano, marjoram or basil

1. Heat the oil in a saucepan and sauté the onion, garlic and bacon, if using, for 5 minutes.

2. Add the chopped tomatoes and sauté for a further 5 minutes, stirring occasionally.

3. Blend the tomato purée/paste with the stock, then pour into the pan, add seasoning and herbs and bring to the boil. Cover with a lid, reduce the heat and simmer for 12–15 minutes until a chunky sauce is formed.

4. Blend in a food processor to form a slightly less chunky sauce and then rub through a fine sieve if a smooth sauce is preferred. Adjust seasoning and use as required.

CURRY SAUCE

Makes 300 ml/½ pint/1¼ cups

1 tbsp sunflower/corn oil
1 onion, peeled and chopped
2–4 garlic cloves, peeled and crushed
1 celery stalk, trimmed and chopped
1–2 red chillies, deseeded and chopped
1 tsp ground coriander
1 tsp ground cumin, ½ tsp turmeric
1 tbsp plain/all-purpose white flour
450 ml/¾ pint/1¾ cups vegetable stock
salt and freshly ground black pepper
1 tbsp freshly chopped coriander/cilantro (optional)

1. Heat the oil in a saucepan and sauté the onion, garlic, celery and chillies for 5–8 minutes or until softened.

2. Add the spices and continue to sauté for a further 3 minutes, stirring frequently.

3. Sprinkle in the flour, cook for 2 minutes, then slowly add the stock and bring to the boil. Cover with a lid, reduce the heat and simmer for 15 minutes, stirring occasionally.

4. Add seasoning to taste and stir in the chopped coriander/cilantro, if using. Use as required.

MINT SAUCE

Ideal with lamb.

Makes 120 ml/4 fl oz/½ cup

15 g/½ oz/¾ cup fresh mint
1 tbsp caster/superfine sugar
3–4 tbsp white wine vinegar or other
    vinegar of choice

1. Discard the stalks from the mint, rinse the leaves and dry. Finely chop and place in a sauceboat or small bowl.

2. Pour over 3–4 tablespoons hot but not boiling water, then stir in the sugar until dissolved. Stir in the vinegar and use as required.

APPLE SAUCE

Ideal with pork.

Makes 300 ml/½ pint/1¼ cups

450 g/1 lb Bramley/tart cooking apples, peeled,
    cored and chopped
15 g/½ oz/1 tbsp butter
2–3 tbsp sugar

1. Place all the ingredients with 2 tablespoons
water in a saucepan and cook over a gentle
heat for 10 minutes, or until the apples are
tender, stirring occasionally.

Take care that the apples do not burn on the base
of the pan.

2. Remove from the heat and either rub through
a sieve to form a smooth purée or beat with a
spoon to give a chunkier sauce.

The apple sauce can be flavoured with 1 tablespoon
finely grated orange or lemon zest and 2–3 whole
cloves, which you should remove before serving.

Alternatively, add 1 lightly bruised cinnamon stick
(remove before serving).

CRANBERRY SAUCE

Ideal with poultry, especially roast turkey.

450 g/1 lb fresh or thawed frozen cranberries
150 ml/¼ pint/⅔ cup orange juice
50 g/2 oz/¼ cup light muscovado/golden brown
    sugar, or to taste
1–2 tbsp port (optional)

1. Rinse the cranberries and place in a saucepan
with the orange juice and sugar. Place over a
gentle heat and cook, stirring occasionally, for
12–15 minutes until the cranberries are soft
and have popped.

2. Remove from the heat and stir in the port,
if using. Use as required.

FRENCH DRESSING

The classic salad vinaigrette.

Makes 175 ml/
6 fl oz/scant ¾ cup

½ tsp dried
    mustard powder
½–1 tsp caster/superfine sugar, or to taste
salt and freshly ground black pepper
3 tbsp white wine vinegar
120 ml/4 fl oz/½ cup extra virgin olive oil

Place all the ingredients in a screw-top jar and shake vigorously. Use as required.

Other flavours can be created by substituting the vinegar: try raspberry, cider or balsamic vinegar with a little clear honey in place of the sugar.

Also, you could try replacing the dried mustard powder with 1 teaspoon wholegrain mustard.

Freshly chopped herbs can also be added to the dressing.

MAYONNAISE

Invaluable and versatile as a salad dressing and sandwich filler, among many other uses.

Makes 175 ml/6 fl oz/scant ¾ cup

1 medium/large egg yolk
¼ tsp dried mustard powder
salt and freshly ground black pepper
½ tsp caster/superfine sugar
150 ml/¼ pint/⅔ cup extra virgin olive oil
1 tbsp white wine vinegar or lemon juice

1. Place the egg yolk in a bowl and stir in the mustard powder with a little seasoning and the sugar. Beat with a wooden spoon until blended.

2. Gradually add the oil, drop by drop, stirring briskly with either a whisk or wooden spoon. If the mixture becomes too thick, beat in a little of the vinegar or lemon juice. If the mayonnaise curdles, place a further egg yolk in a separate bowl, then slowly beat into the curdled mixture.

3. When all the oil has been added, stir in the remaining vinegar or lemon juice and adjust the seasoning. Store, covered, in the refrigerator until required.

TARTARE SAUCE

The classic piquant sauce for fish.

Makes 175 ml/6 fl oz/scant ¾ cup

150 ml/¼ pint/⅔ cup prepared mayonnaise
1 tbsp freshly chopped tarragon
1 tbsp freshly chopped parsley
pinch cayenne pepper (optional)
1 tbsp capers, rinsed and chopped
1 tbsp finely chopped gherkins/pickles
1 tbsp lemon juice

1. Mix all the ingredients together in a small bowl, cover and leave for at least 30 minutes for the flavours to blend. Use as required.

SABAYON SAUCE

Ideal for serving with fruit dishes.

Makes about 150 ml/¼ pint/⅔ cup

50 g/2 oz/¼ cup caster/superfine sugar
4 tbsp water
2 medium/large egg yolks, beaten
juice and grated zest of ½ lemon
1 tbsp sherry
4 tbsp single/light cream

1. Place the sugar into a heavy-based saucepan and add the water. Place over a gentle heat and cook, stirring frequently, until the sugar has dissolved.

2. Bring to the boil and boil for 3 minutes, or until syrupy.

3. Slowly beat the syrup into the eggs, then whisk until pale and frothy. Add the lemon juice and zest with the sherry and continue to whisk for a further 2–3 minutes. Stir in the cream and serve.

BRANDY SAUCE

This sauce is quick and easy to make and is ideal to serve with Christmas pudding and mince pies, as well as steamed and baked fruit puddings.

Makes 600 ml/1 pint/2½ cups

2 tbsp cornflour/cornstarch
600 ml/1 pint/2½ cups milk
15 g/½ oz/1 tbsp butter
25–50 g/1–2 oz/2 tbsp–¼ cup caster/
    superfine sugar
2–3 tbsp brandy

1. Blend the cornflour/cornstarch with 4 tablespoons of the milk to a smooth paste.

2. Heat the remaining milk to almost boiling point.

3. Draw the pan off the heat and stir in the cornflour paste.

4. Return to the heat, bring to the boil and cook for 2–3 minutes, stirring, until smooth and thickened.

5. Remove from the heat and add the butter and caster/superfine sugar. Stir until smooth, then stir in the brandy. Serve.

CHOCOLATE SAUCE

Makes 150 ml/¼ pint/⅔ cup

100 g/3½ oz dark/bittersweet chocolate
15 g/½ oz/1 tbsp butter
1 tsp golden or corn syrup
5 tbsp semi-skimmed/low-fat milk

1. Break the chocolate into small pieces and place in a small heavy-based saucepan.

2. Add the remaining ingredients and place over a gentle heat, stirring occasionally, until smooth. Pour into a small jug and use as required.

BUTTERSCOTCH SAUCE

Makes 300 ml/½ pint/1¼ cups

75 g/3 oz/⅓ cup light muscovado/golden brown sugar
1 tbsp golden or corn syrup
50 g/2 oz/¼ cup (4 tbsp) butter
200 ml/7 fl oz/¾ cup single/light cream

1. Place the sugar, syrup and butter in a heavy-based saucepan and heat gently, stirring occasionally, until blended.

2. Stir in the cream and continue to heat, stirring, until the sauce is smooth. Use as required.

SYRUP SAUCE

Makes 150 ml/¼ pint/⅔ cup

5 tbsp golden or corn syrup
2 tbsp lemon juice
1 tbsp arrowroot

1. Pour the syrup and lemon juice into a small pan and add 3 tablespoons water. Bring to the boil.

2. Blend the arrowroot with 1 tablespoon water, then stir into the boiling syrup. Cook, stirring, until the sauce thickens and clears. Serve.

LEMON SAUCE

Makes 150 ml/¼ pint/⅔ cup

grated zest of 1 large lemon, preferably unwaxed
5 tbsp fresh lemon juice, strained
2 tbsp caster/superfine sugar
1 tbsp arrowroot
knob butter

1. Place the lemon zest and juice in a saucepan with 4 tablespoons water. Stir in the sugar and heat, stirring, until the sugar has dissolved. Bring to the boil.

2. Blend the arrowroot with 1 tablespoon water, then blend into the boiling sauce. Cook, stirring, until the sauce thickens and clears.

3. Add the butter and cook for a further 1 minute. Note that an orange can be used in place of the lemon, or a combination of the two.

MELBA SAUCE

Makes 300 ml/½ pint/1¼ cups

350 g/12 oz/2 cups fresh or thawed
    frozen raspberries

3 tbsp sugar, or to taste
1 tbsp lemon or orange juice

1. Clean the raspberries, if using fresh, then place all the ingredients and 4 tablespoons water in a heavy-based saucepan and place over a gentle heat. Bring to the boil, then reduce the heat and simmer for 5–8 minutes until the fruits are really soft.

2. Remove from the heat, cool slightly, then blend in a food processor to form a purée. Rub through a fine sieve to remove the pips and use as required.

JAM/JELLY SAUCE

Makes 150 ml/¼ pint/⅔ cup

4 tbsp jam/jelly, such as raspberry, apricot,
    strawberry or marmalade
150 ml/¼ pint/⅔ cup fruit juice or water
1 tbsp arrowroot, 1 tbsp lemon juice

1. Place the jam/jelly and the fruit juice or water
in a small pan and heat, stirring, until blended.

2. Rub the mixture through a fine sieve to remove
any pips, return to the pan and bring to the boil.

3. Blend the arrowroot with the lemon juice and stir
into the sauce. Cook, stirring, until the sauce
thickens and clears. For a thicker sauce, use half
the amount of fruit juice or water.

CUSTARD

Makes 300 ml/½ pint/1¼ cups

300 ml/½ pint/1¼ cups milk
2 tbsp plain/all-purpose white flour
1 medium/large egg
few drops vanilla extract

15 g/½ oz/1 tbsp butter
1–2 tbsp caster/superfine sugar, or to taste

1. Heat the milk to lukewarm.

2. Sift the flour into a bowl, make a well in the
centre and add the egg. Beat the egg into the
flour, drawing the flour in from the sides of the
bowl and slowly adding half the warmed milk.
When all the flour has been incorporated, beat
well to remove any lumps, then stir in the
remaining milk.

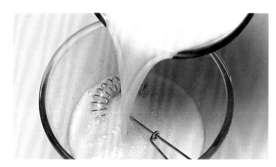

3. Strain into a clean saucepan, place over a gentle
heat and cook, stirring, until the sauce thickens
and coats the back of the wooden spoon.

4. Stir in the vanilla extract, butter and sugar to
taste. Stir until blended and use as required.

Marinades and Butters

Marinades are used to impart flavour as well as to tenderize. In the summer, many people love to eat outside and the most popular food to serve is barbecued. However, some meat can be tough if only cooked for a short period and this is where using a marinade can make a big difference. There are many marinades that are readily available to buy, but for the experienced cook, making their own presents no problem at all. Flavoured butters are used to impart taste and either placed on the food prior to cooking or added just before serving.

WET AND DRY MARINADES

The main ingredients in wet marinades are spices or herbs, which provide flavour, plus a little acidic liquid, such as wine or vinegar. Oil is used to help break down the connective tissue in the meat. If the meat is 'bashed' with a meat mallet, this also helps to tenderize. Popular ingredients are red or white wine vinegar, red or white wine, orange, lemon or lime juice with their zest, plus olive or sunflower/corn oil.

Flavour enhancers can include chopped chillies, garlic, chopped coriander/cilantro, basil, oregano, thyme, whole cloves, ground cumin, ground coriander, saffron, allspice and ginger.

As well as wet marinades, there are also dry marinades, or rubs, so called as they are rubbed over the food. These also use fresh chopped herbs or ground spices. Dry rubs are used to impart a more intense flavour than wet marinades, yet care must be taken not to overpower the natural taste of the food with too powerful a rub. They do not need to be left for as long as a wet marinade and they will also help to tenderize if used on steaks in particular.

How to Make and Use a Wet Marinade

Here is a popular wet marinade that is suitable for fish or meat. This makes enough to marinate 3 chicken breasts.

grated zest and juice of 1 lime
1 mild red chilli, deseeded and finely chopped
small piece root ginger, peeled and coarsely grated
1 tbsp freshly chopped coriander/cilantro
2 tbsp white wine vinegar
1–2 tsp clear honey
5 tbsp olive oil

1. Place all the ingredients in a screw-top jar and shake vigorously.

2. Cut 3 chicken breasts into small bite-size pieces, place in a shallow dish and pour over the marinade. Cover loosely with plastic wrap and leave in the refrigerator until required – for at least 30 minutes, or longer if time permits.

3. Soak 4 wooden kebab sticks for 30 minutes.

4. When ready to cook, drain the chicken, reserving the marinade. Thread the chicken onto the kebab sticks and cook under a grill/broiler or on a barbecue/grill, brushing with the reserved marinade. Once cooked, serve.

How to Make and Use a Dry Rub

Try rubbing pieces of white fish with a rub made from a mix of the following: 2 tablespoons freshly chopped parsley, 1 crushed garlic clove, the grated zest of 1 lemon, freshly ground black pepper and sea salt to taste. Leave for at least 15 minutes, then grill/broil or griddle until cooked.

Alternatively, rub chicken pieces with a mix of 2 finely chopped lemon grass stalks, 1 tablespoon freshly grated root ginger, 2 crushed garlic cloves and ½–1 tablespoon crushed chillies. Leave for 15 minutes, or longer if time permits, then grill or griddle until cooked.

BUTTERS

Herb Butter

1. Place 50 g/2 oz/¼ cup (4 tbsp) softened unsalted butter in a small bowl and add 1 tablespoon chopped herbs, such as parsley or basil.

2. While beating with a wooden spoon, gradually beat in 2 tablespoons lemon juice with 1 crushed garlic clove.

3. Once all the ingredients are well blended, form into a roll and place on a small piece of baking paper. Fold the paper over to encase, then chill until firm.

4. Either place a small pat of the butter onto the food about to be cooked, wrap in baking paper and cook, or, after cooking, place a small pat on top of the food just before serving.

Alternatively, try using ground cinnamon, cumin and coriander or curry powder. Chopped chillies, lemon grass, grated root ginger and chopped coriander/cilantro are all good too. This is such an easy way to flavour food; try experimenting for yourself.

Brandy or Rum Butter

This is ideal to use with Christmas pudding, mince pies or steamed puddings.

75 g/3 oz/⅓ cup (6 tbsp) unsalted
    butter, softened
75 g/3 oz/⅓ cup caster/superfine or light soft
    brown sugar
2–3 tbsp brandy or rum

1. Beat the butter with the sugar until smooth and fluffy.

2. Gradually add the brandy or rum, beating well between each addition. When all the brandy or rum has been added, spoon into a serving dish and, using a fork, make a decorative pattern on top. Chill for 30 minutes before serving.

Key Recipes: Stocks

CHICKEN STOCK

Makes 900 ml/1½ pints/3¾ cups

1 cooked chicken carcass
1 onion, peeled and cut into wedges
1 large carrot, peeled and chopped
1 celery stalk, trimmed and chopped
1 bouquet garni *(see page 78)*
10 peppercorns
4 whole cloves
salt to taste

1. Remove any large pieces of meat from the chicken carcass and reserve to use as required.

2. Break the carcass into small pieces and place in a large saucepan.

3. Add the vegetables, bouquet garni and spices with 1.2 litres/2 pints/1¼ quarts water and bring to the boil.

4. Cover with a lid, reduce the heat and simmer for 2 hours. If the liquid is evaporating too quickly, reduce the heat under the pan.

5. Cool, strain and allow to cool fully before storing, covered, in the refrigerator. Store for up to 3 days. Freeze if desired in small, lidded, freezer-safe tubs.

6. Before using, bring to the boil and simmer for 5 minutes.

BEEF STOCK

Makes 900 ml/1½ pints/3¾ cups

450 g/1 lb beef bones, chopped into small chunks
250 g/9 oz shin of beef, fat discarded, cut into
   small chunks
1 onion, peeled and cut into wedges
1 large carrot, peeled and cut into chunks
1 celery stalk, trimmed and chopped
1 bouquet garni *(see page 78)*
12 black peppercorns
salt to taste

1. Place the bones and beef in a roasting tin/pan and cook in an oven preheated to 200°C/400°F/Gas Mark 6 for 20 minutes, or until sealed and browned.

2. Remove the beef, place in a large saucepan with the remaining ingredients and 1.2 litres/2 pints/1¼ quarts water and bring to the boil. Cover with a lid, reduce the heat and simmer very gently for 4 hours.

3. Strain and add salt to taste. Cool, then skim off any fat that rises to the surface. Store in the refrigerator for up to 3 days, boiling for 5 minutes before using. Alternatively, freeze in small, lidded, freezer-safe tubs.

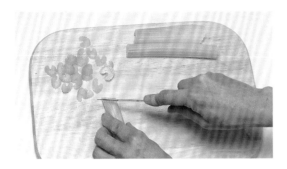

VEGETABLE STOCK

Makes 900 ml/1 ½ pints/3 ¾ cups

1 tbsp sunflower/corn oil
1 onion, peeled and cut into wedges
1 large carrot, peeled and chopped
2 celery stalks, trimmed and chopped
1 small turnip, peeled and chopped (optional)
2 bay leaves, 10 black peppercorns
3 whole cloves, salt to taste

1. Heat the oil in a large saucepan and sauté the vegetables for 8 minutes, stirring frequently.

2. Add the bay leaves with the spices and 1.2 litres/2 pints/1 ¼ quarts water and bring to the boil. Cover with a lid, reduce the heat and simmer for 40 minutes.

3. Strain the stock and add salt to taste. Cool, cover and store in the refrigerator for up to 3 days. Alternatively, freeze in small, lidded, freezer-safe tubs.

FISH STOCK

Makes 600 ml/1 pint/2 ½ cups

fish bones or 1 cod's head
1 onion, peeled and cut into wedges
1 celery stalk, trimmed and chopped
1 bouquet garni *(see page 78)*
salt and freshly ground black pepper

1. Thoroughly wash the fish bones or cod's head and place in a large saucepan with the vegetables and bouquet garni.

2. Add 900 ml/1 ½ pints/3 ¾ cups water and bring to the boil. Cover with a lid, reduce the heat and simmer for 30 minutes.

3. Strain and add seasoning to taste, then cool and store in the refrigerator for up to 2 days, bringing to the boil and simmering steadily for 5 minutes before using. If desired, freeze in small, lidded, freezer-safe tubs.

Key Recipes: Stuffings

 All manner of foods can be stuffed with all kinds of ingredients, and some delicious combinations can easily be achieved. The purpose of stuffing food is threefold: to fill a cavity normally created by boning, which helps to give a good shape; to add flavour; and, in some cases, to make the expensive part of the meal go further. Whether it is chicken breasts, boned chicken legs, pork chops, vegetables, such as peppers, potatoes, marrow or onions, or even apples, peaches or oranges, all are enhanced by a stuffing (also sometimes called 'forcemeat').

Stuffings need a base, which can be quinoa, breadcrumbs, cooked rice or couscous, and then other ingredients to add flavour and interest. These include onion, garlic, spring onions/scallions, chopped chilli, herbs, dried fruits or nuts. All these ingredients then need to be held together by the use of egg or a liquid. It is important that the stuffing is not too wet or too dry, so, when making, squeeze the ingredients together to form a ball to ensure that the stuffing stays together during cooking.

RULES FOR STUFFING

Do not make the stuffing too wet or too dry
Too wet, and it will become stodgy on cooking; too dry, and the stuffing will collapse and fall to pieces.

Do not overstuff Otherwise the stuffing could burst out. If too much stuffing has been made, either cook in a small dish or roll into balls and cook round the food.

Tie up If stuffing a joint, turkey breast fillet or boneless chicken portions, once stuffed, tie with fine twine in several places to encase the stuffing and to keep a good shape.

Stuff the right places If stuffing a whole chicken or turkey, only stuff the neck flap, and do not stuff until you are ready to cook, otherwise toxins may build up. Never stuff the body cavity, as it may prevent full cooking of the bird.

Precook veg If stuffing vegetables, blanch first so that the vegetables cook at the same time as the stuffing.

RICE & PEPPER STUFFING

2 tablespoons olive oil
1 small onion, peeled and chopped
1 garlic clove, crushed
1 green pepper, chopped and deseeded
2 medium tomatoes, skinned and chopped
2 tbsp dried cranberries
salt and freshly ground black pepper
50 g/2 oz/$\frac{1}{3}$ cup cooked white rice

1. Heat the oil and fry the onion for 3 minutes, then remove from the heat.

50 g/2 oz/⅓ cup ready-to-eat dried apricots
75 g/3 oz/⅔ cup fresh breadcrumbs
salt and freshly ground black pepper
1 medium/large egg, beaten

1. Cook the celery and onion in the butter until softened.

2. Add the orange zest and lemon zest and juice, the apricots, breadcrumbs and seasoning to taste.

3. Bind together with the beaten egg and use for chicken or turkey.

2. Stir in the garlic with the green pepper, chopped tomatoes, dried cranberries, seasoning to taste and the cooked rice. Mix together and use as required. Ideal for stuffing vegetables.

CELERY & APRICOT STUFFING

4 celery stalks, washed and chopped
1 medium onion, chopped
40 g/1½ oz/3 tbsp butter
grated zest of 1 medium orange
grated zest and juice of ½ lemon

MINT STUFFING

1 medium onion, chopped
50 g/2 oz/¼ cup (4 bsp) unsalted butter
40 g/1½ oz/⅓ cup toasted pine nuts
grated zest and juice of 1 lemon
50 g/2 oz/1 cup fresh breadcrumbs
50 g/2 oz/⅓ cup sultanas/golden raisins
salt and freshly ground black pepper
2 tbsp freshly chopped mint
1 medium/large egg, beaten

1. Cook the onion in the butter for 5 minutes, or until beginning to soften.

2. Remove from the heat and stir in the pine nuts, grated lemon zest and juice, breadcrumbs and sultanas/golden raisins.

3. Add seasoning to taste along with the mint, and bind together with the beaten egg. Ideal to use with lamb dishes.

CHESTNUT STUFFING

225 g/8 oz/1½ cups chestnuts, cooked and peeled
1 small onion, peeled and cut into chunks
125 g/4 oz pork sausage meat
40 g/1½ oz/1 cup fresh breadcrumbs
2 tbsp chopped herbs
salt and freshly ground black pepper
2 tbsp cranberry sauce *(see page 141)*
a little stock or lemon juice, if necessary

Place the chestnuts and the onion in a food processor and whizz until chopped. Add the sausage meat and whizz again for 1 minute, then add the breadcrumbs, chopped herbs and seasoning to taste. Add the cranberry sauce and whizz again, adding a little stock or lemon juice if too dry. Ideal for poultry.

Cooking with Alcohol

 Wine, beer, cider and some spirits are good when used in cooking; they can transform an ordinary dish into something really special. Alcohol can also help to tenderize meat. Often, a recipe will leave the meat, beef in particular, marinating overnight before cooking, such as in the well-known recipe Beef Bourguignon.

WHICH ALCOHOL?

Normally, wine, beer or cider are combined with stock in meat dishes – try using beer with beef, and cider with pork, sausages or chicken. As for spirits, brandy is the most commonly used spirit for meat.

However, there are a few desserts or sweet recipes where alcohol – usually brandy or other spirits – are used. Puddings such as Christmas pudding or cake are not the same if no spirit has been used. Whisky is often used in Scottish and Irish recipes. Cointreau, Grand Marnier, Kirsch, crème de menthe and other liqueurs are also used; these are not generally set alight. However, there is always the exception, such as Crêpes Suzette *(see opposite)*.

RULES AND TIPS

Use wine you would drink A word of caution: although you should not waste very high-quality wine in your food, it is not worth using wine that you would not drink – using it in cooking will not improve the wine and could seriously impair the finished dish.

Burn off the alcohol When using wine or spirits, it is important to ensure that the dish has the flavour of the wine or spirit rather than simply tasting of alcohol. This is why often, during preparation, the dish is set alight (flambéed). This burns off most of the alcohol content, leaving the flavour. In uncooked dishes where alcohol has been used, the amount is normally less than is used in cooked dishes. Too much alcohol can ruin a dish, not enhance it.

Not for freezing It is not advised to use alcohol in dishes to be frozen, as alcohol freezes at a lower temperature than other liquids, so the thawed dish may separate into the alcohol which has thawed and the rest of the dish which is still semi-frozen.

A last taster To reinforce the flavour, add a splash of the alcohol used in the cooking to the finished dish just before serving.

Avoid waste Buy small quarter bottles of wine to use in cooking rather than opening a bottle especially. If you have any leftover wine after opening, freeze in ice cube trays, then just pop in 1 or 2 cubes to a dish to add a splash of wine to sauces, stocks, stews, casseroles or even soups. No need to thaw if adding to hot food.

Alcohol in milk or cream dishes First, burn off the alcohol before adding the milk or cream, to prevent the dish curdling.

CRÊPES SUZETTE

Makes 8

125 g/4 oz/1 cup plain white/all-purpose flour
pinch salt
3 medium/large eggs
250 ml/8 fl oz/1 cup semi-skimmed/low-fat milk
25 g/1 oz/2 tbsp unsalted butter, melted

For the orange butter:
125 g/4 oz/½ cup (8 tbsp) unsalted butter, softened
75 g/3 oz/¾ cup icing/powdered sugar, sifted
grated zest of 1 lemon
grated zest and juice of 1 small orange
2–3 tbsp Cointreau

1–2 tbsp sunflower oil or clarified butter,
   for cooking
2–3 tbsp brandy
orange zest, to decorate (optional)

1. To make the batter, sift the flour and salt into a mixing bowl and make a well in the centre. Beat the eggs together, then pour into the well together with 2 tablespoons of the milk. Using a wooden spoon, draw the flour in from the sides of the bowl. Gradually add the rest of the milk, beating well after each addition. When all the

milk has been added, allow to stand for 30 minutes before stirring in the melted butter.

2. To make the orange butter, cream the butter and icing/powdered sugar together with the lemon and orange zest until soft and fluffy. Slowly beat in the Cointreau. Spoon into a dish and chill until required.

3. When ready to cook, heat a small teaspoon of oil or a small amount of clarified butter in a crepe pan or small 15 cm/6 inch frying pan. Carefully swirl the pan until lightly coated in the oil or butter and pour off any excess. Add 2 tablespoons of the batter and swirl the pan again so the batter evenly coats the base. Cook for 2–3 minutes until the bubbles on the surface burst. Turn or flip the pancake over and cook for a further 1 minute. Fold into quarters and remove. Keep warm while cooking the other pancakes. Repeat with the remaining batter.

4. When all the pancakes are cooked, place 2 tablespoons of the orange butter in the pan and heat gently. Add 4 of the folded pancakes to the pan and heat gently for 1 minute, then turn the pancakes over and heat for a further minute. Pour in 2–3 teaspoons of the brandy, heat for 20 seconds, then draw the pan off the heat and set alight. When the flames have subsided, serve the

pancakes and repeat with the remaining batter, orange butter and brandy. Decorate with orange zest, if using.

Tip Keep the pancakes warm either on a plate over a pan of gently simmering water or in a warm oven at 160°C/325°F/Gas Mark 3, covered with kitchen foil.

Basic Baking Techniques

There is no mystery to successful baking; it really is easy, providing you follow a few simple rules and guidelines. First, read the recipe right through before commencing. There is nothing more annoying than getting to the middle of a recipe and discovering that you are minus one or two of the ingredients. Until you are confident, follow a recipe; do not try a short cut, otherwise you may find that you have left out a vital step which means that the recipe really cannot work. Most of all, have patience, baking is easy – if you can read, you can bake.

WORKING WITH PASTRY

Pastry dough needs to be kept as cool as possible throughout. Cool hands help, but are not essential. Use cold or iced water, but not too much, as pastry does not need to be wet. Make sure that your fat is not runny or melted but firm (this is why block fat is the best). Avoid using too much flour when rolling out as this alters the proportions, and also avoid handling the dough too much. Chill pastry, wrapped in foil or a plastic bag, for 30 minutes after making the dough. Roll in one direction, as this helps to ensure that the pastry does not shrink. Allow the pastry to rest, preferably in the refrigerator, after rolling. If you follow these guidelines but still your pastry is not as good as you would like it to be, then make in a processor instead.

Lining a Flan Dish/Tart Pan

It is important to choose the right tin or dish to bake with. You will often find that a loose-bottomed metal flan tin/tart pan is the best option, as it conducts heat more efficiently and evenly than a ceramic dish. It also has the added advantage of a removable base, which makes the transfer of the final flan or tart a much simpler process; it simply lifts out, keeping the pastry intact.

1. Roll the pastry dough out on a lightly floured surface, ensuring that it is a few inches larger than the flan tin.

2. Wrap the pastry round the rolling pin, lift and place in the tin. Carefully ease the pastry into the base and sides of the tin, ensuring that there are no gaps or tears in the pastry. Allow to rest for a few minutes.

3. Trim the edge either with a sharp knife or by rolling a rolling pin across the top of the flan tin.

4. Prick the pastry with the tines of a fork to prevent it from rising up during baking and chill before baking.

Baking Blind

The term 'baking blind' means cooking the pastry case/pie crust without the filling, resulting in a crisp pastry shell that is either partially or fully cooked, depending on whether the filling needs any cooking. Pastry shells can be prepared ahead of time, as they last for several days if stored correctly in an airtight container, or longer if frozen.

1. Line a tin or dish with the prepared pastry dough and allow to rest in the refrigerator for 30 minutes. This will help to minimize shrinkage while it is being cooked.

2. Remove from the refrigerator and lightly prick the base all over with a fork (do not do this if the filling is runny). Line the case with a large square of greaseproof paper, big enough to cover both the base and sides of the pastry case.

3. Fill with ceramic baking beans/pie weights, dried beans or rice. Place on a baking sheet and bake in a preheated oven, generally at 200°C/400°F/Gas Mark 6, remembering that ovens can take at least 15 minutes to reach this heat (unless they are fan/convection ovens, *see page 164*). Cook for 10–12 minutes, then remove from the oven, discarding the paper and beans.

4. Return to the oven and continue to cook for a further 5–10 minutes, depending on whether the filling needs cooking. Normally, unless otherwise stated, individual pastry tartlet cases also benefit from baking blind.

Covering a Pie with a Pastry Lid

1. Roll out the pastry dough until it is about 5 cm/2 inches larger than the circumference of the dish.

2. Cut a 2.5 cm/1 inch strip from around the outside of the pastry and then moisten the edge of the pie dish you are using. Place the strip on the edge of the dish and brush with water or beaten egg.

3. Generously fill the pie dish until the surface is slightly rounded. Using the rolling pin, lift the remaining pastry and cover the pie dish. Press together, then seal.

4. Using a sharp knife, trim off any excess pastry from around the edges, then brush the top with beaten egg. Try to avoid brushing the edges of the pastry, especially puff pastry, as this prevents the pastry rising evenly.

5. Before placing in the oven, make a small hole in the centre of the pie to allow the steam to escape.

Decorative Pie Edges

The edges of a pie can be decorated by pressing the back of a fork around the edge or, instead, crimp by pinching the edge of the crust, holding the thumb and index finger of one hand against the edge while gently pushing with the index finger of your other hand. Other ways of finishing the pie are to knock up (achieved by gently pressing your index finger down onto the rim and, at the same time, tapping a knife horizontally along the edge, giving it a flaky appearance), or fluting the edges by pressing your thumb down on the edge of the pastry while gently drawing back an all-purpose knife about 1 cm/$^1/_2$ inch and repeating around the rim. Experiment by putting leaves and berries made out of leftover pastry to finish off the pie, then brush the top of the pie with beaten egg.

GREASING AND LINING CAKE TINS

Most tins/pans will at least need oiling or greasing with butter (butter is better, as oil runs off lining paper). If a recipe states that the tin needs lining, do not be tempted to ignore this. Rich fruit cakes and other cakes that take a long time to cook benefit from the tin being lined so that the edges and base do not burn or dry out. Greaseproof/waxed paper or baking parchment is ideal for this. It is a good idea to have the paper at least double thickness, or preferably 3–4 thicknesses. Sponge cakes and other cakes that are cooked in 30 minutes or less are also better if the bases are lined, as it is far easier to remove them from the tin. Steamed puddings usually need only a disc of greaseproof paper at the bottom of the dish so that it will turn out easily. The best way to line a round or square tin is as follows:

1. Lightly draw around the base and then cut just inside the markings, making it easy to sit in the tin.

2. Next, lightly grease the paper (with butter) so that it will easily peel away from the cake.

3. If the sides of the tin also need to be lined, then cut a strip of paper long enough for the tin. This can be measured by wrapping a piece of string around the rim of the tin.

4. Once again, lightly grease the paper, push against the tin and grease once more, as this will hold the paper to the sides of the tin.

HINTS FOR SUCCESSFUL BAKING

Measurements
Ensure that the ingredients are accurately measured. A cake that has too much flour or insufficient egg will be dry and crumbly. Take care when measuring the raising/leavening agent if used, as too much will mean that the cake will rise too quickly and then sink. Not enough raising agent means the cake will not rise adequately.

Oven Temperature
Ensure that the oven is preheated to the correct temperature; it can take 10 minutes to reach up to 190°C/375°F/Gas Mark 5, and 15 minutes for above that – but ovens vary. You may find that an oven thermometer is a good investment. Cakes are best if cooked in the centre of the preheated oven. Do try to avoid the temptation of opening the oven door at the beginning of cooking, as a draught of cool air can make the cake sink. **Important**: if using a fan/convection oven, then refer to the manufacturer's instructions, as they normally cook 10–20°C/50–68°F hotter than conventional ovens and often do not need preheating. As a general rule, preheat your fan oven to 20 per cent lower than is stated for a non-fan oven – this usually works out at 20°C/68°F lower.

Testing to see When a Cake is Cooked
Check that the cake is thoroughly cooked by removing from the oven and inserting a clean skewer into the cake. Leave for 30 seconds and

remove. If the skewer is completely clean, then the cake is cooked; if there is a little mixture left on the skewer, then return to the oven for a few minutes.

Problems

Other problems that you may encounter while cake-making are insufficient creaming of the fat and sugar or a curdled creamed mixture (which will result in a densely textured and often fairly solid cake). Flour that has not been folded in carefully enough or has not been mixed with enough raising agent may also result in a fairly heavy consistency. It is very

important to try to ensure that the correct size of tin is used, as you may end up either with a flat, hard cake or one which has spilled over the edge of the tin/pan. Another tip to be aware of (especially when cooking with fruit) is that, if the consistency is too soft, the cake will not be able to support the fruit.

Cooling and Storing

Finally, when you take your cake out of the oven, unless the recipe states that it should be left in the tin until cold, leave for a few minutes to settle, then loosen the edges and turn out onto a wire rack to cool. Cakes which are left in the tin for too long will develop a damp, soggy base.

When storing, make sure the cake is completely cold before placing it into an airtight container. Generally, biscuits/cookies and cakes will keep for about 5 days in an airtight container. However, if a cake uses fresh cream, cream cheese frosting or other fresh ingredients such as fruit, it will only last for 1–2 days kept refrigerated (note: do not refrigerate cakes covered with sugarpaste/rolled fondant icing). Cakes with buttercream and similar icings will keep for 2–3 days in a cool place. Light fruit cakes such as Dundee will store for about a week and rich fruit cakes such as Christmas Cake will keep for up to 3 months if fortified with alcohol and wrapped tightly in foil.

Key Recipes: Baking

PASTRY

Shortcrust Pastry

Makes 225 g/8 oz

225 g/8 oz/2 cups plain/all-purpose white flour
pinch salt
50 g/2 oz/4 tbsp white vegetable fat/shortening or lard
50 g/2 oz/¼ cup (4 tbsp) butter or block margarine

1. Sift the flour and salt into a mixing bowl. Cut the fats into small pieces and add to the bowl.

2. Rub the fats into the flour using your fingertips until the mixture resembles fine breadcrumbs.

3. Add 1–2 tablespoons cold water and, using a knife, or your hands if easier, mix to form a soft, pliable dough.

4. Knead gently on a lightly floured surface until smooth and free from cracks, then wrap and chill for 30 minutes before using.

5. When ready to use, roll out on a lightly floured surface and use as required. Cook in a preheated hot oven (200°C/400°F/Gas Mark 6), or as directed.

Sweet Shortcrust Pastry (Pâte Sucrée)

Makes 225 g/8 oz

225 g/8 oz/2 cups plain/all-purpose white flour
150 g/5 oz/⅔ cup (1¼ sticks) unsalted butter, softened
2 tbsp caster/superfine sugar
1 medium/large egg yolk

1. Sift the flour into a mixing bowl, cut the fat into small pieces, add to the bowl and rub into the flour.

2. Stir in the sugar, then mix to form a pliable dough with the egg yolk and about 1 tablespoon cold water. Wrap, chill and use as required.

Chocolate Variation To make chocolate sweet shortcrust pastry, simply sift in 1 tablespoon cocoa powder with the flour after the butter has been rubbed in.

Cheese Pastry

Follow the recipe for sweet shortcrust pastry, but omit the sugar and add 1 teaspoon dried mustard powder and 50 g/2 oz/½ cup mature grated Cheddar cheese.

Rough Puff Pastry

Makes 225 g/8 oz

225 g/8 oz/2 cups plain/all-purpose white flour
pinch salt
150 g/5 oz/⅔ cup (1¼ sticks) butter, block
    margarine or lard
squeeze lemon juice

1. Sift the flour and salt together in a mixing bowl. Cut up the fat and add to the bowl.

2. Add the lemon juice and 6–7 tablespoons cold water. Mix with a fork until it is a fairly stiff mixture.

3. Turn out onto a lightly floured surface. Roll into an oblong. Fold the bottom third up to the centre, bring the top third down to the centre. Gently press the edges together.

4. Give the pastry a half turn, roll the pastry out again into an oblong. Repeat the folding, turning and rolling at least four times.

5. Wrap and leave to rest in a cool place for at least 30 minutes. Cook as directed by your recipe, in a preheated oven at 220°C/425°F/Gas Mark 7.

Choux Pastry

Makes 225 g/8 oz

50 g/2 oz/¼ cup (4 tbsp) butter
75 g/3 oz/¾ cup plain/all-purpose white flour
pinch salt
2 medium/large eggs, beaten

1. Place the butter and 150 ml/¼ pint/⅔ cup water in a heavy-based saucepan. Heat gently, stirring until the butter has melted, and bring to the boil.

2. Draw off the heat and add the flour and salt all at once. Beat with a wooden spoon until the mixture forms a ball in the centre. Cool for 5 minutes.

3. Gradually add the eggs, beating well after each addition, until a stiff mixture is formed.

4. Either place in a piping/decorating bag fitted with a large nozzle/tip, or shape using two spoons. Cook in a preheated oven at 200°C/400°F/Gas Mark 6 for 15–25 minutes, depending on size.

5. Remove and make a small slit in the side, then return to the oven and cook for a further 5 minutes. Remove and cool before filling.

Hot Water Crust Pastry

Makes 450 g/1 lb

450 g/1 lb/4 cups plain/all-purpose white flour
1 tsp salt
125 g/4 oz/½ cup (8 tbsp) lard or white vegetable fat/shortening
150 ml/¼ pint/⅔ cup milk and water, mixed

1. Sift the flour and salt together and reserve.

2. Heat the lard or white vegetable fat/shortening until melted. Bring to the boil.

3. Pour immediately into the flour along with some of the milk and water and, using a wooden spoon,

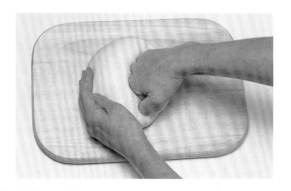

mix together and beat until the mixture comes together and forms a ball, using more milk and water as needed.

4. When cool enough to handle, knead lightly until smooth and pliable.

5. Use as required, covering the dough with a clean cloth before use. Bake in a preheated oven at 220°C/425°F/Gas Mark 7, or as directed.

BATTERS

Pouring Batter for Yorkshire Puddings and Pancakes

125 g/4 oz/1 cup plain/all-purpose white flour
pinch salt
2 medium/large eggs
300 ml/½ pint/1¼ cups whole milk and water, mixed
1 tbsp vegetable oil, for baking the Yorkshire puddings

1. Sift the flour and salt into a mixing bowl and make a well in the centre.

2. Drop the eggs into the well with a little milk. Beat the eggs into the flour, gradually drawing the flour in from the sides of the bowl.

3. Once half the milk has been added, beat well until smooth and free from lumps. Stir in the remaining milk and leave to stand for 30 minutes. Stir before using.

This batter can be used for pancakes and, if liked, 2 tbsp caster/superfine sugar can be added.

To use to make Yorkshire puddings:

1. Heat 1 tablespoon oil in a roasting tin/pan or individual Yorkshire pudding tins/pans in an oven preheated to 220°C/425°F/Gas Mark 7.

2. When the oil is almost smoking, stir the batter, then pour it into the hot oil. Cook for 30–40 minutes for a large pudding and 18–20 minutes for individual puddings.

Coating Batter for Fritters

125 g/4 oz/1 cup plain/all-purpose white flour
pinch salt
1 tbsp sunflower/corn oil
150 ml/¼ pint/⅔ cup water
2 medium/large egg whites

1. Sift the flour and salt into a mixing bowl and make a well in the centre.

2. Add the oil and half the water and beat until smooth and free from lumps.

3. Gradually beat in the remaining water.

4. Just before using, whisk the egg whites until stiff, then stir into the batter and use immediately.

MERINGUES

Meringue is made from egg whites and caster/superfine sugar. As a general rule, allow 1 medium/large egg white to 50 g/2 oz/¼ cup caster sugar. If liked, add a pinch of salt at the start of whisking.

Making Meringue

1. Place the egg whites in a clean mixing bowl (any grease in the bowl will prevent the egg white from whisking).

2. Use a balloon or wire whisk if whisking by hand, or an electric mixer fitted with a balloon whisk if not. Whisk the egg whites until stiff. To test if they are stiff enough, turn the bowl upside down – if the egg white does not move, it is ready.

3. Slowly add half the sugar, 1 teaspoon at a time,

whisking well after each addition. Once half the sugar has been added, add the remaining sugar and gently stir it in with a metal spoon. Take care not to overmix.

4. Spoon the meringue onto a baking sheet lined with nonstick baking parchment. Shape the meringue according to preference or the recipe – such as in a round 'case' – and bake in a preheated oven at 150°C/300°F/Gas Mark 2 for 1½ hours, or until set and firm to the touch.

5. Once cooked, ideally leave the meringue in the oven for a while to cool slowly and dry out properly. Remove from the oven and leave until fully cold before using or storing in an airtight container.

Whipped Cream (to accompany the meringues)

Whipping cream, double/heavy cream or a combination of single/light cream and double cream will all whip. For the combination option, use one third single cream and two thirds double cream. Whipped cream is ideal for using in soufflés, mousses and other cream desserts.

1. Place the cream in a mixing bowl and use a balloon whisk, wire whisk or electric mixer fitted with the balloon whisk attachment. Place the bowl on a damp cloth if whipping by hand.

2. Whip until thickened and soft peaks are formed – this is when the whisk, if dragged gently through the cream and lifted out, leaves soft peaks in the cream.

3. For piping/decorating and to use as a filling, whip for a little longer until the cream is slightly stiffer. If using only double cream, take care that you do not overwhip, as it will curdle.

BASIC RECIPES: ICINGS

Buttercream

125 g/4 oz/½ cup (8 tbsp) unsalted butter or
    margarine, softened
1 tsp vanilla extract
225 g/8 oz/2 cups icing/powdered sugar, sifted
1–2 tbsp slightly cooled boiled water or
    fruit juice (optional)

1. Cream the butter or margarine with the vanilla extract until soft and creamy.

2. Add the icing/powdered sugar, 1 tablespoon at a time, and beat well. Continue until all the icing sugar is incorporated.

3. If liked, to give a smooth, spreadable consistency, beat in 1– 2 tablespoons slightly cooled boiled water or fruit juice.

Chocolate buttercream Melt 50 g/2 oz dark/bittersweet chocolate. Stir into the prepared buttercream, omitting the hot water. Or, if preferred, replace 1 tablespoon of the icing/powdered sugar with 1 tablespoon cocoa.

Orange/lemon buttercream Beat 1 tablespoon finely grated orange or lemon zest into the buttercream and replace the water with fruit juice.

Coffee buttercream Dissolve 1 tablespoon coffee granules in a little very hot water. Omit the vanilla extract and stir in the coffee in place of the hot water.

Mocha buttercream Make the coffee buttercream as above and replace 1 tablespoon of the icing sugar with 1 tablespoon unsweetened cocoa powder, or use melted chocolate.

Glacé Icing

1. Sift 225 g/8 oz/2 cups icing/powdered sugar into a mixing bowl, then slowly stir in 2–3 tablespoons hot water.

2. Blend to form a spreadable consistency – the icing should coat the back of a wooden spoon.

Other flavours can be made by adding 1 tablespoon cocoa to the sugar or 1 tablespoon coffee granules, dissolved in hot water. Or use orange or lemon juice, such as with Bakewell Tart. For a coloured icing, add a few drops of food colouring.

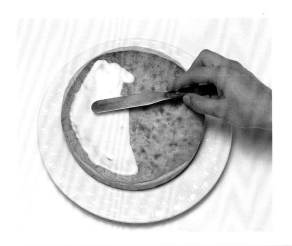

Cooking with Kids

How did your parents learn to cook? Was it by watching their mother in the kitchen and then cooking with her or was it by trial and error once you had left home? It is so important that the love of food and cooking is developed early in life, as it is a skill that will stay for ever. There is nothing to compare with good home-cooked food and the best way to learn this is in the home. Cooking can become both a skill and a hobby lasting the whole of your life. But how does today's busy parent instil this love in her children? Well, in my opinion, it is by encouraging little ones at a very early age to 'play' with food. This has two effects: their love for food means that they are happy to try new tastes, and they are keen to make their own food. So how or where to start?

HOW TO GET KIDS TO EAT THEIR FOOD

First, never push different foods on your child and insist that they eat it 'all up'. This will instantly make them say, 'I don't like it', even if they have never tried it before. Make no fuss; with very young children, once they have progressed from puréed foods, simply give them a little to try and leave it to them. If the food is rejected, remove the offending food but under no circumstances threaten with a punishment, get cross or show any anxiety that they are not eating. Children quickly realize when you are stressed and will then start rejecting other foods in order to get your attention. If they see that you are ignoring the fact that they are not eating, but you are eating, they will be curious and will want to copy you in case they are missing something good. So follow this guideline, and soon your little one will be eating food that you are preparing for the rest of the family. Once the children are a little older and eating reasonably normally, that is the time to let them start playing and to introduce new tastes and flavours on a regular basis.

KIDS IN THE KITCHEN

Kids love copying their parents, and so, when you are cooking, give them the same utensils, except for knives and scissors, that you are using, and if you put a little of the food in another bowl or pan, then they

can copy you and feel they are cooking. At the same time, encourage them to taste what you are preparing (obviously, do not give them raw meat or fish) – this also instils in them the importance of tasting while cooking.

Safety First
As they get older, it will be safe to let them do more. However, it has to be stressed that great care must be taken with safety. There should always be an adult with children in the kitchen, in order to keep an eye open while they are cooking. All cutting should be done by an adult until the child is responsible and able to use a knife correctly. Care must also be taken when the hob/stove top or oven is being used, as there will be hot equipment, saucepans and dishes.

Hygiene in the Kitchen
See pages 37–39 for the few simple rules that children (and everyone) need to learn right from the beginning. Although the list may appear a little long, if the rules are introduced at the start, they will become a way of life and it will be automatic to follow them. Make a game of the rules to make them fun – perhaps rewarding when they are followed with little or no prompting from you.

How to Start?
As with hygiene, there are a few important guidelines that you should be aware of when starting your child on the exciting adventure of learning to cook. If these are followed right from the beginning, cooking will be far easier and more enjoyable for both you and your child.

Start simple Do not expect them to be able to cook a whole meal, even if they have supervision – there are a few simple recipes below to get you started.

Read the recipe Having decided on what to cook, read the recipe before you do anything else. Check that you have all the ingredients and collect the ingredients all together.

Focus on fun Impress on them how much fun this will be, and try to make it so – if a mistake happens, it is not a problem; quietly sort it out and move on. A big drama will be remembered and could put the little one off attempting to cook again.

Highlight health Try to instil a knowledge of a healthy eating plan and, while not banning any particular foods, try to put the emphasis on fresh food and vegetables, rather than biscuits and convenience foods.

Practise techniques First, before starting to cook a particular recipe, have a play at some of the easy techniques they will need to know, even if you have to do the cutting:

- Show how to cream butter and sugar together to make cakes and puddings.

- Make a sauce with butter and flour and let them stir in the liquid.

- Make a basic pastry: show them how to rub some fat into flour, add the water, knead the dough and roll out using a rolling pin. Let them cut out shapes with plastic cutters.

- Grate some cheese.

- Whip some cream using a hand-held whisk or food mixer.

- Make breadcrumbs in a food processor.

- Make some soup, then whizz to form a purée *(see the recipe opposite)*.

- Melt chocolate and make some chocolate crunchy cakes *(see the recipe on page 178)* – and impress on them that this recipe is for special occasions.

DISHES TO COOK WITH KIDS

Try cooking these dishes with your kids, letting them get involved as much or as little as their abilities allow – but all the time they can watch you.

Scrambled Eggs on Toast
An easy dish to start with would be scrambled eggs on toast for you both; ideal for breakfast or supper *(see page 47)*.

Bacon, Tomatoes and Beans

Another very simple dish, again for breakfast or dinner, would be grilled bacon and tomatoes with baked beans.

1. First, line the grill/broiler rack with kitchen foil and switch the grill on. Have handy a pair of oven gloves and a trivet to put anything hot on.

2. Open the baked beans and empty into a small saucepan using a wooden spoon that you will stir with. Place over a gentle heat and stir regularly.

3. Put the bacon on the grill rack. Rinse the tomato and cut in half. Add to the grill rack. Place the grill pan under the grill for 2 minutes.

4. Remove the pan from under the grill and place on the trivet. Using a pair of tongs, turn the bacon over, then return the grill pan under the heat.

5. Continue to grill for a further 2–3 minutes until the bacon and tomatoes are cooked. Do not forget to stir the baked beans while doing this. Once the bacon is cooked, remove from the heat, and switch the heat off. Place all the cooked food on plates and eat.

Vegetable Soup

Soups are some of the simplest dishes to make, especially if you have a few vegetables to hand, and a blender.

2 carrots
1 large baking potato
1 medium onion
1 tablespoon oil
600 ml/1 pint/2½ cups vegetable stock
abour 300 ml/½ pint/1¼ cups semi-skimmed/
    low-fat milk
salt and pepper, to taste
about 1 tbsp parsley, chopped or 25 g/1 oz frozen
    peas, thawed

1. Peel the carrots, potato and onion, and chop into pieces.

2. Take a large saucepan and pour in the oil, then add all the chopped vegetables. Cook over a medium heat, stirring with a wooden spoon until they are all coated in the oil.

3. Pour in the stock and bring to the boil. Reduce the heat to a simmer and cover with a lid. Cook for 12–15 minutes until all the vegetables are tender. Check occasionally that the stock does not evaporate too much; if so, add more.

4. Allow to cool for about 5 minutes, then carefully pour into the bowl of a food processor or blender. Whizz until a smooth purée is formed, then scrape out into the saucepan.

5. Stir in the milk into the pan and add some seasoning to taste. Stir in the parsley or peas. Heat gently until hot, then ladle into warm soup bowls and serve.

Chocolate Crunchy Cakes

An eternal favourite with children, and very easy to make. If liked, 25 g/1 oz/2½ tbsp dried fruits such as raisins, chopped cherries, cranberries or chopped ready-to-eat dried apricots can be added as well.

1. Break 125 g/4 oz good-quality milk/semisweet or dark/bittersweet chocolate into small pieces,

place in a medium-sized heatproof mixing bowl and place over a pan of gently simmering water. (Before doing this, check that the bowl will sit on the rim of the saucepan without lots of space around it, otherwise the water might splash up and go into the bowl and spoil the chocolate.) Have a pair of oven gloves or a very thick towel ready so the bowl can be removed from the water.

2. Once the chocolate is very soft, carefully remove the bowl from the pan and, using a spoon, stir until smooth. Stir in about 25 g/1 oz/1 cup cornflakes, or other crunchy cereal, and stir gently until the cereal is coated with the chocolate. Spoon into fairy cake cases and leave to set.

Fairy Cakes

These little cakes are just as popular as the crunch cakes, and will introduce your child to baking.

125 g/4 oz/½ cup (8 tbsp) unsalted butter or
    margarine, softened
125 g/4 oz/⅔ cup caster/superfine sugar
2 medium/large eggs
125 g/4 oz self-raising flour
1 tsp vanilla extract or 1 tbsp lemon or orange zest,
    finely grated (optional)
125 g/4 oz/1¼ cups icing/powdered sugar,
    for the icing (optional)
dried fruit or little candies, to decorate (optional)

1. First, line a 12-hole muffin tray with paper cases/baking cups and preheat the oven to 180°C/350°F/Gas Mark 4, 10 minutes before baking. Place the butter or margarine in a bowl with the caster/superfine sugar. Beat until very smooth and creamy.

3. Whisk the eggs in a small jug or bowl, then gradually beat into the butter mixture. Add a little of the flour after each addition. When you have added all the eggs, stir in any remaining flour.

4. You can now, if you like, flavour the cakes with either the vanilla extract or the lemon or orange zest.

5. If the mixture is a little stiff, stir in either 1 tablespoon cooled boiled water or lemon or orange juice. (The mixture should drop off the spoon back into the bowl when the spoon is tapped lightly on the side of the bowl.)

6. Spoon the cake mixture into the cake cases, filling them about two-thirds full. Smooth the tops and then put in the preheated oven. Cook for 15–20 minutes until the tops spring back when touched lightly with a finger. Remove from the oven and allow to cool. Serve plain or decorate with a little icing.

7. To make the icing, *see page 173*. Stir well while adding the water to form a smooth icing. Spoon the icing on top of the cakes and, if liked, decorate with some dried fruit or little candies.

Meal
Suggestions

Try out your newly honed skills on this selection of recipes.
For your inspiration, they are organized as **full 'meals'**,
with suggestions for **starters**, **main courses** and **desserts**.

Cream of Pumpkin Soup

4 tbsp olive oil
900 g/2 lb/6 cups pumpkin,
   peeled, deseeded and
   cut into 2.5 cm/1 inch cubes
1 large onion, peeled and
   finely chopped
1 leek, trimmed and
   finely chopped

1 carrot, peeled and diced
2 celery stalks, diced
4 garlic cloves, peeled
   and crushed
1.7 litres/3 pints/1¾
   quarts water
salt and freshly ground
   black pepper

¼ tsp freshly grated nutmeg
150 ml/¼ pint/⅔ cup
   single/light cream
¼ tsp cayenne pepper
warm herby bread, to serve

1. Heat the olive oil in a large saucepan and cook the pumpkin for 2–3 minutes, coating it completely with oil.

2. Add the onion, leek, carrot and celery to the saucepan with the garlic and cook, stirring, for 5 minutes, or until they have begun to soften. Cover the vegetables with the water and bring to the boil. Season with plenty of salt and pepper and the nutmeg, cover and simmer for 15–20 minutes until all of the vegetables are tender.

3. When the vegetables are tender, remove from the heat, cool slightly, then pour into a food processor or blender. Liquidize to form a smooth purée, then pass through a sieve into a clean saucepan.

4. Adjust the seasoning to taste and add all but 2 tablespoons of the cream and enough water to obtain the desired consistency. Bring the soup to boiling point, add the cayenne pepper and serve immediately, swirled with cream and accompanied by warm herby bread.

Steak & Kidney Pie

SERVES 4

4–6 lambs' kidneys, halved
2 tbsp olive oil
1 medium onion, peeled
  and chopped
575 g/1¼ lb braising steak,
  trimmed and chopped

4 medium carrots, peeled
  and chopped
75 g/3 oz/1 cup mushrooms
  (button), wiped and sliced
3 tbsp plain/all-purpose flour
1 tbsp tomato purée/paste

900 ml/1½ pints/1 scant quart
  beef stock
2 fresh bay leaves
freshly ground black pepper
375 g/13 oz puff pastry dough
1 small/medium egg, beaten

1. Preheat the oven to 160°C/325°F/Gas Mark 3, 10 minutes before required. Slice the kidneys. Heat the oil in a large saucepan over a medium heat and add the onion. Cook, stirring, for 5 minutes and transfer to a plate. Add the steak and kidneys to the oil remaining in the pan and cook for 5–8 minutes until sealed. Return the onion to the pan together with the carrots and mushrooms. Sprinkle in the flour and cook for 2 minutes. Blend the tomato purée/paste with a little of the stock and add to the pan. Stir in the remaining stock and the bay leaves. Bring to the boil. Transfer to a casserole dish and cook in the oven for 2 hours, or until tender. Remove from the oven, discard the bay leaves and season with black pepper. Using a slotted spoon, place the mixture into an ovenproof 1.1 litre/2 pint pie dish/pan. Reserve the liquid to use for gravy.

2. Roll the pastry dough out on a lightly floured surface and cut a 2.5 cm/1 inch wide strip long enough to go round the edge of the pie dish. Press firmly onto the rim of the dish. Roll the remaining pastry out to form a lid large enough to cover the pie dish completely. Lightly brush the pastry strip with a little beaten egg and then place the lid on top. Press the two edges firmly together. Trim with a sharp knife. Use any remaining pastry to decorate the top of the pie. Brush lightly with the beaten egg and place on a baking tray. Leave to relax in the refrigerator for 30 minutes. Fifteen minutes before cooking, preheat the oven to 220°C/425°F/Gas Mark 7. Cook the pie in the oven for 30–35 minutes until golden brown. Brush the crust again with the egg halfway through cooking time. Reheat the remaining gravy and serve with the pie.

Eve's Pudding

SERVES 6

450 g/1 lb cooking apples
175 g/6 oz/1½ cups
   blackberries
75 g/3 oz/⅓ cup demerara/
   turbinado sugar
grated zest of 1 lemon

125 g/4 oz/⅔ cup
   caster/superfine sugar
125 g/4 oz/½ cup
   (8 tbsp) butter
few drops vanilla extract
2 eggs, beaten

125 g/4 oz/1 cup
   self-raising flour
1 tbsp icing/powdered sugar
ready-made custard,
   to serve

1. Preheat the oven to 180°C/350°F/Gas Mark 4. Oil a 1.2 litre/2 pint/1¼ quart baking dish. Peel, core and slice the apples and place a layer in the base of the prepared dish. Sprinkle over some of the blackberries, a little demerara/turbinado sugar and lemon zest. Continue to layer the apples and blackberries in this way until all the ingredients have been used.

2. Cream the sugar and butter together until light and fluffy. Beat in the vanilla extract and then the eggs, a little at a time, adding a spoonful of flour after each addition. Fold in the extra flour with a metal spoon or rubber spatula and mix well.

3. Spread the sponge mixture over the top of the fruit and level with the back of a spoon. Place the dish on a baking sheet and bake in the preheated oven for 35–40 minutes until well risen and golden brown. To test if the pudding is cooked, press the cooked sponge lightly with a clean finger – if it springs back, the sponge is cooked. Dust the pudding with a little icing/powdered sugar and serve immediately with custard.

Winter Coleslaw

SERVES 6

175 g/6 oz white cabbage
1 red onion, peeled
175 g/6 oz (about 2½)
   carrots, peeled
175 g/6 oz (1 head)
   celeriac, peeled
2 celery stalks, trimmed

75 g/3 oz/½ cup sultanas/
   golden raisins

**For the yogurt and
herb dressing:**
150 ml/¼ pint/⅔ cup
   natural yogurt

1 garlic clove, peeled
   and crushed
1 tbsp lemon juice
1 tsp clear honey
1 tbsp freshly snipped chives

1. Remove the hard core from the cabbage with a small knife and shred the cabbage finely. Slice the onion finely and coarsely grate the carrots. Place the raw vegetables in a large bowl and mix together.

2. Cut the celeriac into thin strips and simmer in boiling water for about 2 minutes. Drain the celeriac and rinse thoroughly with cold water. Chop the celery and add to the bowl with the celeriac and sultanas/golden raisins and mix well.

3. Make the yogurt and herb dressing by briskly whisking the yogurt, garlic, lemon juice, honey and chives together.

4. Pour the dressing over the top of the salad. Stir the vegetables thoroughly to coat evenly and serve.

Traditional Fish Pie

SERVES 4

450 g/1 lb cod or coley/white fish fillets, skinned
450 ml/¾ pint/1¾ cups milk
1 small onion, peeled and quartered
salt and freshly ground black pepper

6–8 potatoes, peeled and cut into chunks
100 g/3½ oz/7 tbsp butter
125 g/4 oz large prawns/shrimp, peeled
2 large/extra-large eggs, hard-boiled and quartered

198 g/7 oz can sweetcorn, drained
2 tbsp freshly chopped parsley
3 tbsp plain/all-purpose flour
50 g/2 oz/½ cup grated Cheddar cheese

1. Preheat the oven to 200°C/400°F/Gas Mark 6, about 15 minutes before baking. Place the fish in a shallow frying pan, pour over 300 ml/½ pint/1¼ cups of the milk and add the onion. Season to taste with salt and pepper. Bring to the boil and simmer for 8–10 minutes until the fish is cooked. Remove the fish with a slotted spoon and place in a 1.5 litre/2½ pint/1½ quart baking dish. Strain the cooking liquid and reserve.

2. Boil the potatoes until soft, then mash with 40 g/1½ oz/3 tbsp of the butter and 2–3 tablespoons of the remaining milk. Reserve.

3. Arrange the prawns/shrimp and quartered eggs on top of the fish, then scatter the sweetcorn over and sprinkle with the parsley.

4. Melt the remaining butter in a saucepan, stir in the flour and cook gently for 1 minute, stirring. Whisk in the reserved cooking liquid and remaining milk. Cook for 2 minutes, or until thickened, then pour over the fish mixture and cool slightly.

5. Spread the mashed potato over the top of the pie and sprinkle over the grated cheese. Bake in the preheated over for 30 minutes until golden. Serve immediately.

Apple & Cinnamon Brown Betty

SERVES 2

450 g/1 lb cooking apples, peeled, cored and sliced
50 g/2 oz/¼ cup caster/superfine sugar
finely grated zest of 1 lemon
125 g/4 oz/2¾ cups fresh white breadcrumbs

125 g/4 oz/⅔ cup demerara/turbinado sugar
½ tsp ground cinnamon
25 g/1 oz/2 tbsp butter

For the custard:
3 egg yolks

1 tbsp caster/superfine sugar
500 ml/18 fl oz/2 cups milk
1 tbsp cornflour/cornstarch
few drops vanilla extract

1. Preheat the oven to 180°C/350°F/Gas Mark 4. Lightly oil a 900 ml/1½ pint/1 scant quart ovenproof dish. Place the apples in a saucepan with the caster/superfine sugar, lemon zest and 2 tablespoons water. Simmer for 10–15 minutes until soft.

2. Mix the breadcrumbs with the sugar and the cinnamon. Place half the sweetened apples in the base of the prepared dish and spoon over half of the crumb mixture. Place the remaining apples on top and cover with the rest of the crumb mixture. Melt the butter and pour over the surface of the dessert. Cover the dish with nonstick baking parchment and bake in the preheated oven for 20 minutes. Remove the paper and bake for a further 10–15 minutes until golden.

3. Meanwhile, make the custard by whisking the egg yolks and sugar together until creamy. Mix 1 tablespoon of the milk with the cornflour/cornstarch until a paste forms and reserve. Warm the rest of the milk until nearly boiling and pour over the egg mixture with the paste and vanilla extract. Place the bowl over a saucepan of gently simmering water. Stir over the heat until the custard is thickened and can coat the back of a spoon. Strain into a jug and serve hot, poured over the dessert.

Cullen Skink

2 tbsp unsalted butter
1 onion, peeled and chopped
1 fresh bay leaf
3 tbsp plain/all-purpose flour
350 g/12 oz/⅔ cup new
  potatoes, scrubbed and
  cut into small pieces

600 ml/1 pint/2½ cups semi-
  skimmed/low-fat milk
300 ml/½ pint/1¼ cups water
350 g/12 oz undyed smoked
  haddock fillet, skinned
75 g/3 oz/½ cup
  sweetcorn kernels

50 g/2 oz/⅓ cup garden peas
freshly ground black pepper
½ tsp freshly grated nutmeg
2–3 tbsp single/light cream
2 tbsp freshly
  chopped parsley
crusty bread, to serve

1. Melt the butter in a large heavy-based saucepan, add the onion and sauté for 3 minutes, stirring occasionally. Add the bay leaf and stir, then sprinkle in the flour and cook over a low heat for 2 minutes, stirring frequently. Add the potatoes.

2. Take off the heat and gradually stir in the milk and water. Return to the heat and bring to the boil, stirring. Reduce the heat to a simmer and cook for 10 minutes.

3. Meanwhile, discard any pin bones from the fish and cut into small pieces. Add to the pan together with the sweetcorn and peas. Cover and cook gently, stirring occasionally, for 10 minutes, or until the vegetables and fish are cooked.

4. Add pepper and nutmeg to taste, then stir in the cream and heat gently for 1–2 minutes until piping hot. Sprinkle with the parsley and serve with crusty bread.

Shepherd's Pie

SERVES 4

2 tbsp vegetable or olive oil
1 onion, peeled and
   finely chopped
1 carrot, peeled and
   finely chopped
1 celery stalk, trimmed and
   finely chopped
1 tbsp fresh thyme leaves
450 g/1 lb leftover roast
   lamb, finely chopped,
   or fresh lean minced/
   ground lamb

150 ml/¼ pint/⅔ cup red wine
150 ml/¼ pint/⅔ cup lamb or
   vegetable stock, or
   leftover gravy
2 tbsp tomato purée/paste
salt and freshly ground
   black pepper
700 g/1½ lb (3–4 medium)
   potatoes, peeled and
   cut into chunks
25 g/1 oz/2 tbsp butter
6 tbsp milk

1 tbsp freshly chopped
   parsley
fresh herbs, to garnish

1. Preheat the oven to 200°C/400°F/Gas Mark 6, about 15 minutes before baking. If using fresh lamb, dry-fry the meat in a nonstick frying pan over a high heat until well browned, and reserve. Heat the oil in a large saucepan and add the onion, carrot and celery. Cook over a medium heat for 8–10 minutes until softened and starting to brown. Add the thyme and cook briefly, then add the cooked lamb, wine, stock and tomato purée/paste. Season to taste with salt and pepper and simmer gently for 25–30 minutes until reduced and thickened. Remove from the heat to cool slightly and season again.

2. Meanwhile, boil the potatoes in plenty of salted water for 12–15 minutes until tender. Drain and return to the saucepan over a low heat to dry out. Remove from the heat and add the butter, milk and parsley. Mash until creamy, adding a little more milk if necessary. Adjust the seasoning.

3. Transfer the lamb mixture to a shallow ovenproof dish. Spoon the mash over the filling, spreading evenly to cover. Fork the surface, place on a baking sheet, then cook in the preheated oven for 25–30 minutes until the topping is browned and the filling is piping hot. Garnish and serve.

Rich Double-crust Plum Pie

SERVES 4–6

For the pastry:
75 g/3 oz/⅓ cup (6 tbsp) butter
75 g/3 oz/⅓ cup white
    vegetable fat/shortening
225 g/8 oz/2 cups plain/
    all-purpose flour
2 egg yolks

For the filling:
450 g/1 lb/3 cups fresh plums
50 g/2 oz/¼ cup caster/
    superfine sugar
1 tbsp milk
a little extra caster/
    superfine sugar

1. Preheat the oven to 200°C/400°F/Gas Mark 6, 15 minutes before baking. Make the pastry dough by rubbing the butter and white vegetable fat/shortening into the flour until it resembles fine breadcrumbs, or blend in a food processor. Add the egg yolks and enough water to make a soft dough. Knead lightly, then wrap and leave in the refrigerator for about 30 minutes.

2. Meanwhile, prepare the fruit. Rinse and dry the plums, then cut in half and remove the stones. Slice the plums into chunks and cook in a saucepan with 25 g/1 oz/2 tablespoons of the sugar and 2 tablespoons water for 5–7 minutes until slightly softened. Remove from the heat and add the remaining sugar to taste and allow to cool.

3. Roll out half the dough on a lightly floured surface and use to line the base and sides of a 1.2 litre/2 pint/1¼ quart pie dish. Allow the dough to hang over the edge. Spoon in the prepared plums.

4. Roll out the remaining dough to use as the lid and brush the edge with a little water. Wrap the dough around the rolling pin and place over the plums. Press the edges together to seal and mark a decorative edge around the rim by pinching with the thumb and forefinger or using the back of a fork. Brush the lid with milk and make a few slits in the top. Use any trimmings to decorate the top of the pie with dough leaves. Place on a baking sheet and bake in the preheated oven for 30 minutes, or until golden brown. Sprinkle with a little caster/superfine sugar. Serve hot or cold.

Stilton, Tomato & Courgette Quiche

For the shortcrust pastry:
225 g/8 oz/2 cups plain/
    all-purpose flour
pinch salt
50 g/2 oz/¼ cup white vegetable
    fat/shortening or lard
50 g/2 oz/¼ cup (4 tbsp)
    butter or block margarine

For the filling:
25 g/1 oz/2 tbsp butter
1 onion, peeled and finely
    chopped
1 courgette/zucchini,
    trimmed and sliced
125 g/4 oz/1 cup Stilton/blue
    cheese, crumbled

6 cherry tomatoes, halved
2 large eggs, beaten
200 ml/7 fl oz/¾ cup crème
    fraîche/sour cream
salt and freshly ground
    black pepper

1. Preheat the oven to 190°C/375°F/Gas Mark 5, 10 minutes before baking. Sift the flour and salt into a mixing bowl. Cut the fats into small pieces and add to the bowl. Rub the fats into the flour using your fingertips until the mixture resembles fine breadcrumbs. Add 1–2 tablespoons cold water and mix to form a soft, pliable dough. Knead gently on a lightly floured surface until smooth and free from cracks, then wrap and chill for 30 minutes.

2. On a lightly floured surface, roll out the dough and use to line an 18 cm/7 inch lightly oiled flan tin/tart pan, trimming any excess dough with a knife. Prick the base all over with a fork and bake blind in the preheated oven for 15 minutes. Remove the pastry from the oven and brush with a little of the beaten egg. Return to the oven for a further 5 minutes.

3. Heat the butter in a frying pan and fry the onion and courgette/zucchini for about 4 minutes until soft and starting to brown. Transfer into the pastry case/pie crust. Sprinkle the Stilton/blue cheese over evenly and top with the halved cherry tomatoes.

4. Beat together the eggs and crème fraîche/sour cream and season to taste with salt and pepper. Pour into the pastry case and bake in the oven for 35–40 minutes until the filling is golden brown and set in the centre. Serve the quiche hot or cold.

Battered Cod & Chunky Chips

1 tbsp fresh yeast
300 ml/½ pint/1¼ cups beer
225 g/8 oz/2 cups plain/all-
   purpose flour
1 tsp salt
700 g/1½ lb potatoes
450 ml/¾ pint/1¾ cups
   groundnut/peanut oil

4 cod fillets, about 225 g/8 oz
   each, skinned and boned
2 tbsp seasoned plain/all-
   purpose flour

To garnish:
lemon wedges
flat-leaf/Italian parsley sprigs

To serve:
tomato ketchup
vinegar

1. Dissolve the yeast with a little of the beer in a measuring jug and mix to a paste. Pour in the remaining beer, whisking all the time, until smooth. Place the flour and salt in a bowl and gradually pour in the beer mixture, whisking continuously, to make a thick, smooth batter. Cover the bowl and allow the batter to stand at room temperature for 1 hour.

2. Peel the potatoes and cut into thick slices. Cut each slice lengthways to make chunky chips/fries. Place them in a nonstick frying pan and heat, shaking the pan, until all the moisture has evaporated. Turn them onto absorbent paper towels to dry off.

3. Heat the oil to 180°C/350°F, then fry the chips a few at a time for 4–5 minutes until crisp and golden. Drain on absorbent paper towels and keep warm.

4. Pat the cod fillets dry, then coat in the flour. Dip the floured fillets into the reserved batter. Fry for 2–3 minutes until cooked and crisp, then drain. Garnish with lemon wedges and parsley and serve immediately with the chips, tomato ketchup and vinegar.

Summer Pavlova

4 egg whites
225 g/8 oz/1 cup
   caster/superfine sugar
1 tsp vanilla extract
2 tsp white wine vinegar
1½ tsp cornflour/cornstarch

300 ml/½ pint/1 cup
   Greek yogurt
2 tbsp honey
225 g/8 oz/2 cups
   strawberries, hulled
125 g/4 oz/1 cup raspberries

125 g/4 oz/1 cup blueberries
4 kiwis, peeled and sliced
icing/powdered sugar,
   to decorate

1. Preheat the oven to 150°C/300°F/Gas Mark 2. Line a baking tray with a sheet of greaseproof/ waxed paper or baking parchment.

2. Place the egg whites in a clean, grease-free bowl and whisk until very stiff. Whisk in half the sugar, the vanilla extract, vinegar and cornflour/cornstarch and continue whisking until stiff. Gradually whisk in the remaining sugar, a teaspoonful at a time, until the mixture is very stiff and glossy.

3. Using a large spoon, arrange the meringue in a circle on the greaseproof paper or baking parchment.

4. Bake in the preheated oven for 1 hour until crisp and dry. Turn the oven off and leave the meringue in the oven to cool completely. Remove the meringue from the baking sheet and peel away the paper. Mix together the yogurt and honey. Place the pavlova on a serving plate and spoon the yogurt into the centre.

5. Sprinkle with the strawberries, raspberries, blueberries and kiwis. Dust with the icing/powdered sugar and serve.

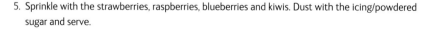

Classic Minestrone

SERVES 4

25 g/1 oz/2 tbsp butter
3 tbsp olive oil
3 slices streaky/fatty bacon
1 large onion, peeled
1 garlic clove, peeled
1 celery stalk, trimmed
2 carrots, peeled
400 g/14 oz can chopped
    tomatoes

1.2 litres/2¼ pints/1¼ quarts
    chicken stock
175 g/6 oz/2½ cups green
    cabbage, finely shredded
50 g/2 oz/½ cup French/
    green beans, trimmed
    and halved
3 tbsp frozen petits pois
50 g/2 oz spaghetti

salt and freshly ground
    black pepper
Parmesan cheese shavings,
    to garnish
crusty bread, to serve

1. Heat the butter and olive oil together in a large saucepan. Chop the bacon and add to the saucepan. Cook for 3–4 minutes, then remove with a slotted spoon and reserve.

2. Finely chop the onion, garlic, celery and carrots and add to the saucepan, one ingredient at a time, stirring well after each addition. Cover and cook gently for 8–10 minutes until the vegetables are softened.

3. Add the chopped tomatoes, with their juice and the stock, bring to the boil, then cover the saucepan with a lid, reduce the heat and simmer gently for about 20 minutes.

4. Stir in the cabbage, beans, petits pois and spaghetti, broken into short pieces. Cover and simmer for a further 20 minutes until all the ingredients are tender. Season to taste with salt and pepper.

5. Return the cooked bacon to the saucepan and bring the soup to the boil. Serve the soup immediately, with Parmesan shavings sprinkled on top and plenty of crusty bread.

Traditional Lasagne

450 g/1 lb lean minced/ground beef
175 g/6 oz/¾ cup pancetta or smoked streaky/fatty bacon, chopped
1 large onion, peeled and chopped
2 celery stalks, trimmed and chopped
125 g/4 oz/1 cup button mushrooms, wiped and chopped

2 garlic cloves, peeled and chopped
100 g/3½ oz/1 cup plain/all-purpose flour
300 ml/½ pint/1¼ cups beef stock
1 tbsp dried mixed herbs
5 tbsp tomato purée/paste
salt and freshly ground black pepper
75 g/3 oz/⅓ cup (6 tbsp) butter
1 tsp English mustard powder

pinch freshly grated nutmeg
900 ml/1½ pints/scant 1 quart milk
125 g/4 oz/1¼ cups Parmesan cheese, grated
125 g/4 oz/1 cup Cheddar cheese, grated
8–12 precooked lasagne sheets

To serve:
crusty bread
fresh green salad leaves

1. Preheat oven to 200°C/400°F/Gas Mark 6, 15 minutes before required. Cook the beef and pancetta in a large saucepan for 10 minutes, stirring to break up any lumps. Add the onion, celery and mushrooms and cook for 4 minutes, or until softened slightly. Stir in the garlic and 1 tablespoon of the flour, then cook for 1 minute. Stir in the stock, herbs and tomato purée/paste. Season to taste. Bring to the boil, then cover, reduce the heat and simmer for 45 minutes.

2. Meanwhile, melt the butter in a small saucepan and stir in the remaining flour, mustard powder and nutmeg until well blended. Cook for 2 minutes. Remove from the heat and gradually blend in the milk until smooth. Return to the heat and bring to the boil, stirring, until thickened. Gradually stir in half the Parmesan and Cheddar cheeses until melted. Season to taste.

3. Spoon half the meat mixture into the base of a large ovenproof dish. Top with a single layer of pasta. Spread over half the sauce and scatter with half the cheese. Repeat layers, finishing with cheese. Bake in the preheated oven for 30 minutes, or until the pasta is cooked and the top is golden brown and bubbly. Serve immediately with crusty bread and a green salad.

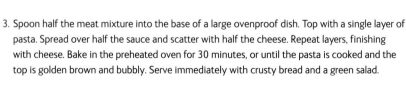

Strawberry Flan

For the sweet pastry:
175 g/6 oz/1⅓ cups plain/
    all-purpose flour
50 g/2 oz/¼ cup
    (4 tbsp) butter
50 g/2 oz/¼ cup white
    vegetable fat/shortening
2 tsp caster/superfine sugar

1 medium/large egg
    yolk, beaten

For the filling:
1 medium/large egg, plus
    1 extra egg yolk
50 g/2 oz/¼ cup
    caster/superfine sugar

25 g/1 oz/3 heaped tbsp
    plain/all-purpose flour
300 ml/½ pint/1¼ cups milk
few drops vanilla extract
450 g/1 lb/3 heaped cups
    strawberries, cleaned
    and hulled
mint leaves, to decorate

1. Preheat the oven to 200°C/400°F/Gas Mark 6, 15 minutes before baking. Place the flour, butter and vegetable fat/shortening in a food processor and blend until the mixture resembles fine breadcrumbs. Stir in the sugar, then, with the machine running, add the egg yolk and enough water to make a fairly stiff dough. Knead lightly, cover and chill in the refrigerator for 30 minutes. Roll out the pastry dough and use to line a 23 cm/9 inch loose-bottomed flan tin/tart pan. Place a piece of greaseproof/waxed paper in the pastry case/pie crust and cover with baking beans/pie weights or rice. Bake in the preheated oven for 15–20 minutes until just firm. Reserve until cool.

2. Make the filling by whisking the eggs and sugar together until thick and pale. Gradually stir in the flour and then the milk. Pour into a small saucepan and simmer for 3–4 minutes, stirring throughout. Add the vanilla extract to taste, then pour into a bowl and leave to cool. Cover with greaseproof paper to prevent a skin from forming.

3. When the filling is cold, whisk until smooth, then pour into the cooked flan case. Slice the strawberries and arrange on top of the filling. Allow to set. Decorate with the mint leaves and serve.

Smoked Haddock Tart

For the shortcrust pastry:
150 g/5 oz/1 heaped cup
   plain/all-purpose flour
pinch salt
25 g/1 oz/2 tbsp lard or white
   vegetable fat/shortening,
   cut into small cubes
40 g/1½ oz/3 tbsp butter
   or hard margarine,
   cut into small cubes

For the filling:
225 g/8 oz/½ lb smoked
   haddock, skinned
   and cubed
2 large/extra-large
   eggs, beaten
300 ml/½ pint/1¼ cups
   double/heavy cream
1 tsp Dijon mustard
freshly ground black pepper

125 g/4 oz/1 heaped cup
   Gruyère/hard Swiss
   cheese, grated
1 tbsp freshly snipped chives

To serve:
lemon wedges
tomato wedges
fresh green salad leaves

1. Preheat the oven to 190°C/375°F/Gas Mark 5, 10 minutes before baking. Sift the flour and salt into a large bowl. Add the fats and mix lightly. With the fingertips, rub into the flour until the mixture resembles breadcrumbs. Sprinkle 1 tablespoon cold water into the mixture. With a knife, start bringing the dough together, using your hands if necessary. If the dough does not form a ball instantly, add a little more water. Put the dough in a polythene/plastic bag and chill for at least 30 minutes.

2. On a lightly floured surface, roll out the dough and use to line an 18 cm/7 inch lightly oiled flan tin/tart pan. Prick the base all over with a fork and bake blind in the preheated oven for 15 minutes. Carefully remove from the oven and brush with a little of the beaten egg.

4. Return the pastry to the oven for a further 5 minutes, then place the fish in the pastry case/pie crust. For the filling, beat together the eggs and cream. Add the mustard, black pepper and cheese and pour over the fish. Sprinkle with the chives and bake for 35–40 minutes until the filling is golden brown and set in the centre. Serve hot or cold with the lemon and tomato wedges and salad leaves.

Lancashire Hotpot

SERVES 4

1 kg/2¼ lb middle end
   neck of lamb, divided
   into cutlets
2 tbsp vegetable oil
2 large onions, peeled
   and sliced
2 tsp plain/all-purpose flour

150 ml/¼ pint/⅔ cup
   vegetable or lamb stock
4–5 waxy potatoes, peeled
   and thickly sliced
salt and freshly ground
   black pepper
1 bay leaf

2 fresh thyme sprigs
1 tbsp melted butter
2 tbsp freshly chopped
   herbs, to garnish
freshly cooked green beans,
   to serve

1. Preheat the oven to 170°C/325°F/Gas Mark 3. Trim any excess fat from the lamb cutlets. Heat the oil in a frying pan and brown the cutlets in batches for 3–4 minutes. Remove with a slotted spoon and reserve.

2. Add the onions to the frying pan and cook for 6–8 minutes until softened and just beginning to colour, then remove and reserve.

3. Stir in the flour and cook for a few seconds, then gradually pour in the stock, stirring well, and bring to the boil. Remove from the heat.

4. Spread the base of a large casserole dish with half the potato slices. Top with half the onions and season well with salt and pepper. Arrange the browned meat in a layer. Season again and add the remaining onions, bay leaf and thyme. Pour in the stock and top with remaining potatoes so that they overlap in a single layer. Brush the potatoes with the melted butter and season again.

5. Cover the saucepan and cook in the preheated oven for 2 hours, uncovering for the last 30 minutes to allow the potatoes to brown. Garnish with chopped herbs and serve immediately with green beans.

Crunchy Rhubarb Crumble

100 g/3½ oz/1 cup plain/
   all-purpose flour
50 g/2 oz/¼ cup (4 tbsp)
   softened butter
50 g/2 oz/⅔ cup rolled oats

50 g/2 oz/¼ cup demerara/
   turbinado sugar
1 tbsp sesame seeds
½ tsp ground cinnamon
450 g/1 lb fresh rhubarb

50 g/2 oz/¼ cup
   caster/superfine sugar
custard or cream, to serve

1. Preheat the oven to 180°C/350°F/Gas Mark 4. Place the flour in a large bowl and cut the
   butter into cubes. Add to the flour and rub in with the fingertips until the mixture looks
   like fine breadcrumbs, or blend for a few seconds in a food processor. Stir in the oats,
   demerara/turbinado sugar, sesame seeds and cinnamon. Mix well and reserve.

2. Prepare the rhubarb by removing the thick ends of the stalks and cut diagonally into
   2.5 cm/1 inch chunks. Wash thoroughly and pat dry with a clean dishtowel. Place the
   rhubarb in a 1 litre/2 pints/1 quart pie dish.

3. Sprinkle the caster/superfine sugar over the rhubarb and top with the reserved crumble/crisp
   mixture. Level the top of the crumble so that all the fruit is well covered and press down
   firmly. If liked, sprinkle the top with a little extra caster sugar.

4. Place on a baking sheet and bake in the preheated oven for 40–50 minutes until the fruit
   is soft and the topping is golden brown. Sprinkle the pudding with some more caster sugar
   and serve hot with custard or cream.

Mozzarella Frittata with Tomato & Basil Salad

SERVES 6

For the salad:
6 ripe but firm tomatoes,
　　thinly sliced
2 tbsp fresh basil leaves
2 tbsp olive oil
1 tbsp fresh lemon juice
1 tsp caster/superfine sugar

freshly ground black pepper

For the frittata:
7 eggs, beaten
salt
300 g/11 oz/2 cups
　　mozzarella cheese, grated

2 spring onions/scallions,
　　trimmed and finely
　　chopped
2 tbsp olive oil
warm crusty bread, to serve

1. To make the tomato and basil salad, place the tomatoes in a dish, tear up the basil leaves and sprinkle over. Make the dressing by whisking the olive oil, lemon juice and sugar together well. Season with black pepper before drizzling the dressing over the salad.

2. To make the frittata, preheat the grill/broiler to a high heat just before starting to cook. Place the eggs in a large bowl with plenty of salt and whisk. Stir the mozzarella into the egg with the finely chopped spring onions/scallions.

3. Heat the oil in a large nonstick frying pan. Pour in the egg mixture, stirring with a wooden spoon to spread the ingredients evenly over the pan. Cook for 5–8 minutes until the frittata is golden brown and firm on the underside. Place the whole pan under the preheated grill and cook for about 4–5 minutes until the top is golden brown. Slide the frittata onto a serving plate, cut into six large wedges and serve immediately with the tomato and basil salad and plenty of warm crusty bread.

Cannelloni

2 tbsp olive oil
175 g/6 oz/¾ cup fresh
    minced/ground pork
75 g/3 oz/⅔ cup chicken
    livers, chopped
1 small onion, peeled
    and chopped
1 garlic clove, peeled
    and chopped

175 g/6 oz/1 cup frozen spinach,
    thawed and chopped
1 tbsp freeze-dried oregano
pinch freshly grated nutmeg
salt and freshly ground
    black pepper
175 g/6 oz/¾ cup ricotta or
    quark cheese
25 g/1 oz/2 tbsp butter

25 g/1 oz/¼ cup plain/
    all-purpose flour
600 ml/1 pt/2½ cups milk
600 ml/1 pt/2½ cups ready-
    made tomato sauce
16 precooked cannelloni tubes
50 g/2 oz/½ cup Parmesan
    cheese, grated
green salad, to serve

1. Preheat the oven to 190°C/375°F/Gas Mark 5, 10 minutes before cooking. Heat the olive oil in a frying pan and cook the pork and chicken livers for about 5 minutes, stirring occasionally, until browned all over. Break up any lumps if necessary with a wooden spoon. Add the onion and garlic and cook for 4 minutes until softened. Add the spinach, oregano and nutmeg and season to taste with salt and pepper. Cook until all the liquid has evaporated, then remove the pan from the heat and allow to cool. Stir in the ricotta or quark cheese.

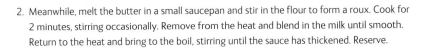

2. Meanwhile, melt the butter in a small saucepan and stir in the flour to form a roux. Cook for 2 minutes, stirring occasionally. Remove from the heat and blend in the milk until smooth. Return to the heat and bring to the boil, stirring until the sauce has thickened. Reserve.

3. Spoon a thin layer of the tomato sauce on the base of a large ovenproof dish. Divide the pork filling between the cannelloni tubes. Arrange on top of the tomato sauce. Spoon over the remaining tomato sauce. Pour over the white sauce and sprinkle with the Parmesan cheese. Bake in the preheated oven for 30–35 minutes until the cannelloni is tender and the top is golden brown. Serve immediately with a green salad.

Hazelnut, Chocolate & Chestnut Meringue Torte

For the chocolate meringue:
1 medium/large egg white
50 g/2 oz/¼ cup
   caster/superfine sugar
2 tbsp cocoa powder

For the hazelnut meringue:
75 g/3 oz/½ cup hazelnuts,
   toasted

2 medium/large egg whites
125 g/4 oz/⅔ cup
   caster/superfine sugar

For the filling:
300 ml/½ pint/1¼ cups
   double/heavy cream
250 g/9 oz can sweetened
   chestnut purée

50 g/2 oz dark/bittersweet
   chocolate, melted
25 g/1 oz dark/bittersweet
   chocolate, grated

1. Preheat the oven to 130°C/250°F/Gas Mark ½. Line three baking sheets with nonstick baking parchment and draw a 20.5 cm/8 inch circle on each. Beat 1 egg white until stiff peaks form. Add 2 tbsp of the sugar and beat until shiny. Mix the cocoa powder with the remaining sugar, adding 1 tablespoon at a time, beating well after each addition, until all the sugar is added and the mixture is stiff and glossy. Spread onto one of the baking sheets within the circle.

2. Put the nuts in a food processor and blend until chopped. In a clean bowl, beat the 2 egg whites until stiff. Add 50 g/2 oz/¼ cup of the sugar and beat. Add the remaining sugar 1 tablespoon at a time, beating until all the sugar is added and the mixture is stiff and glossy. Reserve 2 tablespoons of the nuts, then fold in the remainder and divide between the two remaining baking sheets. Sprinkle one of the hazelnut meringues with the reserved hazelnuts. Bake all three meringues in the oven for 1½ hours. Turn off and leave there until cold.

3. Whip the cream until thick. Beat the chestnut purée in another bowl until soft. Add a spoonful of the cream and fold together before adding the remaining cream and melted chocolate and folding together. Place the plain hazelnut meringue on a serving plate. Top with half the cream and chestnut mixture. Add the chocolate meringue and top with the remaining cream. Add the final meringue. Sprinkle over the grated chocolate and serve.

Beetroot Ravioli with Dill Cream Sauce

For the pasta:
225 g/8 oz/1⅛ cups strong plain bread flour or type 00 pasta flour, plus extra for rolling
1 tsp salt
2 medium/large eggs; 1 medium/large egg yolk
1 tbsp extra virgin olive oil

For the filling:
1 tbsp olive oil
1 small onion, peeled and finely chopped
½ tsp caraway seeds
175 g/6 oz/1 cup cooked beetroot/beets, chopped
175 g/6 oz/¾ cup ricotta cheese
25 g/1 oz/½ cup fresh

white breadcrumbs
1 medium/large egg yolk
2 tbsp grated Parmesan cheese
salt and freshly ground pepper
4 tbsp walnut oil
4 tbsp freshly chopped dill
1 tbsp green peppercorns, drained and chopped
6 tbsp crème fraîche/sour cream

1. To make the pasta dough, sift the flour and salt into a large bowl, make a well in the centre and add the eggs and yolk, the oil and 1 teaspoon water. Gradually mix to form a soft but not sticky dough, adding a little more flour or water as necessary. Turn out on to a lightly floured surface and knead for 5 minutes, or until smooth and elastic. Wrap in clingfilm/plastic wrap and leave to rest at room temperature for about 30 minutes.

2. To make the filling, heat the oil in a large pan, add the onion and seeds and cook over a medium heat for 5 minutes, or until the onion is softened and lightly golden. Stir in the beetroot and cook for 5 minutes. Blend the mixture in a food processor until smooth, then allow to cool. Stir in the ricotta cheese, breadcrumbs, egg yolk and Parmesan. Season to taste with salt and pepper and reserve. Divide the pasta dough into eight pieces. Roll out into long thin sheets. Lay one sheet on a floured surface and place 5 heaped teaspoons of the filling 2.5 cm/1 inch apart. Dampen around the heaps of filling and lay a second sheet over the top. Press around the heaps to seal. Cut into squares. Put the filled pasta onto a floured dishtowel. Bring a large pan of lightly salted water to a rolling boil. Drop the ravioli into the boiling water, return to the boil and cook for 3–4 minutes until *al dente*. Meanwhile, heat the walnut oil in a small pan, then add the chopped dill and green peppercorns. Remove from the heat, stir in the crème fraîche/sour cream and season well. Drain the pasta thoroughly and toss with the sauce. Tip into warmed dishes and serve immediately.

Italian Beef Pot Roast

1.8 kg/4 lb brisket of beef
225 g/8 oz small onions, peeled
3 garlic cloves, peeled
   and chopped
2 celery stalks, trimmed
   and chopped
2 carrots, peeled and sliced
450 g/1 lb ripe tomatoes

300 ml/½ pint/1¼ cups Italian
   red wine
2 tbsp olive oil
300 ml/½ pint/1¼ cups
   beef stock
1 tbsp tomato purée/paste
2 tsp freeze-dried
   mixed herbs

salt and freshly ground
   black pepper
25 g/1 oz/2 tbsp butter
3 tbsp plain/all-purpose flour
freshly cooked vegetables,
   to serve

1. Preheat the oven to 150°C/300°F/Gas Mark 2, 10 minutes before cooking. Place the beef in a bowl. Add the onions, garlic, celery and carrots.

2. Place the tomatoes in a bowl and cover with boiling water. Allow to stand for 2 minutes and drain. Peel away the skins, discard the seeds and chop, then add to the beef mixture along with the red wine. Cover tightly and marinate in the refrigerator overnight.

3. Lift the marinated beef from the bowl and pat dry with paper towels. Heat the olive oil in a large casserole dish and cook the beef until it is browned all over, then remove from the dish.

4. Drain the vegetables from the marinade, reserving the marinade. Add the vegetables to the casserole dish and fry gently for 5 minutes, stirring occasionally, until browned. Return the beef to the dish with the marinade, beef stock, tomato purée/paste and mixed herbs and season with salt and pepper. Bring to the boil, then cover and cook in the preheated oven for 3 hours.

6. Using a slotted spoon, transfer the beef and large chunks of vegetables to a plate and keep warm. Blend the butter and flour to form a paste. Bring the casserole juices to the boil, then gradually stir in the paste. Cook until thickened. Serve with the sauce and freshly cooked vegetables.

Tiramisu

225 g/8 oz/1 cup mascarpone cheese

25 g/1 oz/¼ cup icing/powdered sugar, sifted

150 ml/¼ pint/⅔ cup strong brewed coffee, chilled

300 ml/½ pint/1¼ cups double/heavy cream

3 tbsp coffee liqueur

125 g/4 oz sponge fingers/ladyfingers

50 g/2 oz dark/bittersweet chocolate, grated or curled

unsweetened cocoa powder, for dusting

assorted summer berries, to serve

1. Lightly oil and line a 900 g/2 lb loaf tin/pan with a piece of clingfilm/plastic wrap.

2. Put the mascarpone cheese and icing/powdered sugar into a large bowl and, using a rubber spatula, beat until smooth. Stir in 2 tablespoons chilled coffee and mix thoroughly.

3. Whip the cream with 1 tablespoon of the coffee liqueur until just thickened. Stir a spoonful of the whipped cream into the mascarpone mixture, then fold in the rest. Spoon half of the mascarpone mixture into the prepared loaf tin and smooth the top.

4. Put the remaining coffee and coffee liqueur into a shallow dish just bigger than the sponge fingers/ladyfingers. Using half of them, dip one side of each sponge finger into the coffee mixture, then arrange on top of the mascarpone mixture in a single layer. Spoon the rest of the mascarpone mixture over the sponge fingers and smooth the top. Dip the remaining sponge fingers in the coffee mixture and arrange on top of the mascarpone mixture. Drizzle with any remaining coffee mixture. Cover with clingfilm and chill in the refrigerator for 4 hours.

5. Carefully turn the tiramisu out onto a large serving plate. Sprinkle with the grated chocolate or chocolate curls. Dust with cocoa powder, cut into slices and serve with a few summer berries.

Bruschetta with
Pecorino, Garlic & Tomatoes

SERVES 4

6 ripe but firm tomatoes
125 g/4 oz/1¼ cup pecorino
   cheese, finely grated
1 tbsp oregano leaves,
   chopped
salt and freshly ground
   black pepper
3 tbsp olive oil

3 garlic cloves, peeled
8 slices flat Italian bread,
   such as focaccia
8 thin slices mozzarella
   cheese
marinated black olives,
   to serve

1. Preheat the grill/broiler and line the rack with foil just before cooking. Make a small cross in the tops of the tomatoes, then place in a small bowl and cover with boiling water. Leave to stand for 2 minutes, then drain and remove the skins. Cut into quarters and remove the seeds. Chop the flesh into small cubes.

2. Mix the tomato flesh with the pecorino cheese and 2 teaspoons of the fresh oregano and season to taste with salt and pepper. Add 1 tablespoon of the olive oil and mix thoroughly.

3. Crush the garlic and spread evenly over the slices of bread. Heat 2 tablespoons of the olive oil in a large frying pan and fry the bread slices until they are crisp and golden.

4. Place the fried bread on a lightly oiled baking sheet and spoon on the tomato and cheese topping. Place a little mozzarella on top and place under the preheated grill for 3–4 minutes until golden and bubbling. Garnish with the remaining oregano, then arrange the bruschettas on a serving plate and serve immediately with the olives.

Pea & Prawn Risotto

450 g/1 lb whole raw
  prawns/shrimp
125 g/4 oz/½ cup
  (8 tbsp) butter
1 red onion, peeled
  and chopped
4 garlic cloves, peeled and
  finely chopped

225 g/8 oz/1 heaped cup
  arborio/risotto rice
150 ml/¼ pint/⅔ cup dry
  white wine
1.1 litres/2 pints/1 quart
  vegetable or fish stock
375 g/13 oz/2½ cups
  frozen peas

4 tbsp freshly chopped mint
salt and freshly ground
  black pepper

1. Peel the prawns/shrimp and reserve the heads and shells. Remove the black vein from the back of each prawn, then wash and dry on absorbent paper towels. Melt half the butter in a large frying pan, add the prawns' heads and shells and fry, stirring occasionally, for 3–4 minutes until golden. Strain the butter, discard the heads and shells and return the butter to the pan.

2. Add half of the remaining butter to the pan and fry the onion and garlic for 5 minutes until softened but not coloured. Add the rice and stir the grains in the butter for 1 minute, until they are coated thoroughly. Add the white wine and boil rapidly until the wine is reduced by half.

3. Bring the stock to a gentle simmer and add to the rice, a ladleful at a time. Stir constantly, adding the stock as it is absorbed, until the rice is creamy, but still has a bite in the centre.

4. Melt the remaining butter and stir-fry the prawns for 3–4 minutes. Stir into the rice, along with all the pan juices and the peas. Add the chopped mint and season to taste with salt and pepper. Cover the pan and leave the prawns to infuse for 5 minutes before serving.

Ricotta Cheesecake with Strawberry Coulis

SERVES 6-8

8 digestive biscuits/
  Graham crackers
100 g/3½ oz mixed/candied
  peel, chopped
65 g/2½ oz/5 tbsp
  butter, melted
150 ml/¼ pint/⅔ cup crème
  fraîche/sour cream

375 g/13 oz/1 cup
  ricotta cheese
100 g/3½ oz/½ cup
  caster/superfine sugar
1 vanilla pod, seeds only
2 large/extra-large eggs
225 g/8 oz/1½ cups
  strawberries, hulled

2–4 tbsp caster/superfine
  sugar, to taste
zest and juice of 1 orange

1. Preheat the oven to 170°C/325°F/Gas Mark 3. Line a 20.5 cm/8 inch springform tin/pan with baking parchment. Put the biscuits/crackers in a food processor together with the peel. Blend until the biscuits are crushed and the peel is chopped. Add 50 g/2 oz/¼ cup (4 tbsp) of the melted butter and process until mixed. Tip into the tin and spread firmly and evenly over the bottom.

2. Blend together the crème fraîche/sour cream, ricotta cheese, sugar, vanilla seeds and eggs in a food processor. With the motor running, add the remaining melted butter and blend for a few seconds. Pour the mixture onto the base. Transfer to the preheated oven and cook for about 1 hour until set and risen round the edges, but slightly wobbly in the centre. Switch off the oven and allow to cool there. Chill in the refrigerator for at least 8 hours, or preferably overnight.

3. Wash and drain the strawberries. Put into the food processor along with 2 tablespoons of the sugar and the orange zest and juice. Blend until smooth. Add the remaining sugar to taste. Pass through a sieve to remove seeds and chill in the refrigerator until needed. Cut the cheesecake into wedges, spoon over some of the strawberry coulis and serve.

Peperonata
(Braised Mixed Peppers)

2 green peppers
1 red pepper
1 yellow pepper
1 orange pepper
1 onion, peeled
2 garlic cloves, peeled
2 tbsp olive oil

4 very ripe tomatoes
1 tbsp freshly chopped
    oregano
salt and freshly ground
    black pepper
150 ml/¼ pint/⅔ cup light
    chicken or vegetable stock

fresh oregano sprigs,
    to garnish
focaccia or flat bread,
    to serve

1. Remove the seeds from the peppers and cut into thin strips. Slice the onion into rings and chop the garlic cloves finely.

2. Heat the olive oil in a frying pan and fry the peppers, onions and garlic for 5–10 minutes until soft and lightly coloured. Stir continuously.

3. Make a cross on the tops of the tomatoes, then place in a bowl and cover with boiling water. Allow to stand for about 2 minutes. Drain, then remove the skins and seeds and chop the tomato flesh into cubes.

4. Add the tomatoes and oregano to the peppers and onion and season to taste with salt and pepper. Cover the pan and bring to the boil. Simmer gently for about 30 minutes until tender, adding the chicken or vegetable stock halfway through the cooking time.

5. Garnish with oregano sprigs and serve hot with plenty of freshly baked focaccia or lightly toasted slices of flat bread and pile a spoonful of peperonata onto each plate.

Pappardelle with Smoked Haddock & Blue Cheese Sauce

SERVES 4

350 g/12 oz smoked haddock
2 bay leaves
300 ml/½ pint/1¼ cups milk
400 g/14 oz pappardelle
or tagliatelle
25 g/1 oz/2 tbsp butter
25 g/1 oz/¼ cup plain/all-
purpose flour

150 ml/¼ pint/⅔ cup single/
light cream or extra milk
125 g/4 oz Dolcelatte cheese
or Gorgonzola, cut into
small pieces
¼ tsp freshly grated nutmeg
salt and freshly ground
black pepper

40 g/1½ oz/⅓ cup toasted
walnuts, chopped
1 tbsp freshly
chopped parsley

1. Place the smoked haddock in a saucepan with 1 bay leaf and pour in the milk. Bring to the boil slowly, cover and simmer for 6–7 minutes until the fish is opaque. Remove and roughly flake the fish, discarding the skin and any bones. Strain the milk and reserve.

2. Bring a large pan of lightly salted water to a rolling boil. Add the pasta and cook according to the packet instructions, or until *al dente*.

3. Meanwhile, place the butter, flour and single cream, or milk if preferred, in a pan and stir to mix. Stir in the reserved warm milk and add the remaining bay leaf. Bring to the boil, whisking all the time, until smooth and thick. Gently simmer for 3–4 minutes, stirring frequently. Discard the bay leaf. Add the cheese to the sauce. Heat gently, stirring, until melted. Add the flaked haddock and season to taste with nutmeg, salt and pepper.

4. Drain the pasta thoroughly and return to the pan. Add the sauce and toss gently to coat, taking care not to break up the flakes of fish. Tip into a warmed serving bowl, sprinkle with toasted walnuts and parsley and serve immediately.

Chestnut Cake

175 g/6 oz/¾ cup (1½ sticks)
butter, softened
175 g/6 oz/¾ cup
caster/superfine sugar
250 g/9 oz can sweetened
chestnut purée
3 eggs, lightly beaten
175 g/6 oz/1½ cups plain/
all-purpose flour

1 tsp baking powder
pinch ground cloves
1 tsp fennel seeds, crushed
75 g/3 oz/½ cup raisins
50 g/2 oz/½ cup pine nuts,
toasted
125 g/4 oz/1 cup icing/
powdered sugar
5 tbsp lemon juice

strips pared lemon zest,
to decorate

1. Preheat the oven to 150°C/300°F/Gas Mark 2. Oil and line a 23 cm/9 inch springform tin/pan. Beat together the butter and sugar until light and fluffy. Add the chestnut purée and beat. Gradually add the eggs, beating after each addition. Sift in the flour with the baking powder and cloves. Add the fennel seeds and beat. The mixture should drop easily from a wooden spoon when tapped against the side of the bowl. If not, add a little milk.

2. Beat in the raisins and pine nuts. Spoon the mixture into the prepared tin and smooth the top. Put in the centre of the preheated oven and bake for 55–60 minutes until a skewer inserted in the centre of the cake comes out clean. Remove from the oven and leave in the tin.

3. Meanwhile, mix together the icing/powdered sugar and lemon juice in a small saucepan until smooth. Heat gently until hot but not boiling.

4. Using a cocktail stick/toothpick or skewer, poke holes all over the cake. Pour the hot syrup evenly over the cake and leave to soak in. Decorate with pared strips of lemon zest and serve.

Italian Baked Tomatoes with Curly Endive & Radicchio

1 tsp olive oil
4 beef tomatoes
salt, for sprinkling
50 g/2 oz/1 cup fresh white
   breadcrumbs
1 tbsp freshly snipped chives
1 tbsp freshly chopped
   parsley

125 g/4 oz/1¼ cups
   button/white mushrooms,
   finely chopped
salt and freshly ground
   black pepper
25 g/1 oz/¼ cup fresh
   Parmesan cheese, grated

For the salad:
½ curly endive lettuce
½ small piece radicchio
2 tbsp olive oil
1 tsp balsamic vinegar
salt and freshly ground
   black pepper

1. Preheat the oven to 190°C/375°F/Gas Mark 5, 10 minutes before baking. Lightly oil a baking sheet with the oil. Slice the tops off the tomatoes, remove all the tomato flesh and sieve into a large bowl. Sprinkle a little salt inside the tomato shells. Place them upside down on a plate while the filling is prepared.

2. Mix the sieved tomato with the breadcrumbs, fresh herbs and mushrooms and season well with salt and pepper. Place the tomato shells on the prepared baking sheet and fill with the tomato and mushroom mixture. Sprinkle the cheese on top and bake in the preheated oven for 15–20 minutes until golden brown.

3. Meanwhile, prepare the salad. Arrange the endive and radicchio on individual serving plates and mix the remaining ingredients together in a small bowl to make the dressing. Season to taste.

4. When the tomatoes are cooked, allow to rest for 5 minutes, then place on the prepared plates and drizzle over a little dressing. Serve warm.

Melanzane Parmigiana

SERVES 4

900 g/2 lb (2 medium)
aubergines/eggplants
salt and freshly ground
black pepper
5 tbsp olive oil
1 red onion, peeled and
chopped
½ tsp mild paprika

150 ml/¼ pint/⅔ cup dry
red wine
150 ml/¼ pint/⅔ cup
vegetable stock
400 g/14 oz can chopped
tomatoes
1 tsp tomato purée/paste

1 tbsp freshly chopped
oregano
175 g/6 oz/1½ cups
mozzarella cheese, thinly
sliced
40 g/1½ oz/½ cup coarsely
grated Parmesan cheese
fresh basil sprig, to garnish

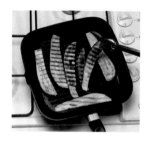

1. Preheat the oven to 200˚C/400˚F/Gas Mark 6, 15 minutes before baking. Cut the aubergines/eggplants lengthways into thin slices. Sprinkle with salt and leave to drain in a colander over a bowl for 30 minutes.

2. Meanwhile, heat 1 tablespoon of the oil in a saucepan and fry the onion for 10 minutes until softened. Add the paprika and cook for 1 minute. Stir in the wine, stock, tomatoes and tomato purée/ paste. Simmer uncovered for 25 minutes, or until fairly thick. Stir in the oregano and season to taste. Remove from the heat.

3. Rinse the aubergine slices thoroughly under cold water. Pat dry on absorbent paper towels. Heat 2 tablespoons of the oil in a griddle pan and cook the aubergines in batches (using the remaing oil where required), for 3 minutes on each side, until golden. Drain well on absorbent paper towels.

4. Pour half of the tomato sauce into the base of a large ovenproof dish. Cover with half the aubergine slices, then top with the mozzarella. Cover with the remaining aubergine and pour over the remaining tomato sauce. Sprinkle with the grated Parmesan. Bake in the preheated oven for 30 minutes, or until the aubergines are tender and the sauce is bubbling. Garnish with a sprig of basil and cool for a few minutes before serving.

Almond & Pine Nut Tart

250 g/9 oz/1¼ cups ready-made sweet shortcrust pastry dough (*see* page 166)
75 g/3 oz/¾ cup blanched almonds
75 g/3 oz/⅓ cup caster/superfine sugar

pinch salt
2 eggs
1 tsp vanilla extract
2–3 drops almond extract
125 g/4 oz/½ cup (8 tbsp) unsalted butter, softened
2 tbsp plain/all-purpose flour
½ tsp baking powder

3–4 tbsp raspberry jam/jelly
50 g/2 oz/½ cup pine nuts
icing/powdered sugar, to decorate
whipped cream, to serve

1. Preheat the oven to 200°C/400°F/Gas Mark 6, 15 minutes before baking. Roll out the pastry dough and use to line a 23 cm/9 inch fluted flan tin/tart pan. Chill in the refrigerator for 10 minutes, then line with greaseproof/waxed paper and baking beans/pie weights. Bake blind in the preheated oven for 10 minutes. Remove the paper and beans. Bake for a further 10–12 minutes until cooked. Leave to cool. Reduce the temperature to 190°C/375°F/Gas Mark 5.

2. Grind the almonds in a food processor until fine. Add the sugar, salt, eggs and vanilla and almond extracts and blend. Add the butter, flour and baking powder and blend until smooth.

3. Spread a thick layer of the raspberry jam/jelly over the cooled pastry case/pie crust, then pour in the almond filling. Sprinkle the pine nuts evenly over the top and bake for 30 minutes, or until firm and browned. Remove the tart from the oven and leave to cool.

4. Dust generously with icing/powdered sugar and serve cut into wedges with whipped cream.

Sesame Prawn Toasts

SERVES 4

125 g/4 oz peeled cooked
prawns/shrimp
1 tbsp cornflour/cornstarch
2 spring onions/scallions,
peeled and roughly
chopped
2 tsp freshly grated
root ginger

2 tsp dark soy sauce
pinch Chinese five-spice
powder
1 small/medium egg, beaten
salt and freshly ground
black pepper
6 thin slices day-old
white bread

5 tbsp sesame seeds
vegetable oil, for deep-frying
chilli sauce, to serve

1. Place the prawns/shrimp in a food processor or blender with the cornflour/cornstarch, spring onions/scallions, ginger, soy sauce and Chinese five-spice powder. Blend to a fairly smooth paste. Spoon into a bowl and stir in the beaten egg. Season to taste with salt and pepper.

2. Cut the crusts off the bread. Spread the prawn paste in an even layer on one side of each slice. Sprinkle over the sesame seeds and press down lightly. Cut each slice diagonally into four triangles, then place on a board and chill in the refrigerator for 30 minutes.

3. Pour oil into a heavy-based saucepan or deep-fat fryer so that it is one-third full. Heat until it reaches a temperature of 180°C/350°F. Cook the toasts in batches of five or six, carefully lowering them, seeded-side down, into the oil. Deep-fry for 2–3 minutes until lightly browned, then turn over and cook for 1 minute more. Using a slotted spoon, lift out the toasts and drain on absorbent paper towels. Keep warm while frying the remaining toasts. Arrange on a warmed platter and serve immediately with chilli sauce for dipping.

Pork Fried Noodles

125 g/4 oz dried thread egg
noodles
125 g/4 oz/1 cup broccoli
florets
4 tbsp groundnut/
peanut oil
350 g/12 oz pork tenderloin,
cut into slices
3 tbsp soy sauce
1 tbsp lemon juice

pinch sugar
1 tsp chilli sauce
1 tbsp sesame oil
2.5 cm/1 inch piece fresh
root ginger, peeled and
cut into sticks
1 garlic clove, peeled
and chopped
1 green chilli, deseeded
and sliced

125 g/4 oz/¾ cup mangetout/
snow peas, halved
2 eggs, lightly beaten
227 g/8 oz can water
chestnuts, drained
and sliced

To garnish:
radish rose
spring onion/scallion tassels

1. Place the noodles in a bowl and cover with boiling water. Leave to stand for 20 minutes, stirring occasionally, or until tender. Drain and reserve. Meanwhile, blanch the broccoli in a saucepan of lightly salted boiling water for 2 minutes. Drain, refresh under cold running water and reserve.

2. Heat a large wok or frying pan, add the groundnut/peanut oil and heat until just smoking. Add the pork and stir-fry for 5 minutes, or until browned. Using a slotted spoon, remove the pork slices and reserve.

3. Mix together the soy sauce, lemon juice, sugar, chilli sauce and sesame oil and reserve.

4. Add the ginger to the wok and stir-fry for 30 seconds. Add the garlic and chilli and stir-fry for 30 seconds. Add the reserved broccoli and stir-fry for 3 minutes. Stir in the mangetout/snow peas, pork and reserved noodles with the beaten eggs and water chestnuts and stir-fry for 5 minutes, or until heated through. Pour over the reserved chilli sauce, toss well and turn into a warmed serving dish. Garnish and serve immediately.

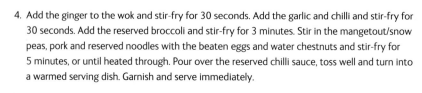

Hot Cherry Fritters

50 g/2 oz/¼ cup (4 tbsp) butter
pinch salt
2 tbsp caster/superfine sugar
125 g/4 oz/1 cup plain/all-
   purpose flour, sifted

¼ tsp ground cinnamon
25 g/1 oz ground almonds
3 eggs, lightly beaten
175 g/6 oz cherries, stoned
sunflower/corn oil, for frying

2 tbsp icing/powdered sugar
1 tsp unsweetened cocoa
   powder
fresh mint sprigs,
   to decorate

1. Place the butter, salt and sugar in a small saucepan with 250 ml/8 fl oz/1 cup water.
   Heat gently until the butter has melted, then add the flour and ground cinnamon and
   beat over a low heat until the mixture leaves the sides of the pan.

2. Remove the saucepan from the heat and beat in the ground almonds. Gradually add the
   eggs, beating well after each addition. Finally stir in the cherries.

3. Pour 5 cm/2 inches depth of oil in a wok and heat until it reaches 180°C/350°F on a sugar
   thermometer. Drop in heaped teaspoons of the mixture, cooking 4 or 5 at a time for about
   2 minutes or until lightly browned and crisp. Remove the fritters from the pan with a slotted
   spoon and drain on absorbent paper towels. Keep warm in a low oven while cooking the
   remaining fritters. Arrange on a warmed serving plate, dust with the icing/powdered sugar and
   cocoa powder. Decorate with mint; serve hot.

Wonton Noodle Soup

SERVES 4

4 shiitake mushrooms, wiped
125 g/4 oz raw prawns/
   shrimp, peeled and
   finely chopped
125 g/4 oz minced/
   ground pork
4 water chestnuts,
   finely chopped

4 spring onions/scallions,
   trimmed and finely sliced
1 egg white
salt and freshly ground
   black pepper
1½ tsp cornflour/cornstarch
1 packet fresh wonton
   wrappers

1.2 litres/2¼ pints/1¼ quarts
   chicken stock
2 cm/¾ inch piece root
   ginger, peeled and sliced
75 g/3 oz fine egg noodles
125 g/4 oz/1½ cups shredded
   pak choi/bok choy

1. Place the mushrooms in a bowl, cover with warm water and leave to soak for 1 hour. Drain, remove and discard the stalks and finely chop the mushrooms. Return to the bowl with the prawns/shrimp, pork, water chestnuts, 2 of the spring onions/scallions and egg white. Season to taste with salt and pepper. Mix well.

2. Mix the cornflour/cornstarch with 1 tablespoon cold water to make a paste. Place a wonton wrapper on a board and brush the edges with the paste. Drop a little less than 1 teaspoon of the pork mixture in the centre. Fold in half to make a triangle, pressing the edges together. Bring the two outer corners together, fixing together with a little more paste. Continue until all the pork mixture is used; you should have 16–20 wontons.

3. Pour the stock into a large, wide saucepan, add the ginger slices and bring to the boil. Add the wontons and simmer for about 5 minutes. Add the noodles and cook for 1 minute. Stir in the pak choi/bok choy and cook for a further 2 minutes, or until the noodles and pak choi are tender and the wontons have floated to the surface and are cooked through.

4. Ladle the soup into warmed bowls, discarding the ginger. Sprinkle with the remaining sliced spring onions and serve immediately.

Fish Balls in
Hot Yellow Bean Sauce

450 g/1 lb skinless white fish
  fillets, such as cod or
  haddock, cut into pieces
½ tsp salt
1 tbsp cornflour/cornstarch
2 spring onions/scallions,
  trimmed and chopped
1 tbsp freshly chopped
  coriander/cilantro

1 tsp soy sauce
1 medium/large egg white
freshly ground black pepper
tarragon sprig, to garnish
freshly cooked rice, to serve

For the yellow bean sauce:
75 ml/3 fl oz/scant ⅓ cup fish
  or chicken stock

1–2 tsp yellow bean sauce
2 tbsp soy sauce
1–2 tbsp Chinese rice wine
  or dry sherry
1 tsp chilli bean sauce,
  or to taste
1 tsp sesame oil
1 tsp sugar (optional)

1. Put the fish pieces, salt, cornflour/cornstarch, spring onions/scallions, coriander/cilantro, soy sauce and egg white into a food processor.

2. Season to taste with pepper, then blend until a smooth paste forms, scraping down the sides of the food processor bowl occasionally.

3. With dampened hands, shape the mixture into 2.5 cm/1 inch balls. Transfer to a baking tray and chill in the refrigerator for at least 30 minutes.

4. Bring a large saucepan of water to simmering point. Working in two or three batches, drop in the fish balls and poach gently for 3–4 minutes until they float to the top. Transfer to absorbent paper towels to drain.

5. Put all the sauce ingredients in a wok or large frying pan and bring to the boil. Add the fish balls to the sauce and stir-fry gently for 2–3 minutes until piping hot. Transfer to a warmed serving dish, garnish with tarragon sprigs and serve immediately with freshly cooked rice.

Orange Freeze

SERVES 4

4 large oranges
about 300 ml/½ pint/1¼ cups
    vanilla ice cream
225 g/8 oz/2 cups raspberries

75 g/3 oz/⅔ cup icing/
    powdered sugar, sifted,
    plus extra for dusting
redcurrant sprigs, to decorate

1. Set the freezer to rapid freeze. Using a sharp knife, carefully cut the top off each orange. Scoop out the flesh from the orange, discarding any pips and thick pith. Place the shells and lids in the freezer and chop any remaining orange flesh.

2. Whisk together the orange juice, orange flesh and vanilla ice cream until well blended. Cover and freeze for about 2 hours, occasionally breaking up the ice crystals with a fork or a whisk. Stir the mixture from around the edge of the container into the centre, then level and return to the freezer. Do this two or three times, then leave until almost frozen solid.

3. Place a large scoop of the ice cream mixture into the frozen shells. Add another scoop on top, so that there is plenty outside of the orange shell, and return to the freezer for 1 hour. Arrange the lids on top and freeze for a further 2 hours until the filled orange shell is completely frozen solid.

4. Using a nylon sieve, press the raspberries into a bowl using the back of a wooden spoon and mix the icing/powdered sugar into the bowl. Spoon the raspberry coulis onto four serving plates and place an orange at the centre of each. Dust with icing sugar and serve decorated with the redcurrants. (Remember to return the freezer to its normal setting.)

Spicy Beef Pancakes

SERVES 4

50 g/2 oz/scant ½ cup
 plain/all-purpose flour
pinch salt
½ tsp Chinese five-spice
 powder
1 large/extra-large egg yolk
150 ml/¼ pint/⅔ cup milk
4 tsp sunflower/corn oil
spring onion/scallion slices,
 to garnish

For the spicy beef filling:
1 tbsp sesame oil
4 spring onions/
 scallions, sliced
1 cm/½ inch piece fresh root
 ginger, peeled and grated
1 garlic clove, peeled and
 crushed
300 g/11 oz sirloin steak,
 trimmed and cut into strips

1 red chilli, deseeded and
 finely chopped
1 tsp sherry vinegar
1 tsp soft dark brown sugar
1 tbsp dark soy sauce

1. Sift the flour, salt and Chinese five-spice powder into a bowl and make a well in the centre.
   Add the egg yolk and a little of the milk. Gradually beat in, drawing in the flour to make a smooth
   batter. Whisk in the rest of the milk.

2. Heat 1 teaspoon of the sunflower/corn oil in a small heavy-based frying pan. Pour in just enough
   batter to thinly coat the base of the pan. Cook over a medium heat for 1 minute, or until the
   underside of the pancake is golden brown. Turn or toss the pancake and cook for 1 minute, or
   until the other side of the pancake is golden brown. Make seven more pancakes with the
   remaining batter. Stack them on a warmed plate as you make them, with greaseproof paper
   between each pancake. Cover with kitchen foil and keep warm in a low oven.

3. Make the filling. Heat a wok or large frying pan, add the sesame oil and, when hot, add the spring
   onions/scallions, ginger and garlic and stir-fry for 1 minute. Add the beef, stir-fry for 3–4 minutes,
   then stir in the chilli, vinegar, sugar and soy sauce. Cook for 1 minute, then remove from the heat.
   Spoon one eighth of the filling over one half of each pancake. Fold the pancakes in half, then fold
   in half again. Garnish with a few slices of spring onion and serve immediately.

Sweet-&-Sour Fish

SERVES 4

For the sauce:
2 tsp cornflour/cornstarch
300 ml/½ pint/1¼ cups fish or chicken stock
4 cm/1½ inch piece fresh root ginger, peeled and finely sliced
2 tbsp soy sauce
2 tbsp rice wine vinegar or dry sherry
2 tbsp ketchup

2 tbsp Chinese rice vinegar or cider vinegar
1½ tbsp soft light brown sugar

1 small carrot, peeled and cut into julienne strips
1 small red or green pepper
125 g/4 oz/1 cup mangetout/ snow peas, cut in half
125 g/4 oz/1 cup frozen peas, thawed

2–3 spring onions/scallions, trimmed and sliced diagonally into 5 cm/2 inch pieces
450 g/1 lb small thin skinless plaice/flounder fillets
1½–2 tbsp cornflour/ cornstarch
vegetable oil, for frying
fresh coriander/cilantro sprigs, to garnish

1. Make the sauce. Place the cornflour/cornstarch in a saucepan and gradually whisk in the stock. Stir in the remaining sauce ingredients and bring to the boil, stirring, until the sauce thickens. Simmer for 2 minutes, then remove from the heat and reserve.

2. Bring a saucepan of water to the boil. Add the carrot, return to the boil and cook for 3 minutes. Add the pepper and cook for 1 minute. Add the mangetout/snow peas and peas and cook for 30 seconds. Drain, rinse under cold running water and drain again, then add to the sweet-and-sour sauce with the spring onions/scallions.

3. Using a sharp knife, make crisscross slashes across the top of each fish fillet, then lightly coat on both sides with the cornflour. Pour enough oil into a large wok to come 5 cm/2 inches up the side. Heat to 190°C/375°F, or until a cube of bread browns in 30 seconds. Fry the fillets, 2 at a time, for 3–5 minutes until crisp and golden, turning once. Using a fish slice, remove and drain on absorbent paper towels. Arrange the fish on a platter and keep warm.

4. Bring the sauce to the boil, stirring, then pour over the fish. Garnish and serve immediately.

Caramelized Oranges in an Ice Bowl

SERVES 4

For the iced bowl:
about 36 ice cubes
fresh flowers and fruits

For the caramelized oranges:
8 oranges

225 g/8 oz/1 cup sugar
4 tbsp Grand Marnier or Cointreau

1. Set the freezer to rapid freeze. Place a few ice cubes in the base of a 1.7 litre/3 pint/1¾ quart freezable glass bowl. Place a 900 ml/1½ pint/1 quart glass bowl on top of the ice cubes. Arrange the flower heads and fruits in between the two bowls, wedging in position with the ice cubes.

2. Weigh down the smaller bowl with some heavy weights, then carefully pour cold water between the two bowls, making sure that the flowers and the fruit are covered. Freeze for at least 6 hours, or until the ice is frozen solid.

3. When ready to use, remove the weights and, using a hot, damp cloth, rub the inside of the smaller bowl with the cloth until it loosens sufficiently for you to remove the bowl. Place the larger bowl in the sink or washing-up bowl, half filled with very hot water. Leave for about 30 seconds until the ice loosens. Take care not to leave the bowl in the water for too long, otherwise the ice will melt. Remove the bowl and leave in the refrigerator. Return the freezer to its normal setting.

4. Thinly pare the rind from 2 oranges and then cut into julienne strips. Using a sharp knife, cut away the rind and pith from all the oranges, holding over a bowl to catch the juices. Slice the oranges, discarding any pips, and reform each orange back to its original shape. Secure with cocktail sticks/toothpicks, then place in a bowl.

5. Heat 300 ml/½ pint/1¼ cups water with the orange rind and sugar in a pan. Stir the sugar until dissolved and bring to the boil. Boil for 15 minutes until a caramel colour and remove the pan from the heat. Stir in the liqueur and pour over the oranges. Allow to cool. Chill for 3 hours, turning the oranges occasionally. Spoon into the ice bowl and serve.

Crispy Prawns with Chinese Dipping Sauce

450 g/1 lb medium-sized raw
prawns/shrimp, peeled
¼ tsp salt
6 tbsp groundnut/peanut oil
2 garlic cloves, peeled and
finely chopped
2.5 cm/1 inch piece fresh
root ginger, peeled and
finely chopped

1 green chilli, deseeded and
finely chopped
4 stems fresh coriander/
cilantro, leaves and stems
roughly chopped

For the dipping sauce:
3 tbsp dark soy sauce
3 tbsp rice wine vinegar
1 tbsp caster/superfine sugar
2 tbsp chilli oil
2 spring onions/scallions,
finely shredded

1. Using a sharp knife, remove the black vein along the back of the prawns/shrimp. Sprinkle the prawns with the salt and leave to stand for 15 minutes. Pat dry on absorbent paper towels.

2. Heat a wok or large frying pan, add the groundnut/peanut oil. When hot, add the prawns. Stir-fry in 2 batches for about 1 minute until they turn pink and are almost cooked. Remove with a slotted spoon and keep warm in a low oven.

3. Drain the oil from the wok, leaving 1 tablespoon. Add the garlic, ginger and chilli and cook for about 30 seconds. Add the coriander/cilantro, return the prawns and stir-fry for 1–2 minutes until the prawns are cooked through and the garlic is golden. Turn into a warmed serving dish.

4. For the dipping sauce, using a fork, beat together the soy sauce, rice wine vinegar, caster/superfine sugar and chilli oil in a small bowl. Stir in the spring onions/scallions and serve immediately with the hot prawns.

Hoisin Duck & Greens Stir-fry

350 g/12 oz/¾ lb skinned
  duck breast fillets,
  cut into strips
1 egg white, beaten
½ tsp salt
1 tsp sesame oil
2 tsp cornflour/cornstarch
2 tbsp groundnut/peanut oil

2 tbsp freshly grated root
  ginger
50 g/2 oz/⅓ cup bamboo
  shoots
50 g/2 oz/½ cup fine green
  beans, trimmed
50 g/2 oz/1¼ cups pak
  choi/bok choy, trimmed

2 tbsp hoisin sauce
1 tsp Chinese rice wine or
  dry sherry
zest and juice of ½ orange
orange zest strips, to garnish
freshly steamed egg
  noodles, to serve

1. Place the duck strips in a shallow dish, then add the egg white, salt, sesame oil and cornflour/cornstarch. Stir lightly until the duck is coated in the mixture. Cover and chill in the refrigerator for 20 minutes.

2. Heat the wok until very hot and add the oil. Remove the wok from the heat and add the duck, stirring continuously to prevent the duck from sticking to the wok. Add the ginger and stir-fry for 2 minutes. Add the bamboo shoots, the green beans and the pak choi/bok choy and stir-fry for 1–2 minutes until wilted.

3. Mix together the hoisin sauce, the Chinese rice wine or sherry and the orange zest and juice. Pour into the wok and stir to coat the duck and vegetables. Stir-fry for 1–2 minutes until the duck and vegetables are tender. Garnish with the strips of orange zest and serve immediately with freshly steamed egg noodles.

Raspberry Sorbet Crush

225 g/8 oz/2 cups raspberries,
    thawed if frozen
grated zest and juice
    of 1 lime

300 ml/½ pint/1¼ cups
    orange juice
225 g/8 oz/1 cup sugar
2 egg whites

1. Set the freezer to rapid freeze. If using fresh raspberries, pick over and lightly rinse.

2. Place the raspberries in a dish and, using a masher, mash to a chunky purée.

3. Place the lime zest and juice, orange juice and half the sugar in a large heavy-based saucepan. Heat gently, stirring frequently, until the sugar is dissolved. Bring to the boil and boil rapidly for about 5 minutes.

4. Remove the pan from the heat and pour carefully into a freezable container.

5. Leave to cool, then place in the freezer and freeze for 2 hours, stirring occasionally to break up the ice crystals.

6. Fold the ice mixture into the raspberry purée with a metal spoon and freeze for a further 2 hours, stirring occasionally.

7. Whisk the egg whites until stiff, then gradually whisk in the remaining sugar a tablespoonful at a time until the egg white mixture is stiff and glossy.

8. Fold into the raspberry sorbet with a metal spoon and freeze for 1 hour. Spoon into tall glasses and serve immediately. Remember to return the freezer to its normal setting.

Spring Rolls

For the filling:
15 g/½ oz dried shiitake
    mushrooms
50 g/2 oz rice vermicelli
1–2 tbsp groundnut/peanut oil
1 small onion, peeled and
    finely chopped
3–4 garlic cloves, peeled and
    finely chopped
4 cm/1½ inch piece fresh
    root ginger, peeled
    and chopped

225 g/8 oz fresh
    minced/ground pork
2 spring onions/scallions,
    trimmed and
    finely chopped
75 g/3 oz/¾ cup beansprouts
4 water chestnuts, chopped
2 tbsp freshly snipped chives
175 g/6 oz cooked peeled
    prawns/shrimp, chopped
1 tsp oyster sauce
1 tsp soy sauce

salt and freshly ground
    black pepper
spring onion/scallion tassels,
    to garnish

For the wrappers:
4–5 tbsp plain/all-purpose
    flour
26–30 spring roll wrappers
300 ml/½ pint/1¼ cups
    vegetable oil,
    for deep frying

1. Soak the shiitake mushrooms in almost boiling water for 20 minutes. Remove and squeeze out the liquid. Discard any stems, slice and reserve. Soak the rice vermicelli as per the packet instructions. Heat a large wok and, when hot, add the oil. Heat, then add the onion, garlic and ginger and stir-fry for 2 minutes. Add the pork, spring onions/scallions and mushrooms and stir-fry for 4 minutes. Stir in the beansprouts, water chestnuts, chives, prawns/shrimp and sauces. Season to taste with salt and pepper and spoon into a bowl. Drain the noodles well, add to the bowl and toss until well mixed, then leave to cool.

2. Blend the flour to a smooth paste with 3–4 tablespoons water. Soften a wrapper in a plate of warm water for 1–2 seconds, then drain. Put 2 tablespoons of the filling near one edge of the wrapper, fold the edge over the filling, then fold in each side and roll up. Seal with a little flour paste and transfer to a baking sheet, seam-side down. Repeat with the remaining wrappers. Heat the oil in a large wok to 190°C/375°F, or until a cube of bread browns in 30 seconds. Fry the spring rolls, a few at a time, until golden. Remove and drain on absorbent paper towels. Arrange on a serving plate and garnish with spring onion tassels. Serve immediately.

Sweet-&-Sour Turkey

SERVES 4

2 tbsp groundnut/peanut oil
2 garlic cloves, peeled
　and chopped
1 tbsp freshly grated
　root ginger
4 spring onions/scallions,
　trimmed and cut into
　4 cm/1½ inch lengths
450 g/1 lb skinless turkey
　breast fillets, cut into strips

1 red pepper, deseeded
　and cut into 2.5 cm/
　1 inch squares
225 g/8 oz canned water
　chestnuts, drained
150 ml/¼ pint/⅔ cup
　chicken stock
2 tbsp Chinese rice wine
3 tbsp light soy sauce
2 tsp dark soy sauce

2 tbsp tomato purée/paste
2 tbsp white wine vinegar
1 tbsp sugar
egg-fried rice, to serve

1. Heat a wok over a high heat, add the oil and, when hot, add the garlic, ginger and spring onions/scallions. Stir-fry for 20 seconds.

2. Add the turkey to the wok and stir-fry for 2 minutes, or until beginning to colour. Add the peppers and water chestnuts and stir-fry for a further 2 minutes.

3. Mix the chicken stock, Chinese rice wine, light and dark soy sauces, tomato purée/paste, white wine vinegar and the sugar together in a small measuring jug or bowl. Add the mixture to the wok, stir and bring the sauce to the boil.

4. Mix together the cornflour/cornstarch with 2 tablespoons water and add to the wok. Reduce the heat and simmer for 3 minutes, or until the turkey is cooked thoroughly and the sauce is slightly thickened and glossy. Serve immediately with egg-fried rice.

Fruit Salad

125 g/4 oz/⅔ cup
   caster/superfine sugar
3 oranges
700 g/1½ lb lychees, peeled
   and stoned
1 small mango

1 small pineapple
1 papaya
4 pieces stem ginger in syrup
4 tbsp stem ginger syrup
125 g/4 oz/¾ cup Cape
   gooseberries

125 g/4 oz/1 cup
   strawberries, hulled
½ tsp almond extract

To decorate:
mint leaves and lime zest

1. Place the sugar and 300 ml/½ pint/1¼ cups water in a small pan and heat, stirring gently, until the sugar has dissolved. Bring to the boil and simmer for 2 minutes. Once a syrup has formed, remove from the heat and allow to cool.

2. Using a sharp knife, cut away the skin from the oranges, then slice thickly. Cut each slice in half and place in a serving dish with the syrup and lychees.

3. Peel the mango, then cut into thick slices around each side of the stone. Discard the stone, cut the slices into bite-size pieces and add to the syrup. Using a sharp knife again, carefully cut away the skin from the pineapple. Remove the central core using the knife or an apple corer, then cut the pineapple into segments and add to the syrup.

4. Peel the papaya, then cut in half and remove the seeds. Cut the flesh into chunks, slice the ginger into matchsticks and add with the ginger syrup to the fruit in the syrup.

5. Prepare the Cape gooseberries by removing the thin papery skins and rinsing lightly.

6. Halve the strawberries, add to the fruit with the almond extract and chill for 30 minutes. Scatter with mint leaves and lime zest to decorate and serve.

Sweetcorn Fritters

4 tbsp groundnut/peanut oil
1 small onion, peeled and
finely chopped
1 red chilli, deseeded and
finely chopped
1 garlic clove, peeled

and crushed
1 tsp ground coriander
325 g/11½ oz can sweetcorn
6 spring onions/scallions,
trimmed and finely sliced
1 egg, lightly beaten

salt and freshly ground
black pepper
3 tbsp plain/all-purpose flour
1 tsp baking powder
spring onion/scallion curls
Thai-style chutney, to serve

1. Heat 1 tablespoon of the oil in a frying pan, add the onion and cook gently for 7–8 minutes until beginning to soften. Add the chilli, garlic and ground coriander and cook for 1 minute, stirring continuously. Remove from the heat.

2. Drain the sweetcorn and tip into a mixing bowl. Lightly mash to break down the corn a little. Add the cooked onion mixture to the bowl with the spring onions/scallions and beaten egg. Season to taste with salt and pepper, then stir to mix together. Sift the flour and baking powder over the mixture and stir in.

3. Heat 2 tablespoons of the oil in a large frying pan. Drop 4 or 5 teaspoonfuls of the sweetcorn mixture into the pan and, using a spatula, flatten each to make a 1 cm/½ inch thick fritter.

4. Fry the fritters for 3 minutes, or until golden brown on the underside, turn over and fry for a further 3 minutes, or until cooked through and crisp.

5. Remove the fritters from the pan and drain on absorbent paper towels. Keep warm while cooking the remaining fritters, adding a little more oil if needed. Garnish with spring onion curls and serve immediately with a Thai-style chutney.

Fragrant Thai Swordfish with Peppers

For the marinade:
1 tbsp soy sauce
1 tbsp Chinese rice wine
  or dry sherry
1 tbsp sesame oil
1 tbsp cornflour/cornstarch

550 g/1¼ lb swordfish, cut
  into 5 cm/2 inch strips
2 tbsp vegetable oil
2 lemon grass stalks, peeled,
  bruised and cut into
  2.5 cm/1 inch pieces
2.5 cm/1 inch piece fresh
  root ginger, peeled and
  thinly sliced
4–5 shallots, peeled and
  thinly sliced
2–3 garlic cloves, peeled and
  thinly sliced

1 small red pepper,
  deseeded and thinly sliced
1 small yellow pepper,
  deseeded and thinly sliced
2 tbsp soy sauce
2 tbsp Chinese rice wine
  or dry sherry
1–2 tsp sugar
1 tsp sesame oil
1 tbsp Thai basil, shredded
salt and freshly ground
  black pepper
1 tbsp toasted sesame seeds

1. Blend all the marinade ingredients together in a shallow, nonmetallic baking dish. Add the swordfish and spoon the marinade over the fish. Cover and leave to marinate in the refrigerator for at least 30 minutes.

2. Using a slotted spatula or spoon, remove the swordfish from the marinade and drain briefly on absorbent paper towels. Heat a wok or large frying pan, add the oil and, when hot, add the swordfish and stir-fry for 2 minutes, or until it begins to brown. Remove the swordfish and drain on paper towels. Add the lemon grass, ginger, shallots and garlic to the wok and stir-fry for 30 seconds. Add the peppers, soy sauce, rice wine or sherry and sugar and stir-fry for 3–4 minutes.

3. Return the swordfish to the wok and stir-fry gently for 1–2 minutes until heated through and coated with the sauce. If necessary, moisten the sauce with a little of the marinade or some water. Stir in the sesame oil and the basil and season to taste with salt and pepper. Tip into a warmed serving bowl, sprinkle with sesame seeds and serve immediately.

Iced Chocolate
& Raspberry Mousse

SERVES 4

12 sponge finger
  biscuits/ladyfingers
juice of 2 oranges
2 tbsp Grand Marnier/
  orange-flavoured liqueur
300 ml/½ pint/1 cup
  double/heavy cream

175 g/6 oz dark/
  bittersweet chocolate,
  broken into small pieces
225 g/8 oz/2 cups frozen
  raspberries
6 tbsp icing/powdered
  sugar, sifted

unsweetened cocoa powder,
  for dusting

To decorate:
few fresh whole raspberries
few mint leaves
grated white chocolate

1. Break the sponge finger biscuits/ladyfingers into small pieces and divide between four individual glass dishes. Blend together the orange juice and Grand Marnier, then drizzle evenly over the sponge fingers. Cover with clingfilm/plastic wrap and chill in the refrigerator for 30 minutes.

2. Place the cream in a small heavy-based saucepan and heat gently, stirring occasionally until boiling. Remove the saucepan from the heat, then add the pieces of dark/bittersweet chocolate and leave to stand untouched for about 7 minutes. Using a whisk, whisk the chocolate and cream together, until the chocolate has melted and is well blended and completely smooth. Leave to cool slightly.

3. Place the frozen raspberries and icing/powdered sugar into a food processor or blender and blend until roughly crushed.

4. Fold the crushed raspberries into the cream and chocolate mixture and mix lightly until well blended. Spoon over the chilled sponge fingers. Lightly dust with a little cocoa powder and decorate with whole raspberries, mint leaves and grated white chocolate. Serve immediately.

Thai Hot-&-Sour Prawn Soup

SERVES 6

700 g/1½ lb large raw
 prawns/shrimp
2 tbsp vegetable oil
3–4 stalks lemon grass,
 outer leaves discarded,
 coarsely chopped
2.5 cm/1 inch piece fresh
 root ginger, peeled and
 finely chopped
2–3 garlic cloves,
 peeled and crushed

small bunch fresh coriander/
 cilantro, leaves stripped
 and reserved, and stems
 finely chopped
½ tsp freshly ground
 black pepper
1.8 litres/3¼ pints/
 1¾ quarts water
1–2 small red chillies,
 deseeded and
 thinly sliced

1–2 small green chillies,
 deseeded and
 thinly sliced
6 kaffir lime leaves,
 thinly shredded
4 spring onions/scallions,
 trimmed and
 diagonally sliced
1–2 tbsp Thai fish sauce
1–2 tbsp freshly squeezed
 lime juice

1. Remove the heads from the prawns/shrimp by twisting away from the body, and reserve. Peel the prawns, leaving the tails on. Reserve the shells with the heads. Using a sharp knife, remove the black vein from the back of the prawns. Rinse and dry the prawns and reserve. Rinse and dry the heads and shells.

2. Heat a wok and add the oil. When hot, add the prawn heads and shells, the lemon grass, ginger, garlic, coriander/cilantro stems and black pepper. Stir-fry for 2–3 minutes until the prawn heads and shells turn pink and all ingredients are coloured.

3. Carefully add the water to the wok. Return to the boil, skimming off any scum from the surface. Simmer over a medium heat for 10 minutes, or until slightly reduced. Strain through a fine sieve and return the clear prawn stock to the wok.

4. Bring the stock back to the boil. Add the reserved prawns, chillies, lime leaves and spring onions/scallions and simmer for 3 minutes, or until the prawns turn pink. Season with the fish sauce and lime juice. Spoon into soup bowls, sharing the prawns evenly. Garnish with a few coriander leaves.

Thai Coconut Chicken

SERVES 4

1 tsp cumin seeds
1 tsp mustard seeds
1 tsp coriander seeds
1 tsp turmeric
1 bird's-eye chilli, deseeded
 and finely chopped
1 tbsp freshly grated
 root ginger
2 garlic cloves, peeled and
 finely chopped

125 ml/4 fl oz/½ cup
 double/heavy cream
8 skinless chicken thighs
2 tbsp groundnut/peanut oil
1 onion, peeled and
 finely sliced
200 ml/7 fl oz/¾ cup
 coconut milk
salt and freshly ground
 black pepper

4 tbsp freshly chopped
 coriander/cilantro
freshly cooked Thai fragrant
 rice, to serve
2 spring onions/scallions,
 shredded, to garnish

1. Heat a wok and add the cumin, mustard and coriander seeds. Dry-fry over a low to medium heat for 2 minutes, or until the fragrance becomes stronger and the seeds start to pop. Add the turmeric and leave to cool slightly. Grind the spices using a pestle and mortar, or blend to a fine powder in a food processor.

2. Mix the chilli, ginger, garlic and cream together in a small bowl, add the ground spices and mix. Place the chicken thighs in a shallow dish and spread the spice paste over the thighs.

3. Heat the wok over a high heat, add oil and, when hot, add the onion and stir-fry until golden brown. Add the chicken and spice paste. Cook for 5–6 minutes, stirring occasionally, until evenly coloured. Add the coconut milk and season with salt and pepper.

4. Simmer the chicken for 15–20 minutes until the thighs are cooked through, taking care not to allow the mixture to boil. Stir in the chopped coriander/cilantro and serve immediately with the freshly cooked rice sprinkled with shredded spring onions/scallions.

Chocolate Ice Cream

MAKES 1 LITRE/2 PINTS/1 QUART

450 ml/¾ pint/1¾ cups
  single/light cream
200 g/7 oz dark/bittersweet
  chocolate

2 medium/large eggs
2 medium/large egg yolks
125 g/4 oz/⅔ cup caster/
  superfine sugar

1 tsp vanilla extract
300 ml/½ pint/1¼ cups
  double/heavy cream

1. Set the freezer to rapid freeze 2 hours before freezing. Place the single/light cream and chocolate in a heavy-based saucepan and heat gently until the chocolate has melted. Stir until smooth. Take care not to let the mixture boil. Remove from the heat.

2. Whisk the eggs, egg yolks and all but 1 tablespoon of the sugar together in a bowl until thick and pale. Whisk the warmed single cream and chocolate mixture with the vanilla extract into the egg custard mixture. Place the bowl over a saucepan of simmering water and continue whisking until the mixture thickens and will coat the back of a spoon. To test, lift the spoon out of the mixture and draw a clean finger through the mixture on the spoon, if it leaves a clean line, then it is ready.

3. Stand the bowl in cold water to cool. Sprinkle the surface with the reserved sugar to prevent a skin forming while it is cooling. Whip the double/heavy cream until soft peaks form, then whisk into the cooled chocolate custard.

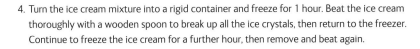

4. Turn the ice cream mixture into a rigid container and freeze for 1 hour. Beat the ice cream thoroughly with a wooden spoon to break up all the ice crystals, then return to the freezer. Continue to freeze the ice cream for a further hour, then remove and beat again.

5. Repeat this process once or twice more, then leave the ice cream in the freezer until firm. Leave to soften in the refrigerator for at least 30 minutes before serving. Turn the freezer back to its normal setting.

Mixed Satay Sticks

12 raw large prawns/
   jumbo shrimp
350 g/¾ lb beef rump steak
1 tbsp lemon juice
1 garlic clove, peeled
   and crushed
pinch salt
2 tsp soft dark brown sugar
1 tsp ground cumin

1 tsp ground coriander
¼ tsp ground turmeric
1 tbsp groundnut/peanut oil
fresh coriander/cilantro
   leaves, to garnish

For the spicy peanut sauce:
1 shallot, peeled and very
   finely chopped

1 tsp demerara/
   turbinado sugar
50 g/2 oz/¼ cup creamed
   coconut, chopped
pinch chilli powder
1 tbsp dark soy sauce
125 g/4 oz/½ cup crunchy
   peanut butter

1. Preheat the grill/broiler on high just before required. Soak eight bamboo skewers in cold water for at least 30 minutes. Peel the prawns/shrimp, leaving the tails on. Using a sharp knife, remove the black vein along the back of the prawns. Cut the beef into 1 cm/½ inch wide strips. Place the prawns and beef in separate bowls and sprinkle each with ½ tablespoon of the lemon juice.

2. Mix together the garlic, pinch salt, sugar, cumin, coriander, turmeric and oil to make a paste. Lightly brush over the prawns and beef. Cover and place in the refrigerator to marinate for at least 30 minutes. To make the sauce, pour 125 ml/4 fl oz/½ cup of water into a small saucepan and add the shallot and sugar. Heat gently until the sugar has dissolved. Stir in the creamed coconut and chilli powder. When melted, remove from the heat and stir in the soy sauce and peanut butter. Leave to cool slightly. Spoon into a serving dish.

3. Thread 3 prawns each onto four skewers. Divide the sliced beef between the remaining skewers. Cook the skewers under the preheated grill for 4–5 minutes, turning occasionally. The prawns should be opaque and pink, the beef browned on the outside but pink in the centre. Transfer to individual serving plates and garnish with a few fresh coriander/cilantro leaves. Serve with the warm peanut sauce.

Red Prawn Curry with Jasmine-scented Rice

SERVES 4

½ tbsp coriander seeds
1 tsp cumin seeds
1 tsp black peppercorns
½ tsp salt
1–2 dried red chillies
2 shallots, peeled and chopped
3–4 garlic cloves
2.5 cm/1 inch piece fresh galangal or root ginger, peeled and chopped
1 kaffir lime leaf or 1 tsp kaffir lime rind

½ tsp red chilli powder
½ tbsp prawn/shrimp paste
1–1½ lemon grass stalks, thinly sliced after removing outer leaves
750 ml/1¼ pints/3¼ cups coconut milk
1 red chilli, deseeded and thinly sliced
2 tbsp Thai fish sauce
2 tsp soft brown sugar
1 red pepper, deseeded and thinly sliced

550 g/1¼ lb large peeled tiger prawns/jumbo shrimp
2 fresh lime leaves, shredded (optional)
2 tbsp fresh mint leaves, shredded
2 tbsp Thai or Italian basil leaves, shredded
freshly cooked Thai fragrant rice, to serve

1. Using a pestle and mortar or a spice grinder, grind the coriander and cumin seeds, peppercorns and salt to a fine powder. Add the dried chillies one at a time and grind to a fine powder.

2. Place the shallots, garlic, galangal or ginger, kaffir lime leaf or rind, chilli powder and prawn/shrimp paste in a food processor. Add the ground spices and process until a thick paste forms.

3. Scrape down the bowl once or twice, adding a few drops of water if the mixture is too thick and not forming a paste. Stir in the lemon grass.

4. Transfer the paste to a large wok. Cook over a medium heat for 2–3 minutes until fragrant. Stir in the coconut milk and bring to the boil. Lower the heat and simmer for about 10 minutes. Add the chilli, fish sauce, sugar and red pepper and simmer for 15 minutes. Stir in the prawns/shrimp and cook for 5 minutes, or until the prawns are pink and tender. Stir in the shredded herbs, heat for a further minute and serve immediately with the cooked rice.

Stir-fried Bananas & Peaches with Rum Butterscotch Sauce

SERVES 4

2 medium-firm bananas,
   peeled and cut into 2.5 cm/
   1 inch diagonal slices
1 tbsp caster/superfine sugar
2 tsp lime juice
4 firm ripe peaches or
   nectarines
1 tbsp sunflower oil

For the sauce:
50 g/2 oz/¼ cup (4 tbsp)
   unsalted butter
50 g/2 oz/¼ cup soft light
   brown sugar
125 g/4 oz/⅔ cup demerara/
   turbinado sugar

300 ml/½ pint/1¼ cups
   double/heavy cream
2 tbsp dark rum

1. Place the bananas in a bowl, sprinkle with the caster/superfine sugar and lime juice and stir until lightly coated. Reserve.

2. Place the peaches or nectarines in a large bowl and pour over boiling water to cover. Leave for 30 seconds, then plunge them into cold water and peel off their skins. Cut each one into eight thick slices, discarding the stones.

3. Heat a wok, add the oil and swirl it round the wok to coat the sides. Add the fruit and cook for 3–4 minutes, shaking the wok and gently turning the fruit until lightly browned. Spoon the fruit into a warmed serving bowl and clean the wok with absorbent paper towels.

4. Add the butter and sugars to the wok and stir continuously over a very low heat until the sugar has dissolved. Remove from the heat and leave to cool for 2–3 minutes.

5. Stir the cream and rum into the sugar syrup and return to the heat. Bring to the boil and simmer for 2 minutes, stirring continuously, until smooth. Leave for 2–3 minutes to cool slightly, then serve warm with the stir-fried peaches and bananas.

Vegetable Thai Spring Rolls

50 g/2 oz cellophane
  vermicelli
4 dried shiitake mushrooms
1 tbsp groundnut/peanut oil
2 carrots, peeled and cut into
  fine matchsticks
125 g/4 oz/1 cup mangetout/
  snow peas, cut into fine strips

3 spring onions/scallions,
  trimmed and chopped
125 g/4 oz/½ cup canned
  bamboo shoots, cut into
  matchsticks
1 cm/½ inch piece fresh root
  ginger, peeled and grated
1 tbsp light soy sauce

1 egg, separated
salt and freshly ground
  black pepper
20 spring roll wrappers
vegetable oil, for deep-frying
spring onion/scallion tassels,
  to garnish

1. Place the vermicelli in a bowl and pour over enough boiling water to cover. Leave to soak for 5 minutes, or until softened, then drain. Cut into 7.5 cm/3 inch lengths. Soak the shiitake mushrooms in almost-boiling water for 15 minutes, then drain, discard the stalks and slice thinly.

2. Heat a wok or large frying pan, add the nut oil and, when hot, add the carrots and stir-fry for 1 minute. Add the mangetout/snow peas and spring onions/scallions and stir-fry for 2–3 minutes until tender. Tip the vegetables into a bowl and leave to cool. Stir the vermicelli and shiitake mushrooms into the cooled vegetables with the bamboo shoots, ginger, soy sauce and egg yolk. Season to taste with salt and pepper and mix thoroughly.

3. Brush the edges of a spring roll wrapper with a little beaten egg white. Spoon 2 teaspoons of the filling onto the wrapper in a 7.5 cm/3 inch log shape 2.5 cm/1 inch from one edge. Fold the edge over the filling, then fold in the right and left sides. Brush the folded edges with more egg white and roll up neatly. Place on an oiled baking sheet seam-side down and make the rest.

4. Heat the oil in a heavy-based saucepan or deep-fat fryer to 180°C/350°F. Deep-fry the spring rolls, six at a time, for 2–3 minutes until golden brown and crisp. Drain on absorbent paper towels. Arrange on a warmed platter. Garnish with spring onion tassels. Serve immediately.

Thai-style Cauliflower & Potato Curry

9–12 new potatoes, peeled and halved or quartered
350 g/12 oz/1¼ cups cauliflower florets
3 garlic cloves, peeled and crushed
1 onion, peeled and finely chopped
40 g/1½ oz/½ cup ground almonds

1 tsp ground coriander
½ tsp ground cumin
½ tsp turmeric
3 tbsp groundnut/peanut oil
salt and freshly ground black pepper
50 g/2 oz/6 tbsp creamed coconut, broken into small pieces

200 ml/7 fl oz/¾ cup vegetable stock
1 tbsp mango chutney
fresh coriander/cilantro sprigs, to garnish
freshly cooked long-grain rice, to serve

1. Bring a saucepan of lightly salted water to the boil, add the potatoes and cook for 15 minutes, or until just tender. Drain and leave to cool. Boil the cauliflower for 2 minutes, then drain and refresh under cold running water. Drain again and reserve.

2. Meanwhile, blend the garlic, onion, ground almonds and spices with 2 tablespoons of the oil and salt and pepper to taste in a food processor until a smooth paste is formed. Heat a wok, add the remaining oil and, when hot, add the spice paste and cook for 3–4 minutes, stirring continuously.

2. Dissolve the creamed coconut in 6 tablespoons boiling water and add to the wok. Pour in the stock, cook for 2–3 minutes, then stir in the cooked potatoes and cauliflower.

3. Stir in the mango chutney and heat through for 3–4 minutes until piping hot. Tip into a warmed serving dish, garnish with coriander/cilantro sprigs and serve immediately with freshly cooked rice.

Passion Fruit & Pomegranate Citrus Tart

SERVES 4

For the pastry:
175 g/6 oz/1⅓ cups plain/
  all-purpose flour
pinch salt
125 g/4 oz/½ cup
  (8 tbsp) butter
4 tsp caster/superfine sugar

1 small egg, separated

For the filling:
2 passion fruit
175 g/6 oz/1 scant cup
  caster/superfine sugar
4 large/extra-large eggs

175 ml/6 fl oz/scant ¾ cup
  double/heavy cream
3 tbsp lime juice
1 pomegranate
icing/powdered sugar,
  for dusting

1. Preheat the oven to 200°C/400°F/Gas Mark 6, 15 minutes before baking. Sift the flour and salt into a large bowl and rub in the butter until the mixture resembles breadcrumbs. Stir in the sugar.

2. Whisk the egg yolk and add to the dry ingredients. Mix well to form a smooth, pliable dough. Knead gently on a lightly floured surface until smooth. Wrap the pastry in clingfilm/plastic wrap and leave to rest in the refrigerator for 30 minutes.

3. Roll out the pastry on a lightly floured surface and use to line a 25.5 cm/10 inch loose-based flan tin/tart pan. Line the pastry case/pie crust with greaseproof/waxed paper and baking beans/pie weights. Brush the edges of the pastry with the egg white and bake blind in the preheated oven for 15 minutes. Remove the paper and beans and bake for 5 minutes. Remove and reduce the temperature to 180°C/350°F/Gas Mark 4.

4. Halve the passion fruit and spoon the flesh into a bowl. Whisk the sugar and eggs together in a bowl. When mixed thoroughly, stir in the double/heavy cream with the passion fruit and the lime juice. Pour the mixture into the pastry case and bake for 30–40 minutes until the filling is just set. Remove and cool slightly, then chill in the refrigerator for 1 hour. Cut the pomegranate in half and scoop the seeds into a sieve. Spoon the drained seeds over the top and, just before serving, dust with icing/powdered sugar.

Coconut Chicken Soup

2 lemon grass stalks
3 tbsp vegetable oil
3 onions, peeled and
 finely sliced
3 garlic cloves, peeled and
 crushed
2 tbsp fresh root ginger,
 finely grated
2–3 kaffir lime leaves

1½ tsp turmeric
1 red pepper, deseeded
 and diced
400 ml/13½ fl oz can
 coconut milk
1.25 litres/2¼ pints/1¼ quarts
 vegetable or chicken stock
275 g/10 oz/1½ cups easy-
 cook long-grain rice

275 g/10 oz cooked
 chicken meat
285 g/9½ oz can sweetcorn,
 drained
3 tbsp freshly chopped
 coriander/cilantro
1 tbsp Thai fish sauce
freshly chopped pickled
 chillies, to serve

1. Discard the outer leaves of the lemon grass stalks. Place on a chopping board and, using a rolling pin, pound gently to bruise; reserve.

2. Heat the vegetable oil in a large saucepan and cook the onions over a medium heat for about 10–15 minutes until soft and beginning to change colour.

3. Lower the heat, stir in the garlic, ginger, lime leaves and turmeric and cook for 1 minute.

4. Add the red pepper, coconut milk, stock, lemon grass and rice. Bring to the boil, cover and simmer gently over a low heat for about 10 minutes.

5. Cut the chicken into bite-size pieces, then stir into the soup with the sweetcorn and the freshly chopped coriander/cilantro. Add the Thai fish sauce to taste, then reheat gently, stirring frequently. Serve with a few chopped pickled chillies to sprinkle on top.

Thai Beef Curry
(with Lemon and Arborio Rice)

450 g/1 lb beef fillet
1 tbsp olive oil
2 tbsp Thai green curry
   paste
1 green and 1 red pepper,
   deseeded and cut
   into strips

1 celery stalk, trimmed
   and sliced
juice of 1 fresh lemon
2 tsp Thai fish sauce
2 tsp demerara/
   turbinado sugar
225 g/8 oz/1 cup risotto rice

15 g/½ oz/1 tbsp butter
2 tbsp freshly chopped
   coriander/cilantro
4 tbsp crème fraîche/
   sour cream

1. Trim the beef fillet, discarding any fat, then cut across the grain into thin slices. Heat a wok, add the oil and, when hot, add the green curry paste and cook for 30 seconds. Add the beef strips and stir-fry for 3–4 minutes.

2. Add the sliced peppers and the celery and continue to stir-fry for 2 minutes. Add the lemon juice, Thai fish sauce and sugar and cook for a further 3–4 minutes until the beef is tender and cooked to personal preference.

3. Meanwhile, cook the risotto rice in a saucepan of lightly salted boiling water for 15–20 minutes until tender. Drain, rinse with boiling water and drain again. Return to the saucepan, add the butter. Cover and allow the butter to melt before turning it out onto a large serving dish. Sprinkle the cooked curry with the chopped coriander/cilantro.

4. Serve with the rice and crème fraîche/sour cream.

Chocolate & Lemon Grass Mousse

SERVES 4

3 lemon grass stalks, outer
   leaves removed
200 ml/7 fl oz/¾ cup milk
2 sheets gelatine
150 g/5 oz milk/semisweet

chocolate, broken into
   small pieces
2 egg yolks
50 g/2 oz/¼ cup caster/
   superfine sugar

150 ml/¼ pint/⅔ cup
   double/heavy cream
juice of 2 lemons
1 tbsp caster/superfine sugar
lemon zest, to decorate

1. Use a wooden spoon to bruise the lemon grass, then cut in half. Pour the milk into a large heavy-based saucepan, add the lemon grass and bring to the boil. Remove from the heat, leave to infuse for 1 hour, then strain. Place the gelatine in a shallow dish, pour over cold water to cover and leave for 15 minutes. Squeeze out excess moisture before use.

2. Place the chocolate in a small bowl set over a saucepan of gently simmering water and leave until melted. Make sure the water does not touch the bowl.

3. Whisk the egg yolks and sugar together until thick, then whisk in the flavoured milk. Pour into a clean saucepan and cook gently, stirring continuously, until the mixture starts to thicken. Remove from the heat, stir in the melted chocolate and gelatine and leave to cool for a few minutes.

4. Whisk the double/heavy cream until soft peaks form, then stir into the cooled milk mixture to form a mousse. Spoon into individual ramekins or moulds and leave in the refrigerator for 2 hours, or until set.

5. Just before serving, pour the lemon juice into a small saucepan, bring to the boil, then simmer for 3 minutes, or until reduced. Add the sugar and heat until dissolved, stirring continuously. Serve the mousse drizzled with the lemon sauce and decorated with lemon zest.

Spinach Dhal

SERVES 4-6

125 g/4 oz/½ cup split red lentils
2 onions, peeled and chopped
1 medium potato, peeled and cut into small chunks

1 green chilli, deseeded and chopped
150 ml/¼ pint/⅔ cup water
1 tsp turmeric
175 g/6 oz/6 cups fresh spinach

2 tomatoes, chopped
2 tbsp vegetable oil
1 tsp mustard seeds
few curry leaves

1. Rinse the lentils and place in a saucepan with the onions, potato, chilli, water and turmeric. Bring to the boil, then reduce the heat, cover and simmer for 15 minutes, or until the lentils are tender and most of the liquid has been absorbed.

2. Chop the spinach and add to the pan with the tomatoes and cook for a further 5 minutes, or until the spinach has wilted.

3. Heat the oil in a frying pan, add the mustard seeds and fry for 1 minute, or until they pop. Add the curry leaves, stir well, then stir into the dhal and serve.

Kerala Pork Curry

SERVES 4-6

450 g/1 lb pork loin, trimmed
2 tbsp vegetable oil or ghee
1 tbsp desiccated/
   shredded coconut
1 tsp mustard seeds
1 tsp fennel seeds
1 cinnamon stick, bruised
1 tsp ground cumin

1 tsp ground coriander
1–2 red chillies, deseeded
   and chopped
2–3 garlic cloves, peeled
   and chopped
2 onions, peeled
   and chopped
½ tsp saffron strands

300 ml/½ pint/1¼ cups
   coconut milk
150 ml/¼ pint/⅔ cup water
100 g/3½ oz/⅚ cup
   frozen peas
freshly cooked basmati rice,
   to serve

1. Cut the pork into small chunks and reserve. Heat 1 teaspoon of the oil or ghee in a frying pan, add the coconut and fry for 30 seconds, stirring, until lightly toasted. Reserve.

2. Add the remaining oil or ghee to the pan, add the seeds and fry for 30 seconds, or until they pop. Add the remaining spices and cook, stirring, for 2 minutes. Add the pork and fry for 5 minutes, or until sealed.

3. Add the chillies, garlic and onions and continue to fry for 3 minutes before stirring in the saffron strands. Stir, then pour in the coconut milk and water.

4. Bring to the boil ,then reduce the heat, cover and simmer, stirring occasionally, for 30 minutes. Add a little more water if the liquid is evaporating quickly. Turn the heat down slightly, then add the peas and cook for a further 10 minutes before serving with freshly cooked basmati rice.

Chocolate & Saffron Cheesecake

SERVES 6

¼ tsp saffron threads
175 g/6 oz/1⅓ cups plain/
   all-purpose flour
pinch salt
75 g/3 oz/⅓ cup (6 tbsp) butter
1 tbsp caster/superfine sugar

1 medium/large egg yolk
350 g/12 oz/1½ cups curd
   cheese/sieved
   cottage cheese
75 g/3 oz/⅓ cup of golden/
   unrefined granulated sugar

125 g/4 oz dark/bittersweet
   chocolate, melted and cooled
6 tbsp milk
3 medium/large eggs
1 tbsp icing/powdered sugar,
   sifted, to decorate

1. Preheat the oven to 200°C/400°F/Gas Mark 6, 15 minutes before baking. Lightly oil a 20.5 cm/8 inch fluted flan tin/tart pan. Soak the saffron threads in 1 tablespoon of hot water for 20 minutes. Sift the flour and salt into a bowl. Cut the butter into small dice, then add to the flour and, using your fingertips, rub in the butter until the mixture resembles breadcrumbs. Stir in the sugar.

2. Beat the egg yolk with 1 tablespoon cold water, add to the mixture and mix until a smooth and pliable dough is formed. Add a little extra water if necessary. Knead on a lightly floured surface until free from cracks, then wrap in clingfilm/plastic wrap and chill in the refrigerator for 30 minutes.

3. Roll the pastry dough out on a lightly floured surface and use to line the flan tin. Prick the pastry base and sides with a fork and line with nonstick baking parchment and baking beans/pie weights. Bake blind in the preheated oven for 12 minutes. Remove the beans and baking parchment and continue to bake blind for 5 minutes.

4. Beat together the cheese and granulated sugar, then beat in the melted chocolate, saffron liquid, milk and eggs; mix until blended thoroughly. Pour into the cooked pastry case/pie crust and place on a baking sheet. Reduce the oven to 190°C/375°F/Gas Mark 5 and bake for 15 minutes, then reduce to 180°C/350°F/Gas Mark 4 and continue to bake for 20–30 minutes until set. Remove from the oven and leave for 10 minutes before removing from the tin, if serving warm. If serving cold, leave in the tin to cool before removing. Sprinkle with icing/powdered sugar before serving.

Spicy Filled Naan Bread

SERVES 6

400 g/14 oz/3½ cups strong
   white/bread flour
1 tsp salt
1 tsp easy-blend dried yeast
15 g/½ oz/1 tbsp ghee or
   melted unsalted butter
1 tsp clear honey
200 ml/7 fl oz/¾ cup
   warm water

For the filling:
25 g/1 oz/2 tbsp ghee or
   unsalted butter
1 small onion, peeled
   and finely chopped
1 garlic clove, peeled
   and crushed
1 tsp ground coriander
1 tsp ground cumin

2 tsp grated fresh root ginger
pinch chilli powder
pinch ground cinnamon
salt and freshly ground
   black pepper

1. Preheat the oven to 230°C/450°F/Gas Mark 8, 15 minutes before baking and place a large baking sheet in to heat up. Sift the flour and salt into a large bowl. Stir in the yeast and make a well in the centre. Add the ghee or melted butter, honey and warm water and mix to a soft dough. Knead the dough on a lightly floured surface until smooth and elastic. Put in a lightly oiled bowl, cover with clingfilm/plastic wrap and leave to rise for 1 hour, or until doubled in size.

2. For the filling, melt the ghee or butter in a frying pan and gently cook the onion for about 5 minutes. Stir in the garlic and spices and season to taste with salt and pepper. Cook for a further 6–7 minutes until soft. Remove from the heat, stir in 1 tablespoon water and leave to cool.

3. Briefly knead the dough, then divide into six pieces. Roll out each piece of dough to 12.5 cm/ 5 inch rounds. Spoon the filling onto one half of each round. Fold over and press the edges together to seal. Re-roll to shape into flat ovals, about 16 cm/6½ inches long. Cover with oiled clingfilm and leave to rise for about 15 minutes.

4. Transfer the breads to the hot baking sheet and cook in the preheated oven for 10–12 minutes until puffed up and lightly browned. Serve hot.

Pumpkin & Chickpea Curry

SERVES 4

1 tbsp vegetable oil
1 small onion, peeled and
sliced
2 garlic cloves, peeled and
finely chopped
2.5 cm/1 inch piece root
ginger, peeled and grated
1 tsp ground coriander
½ tsp ground cumin
½ tsp ground turmeric
¼ tsp ground cinnamon

2 tomatoes, chopped
2 red bird's-eye chillies,
deseeded and finely
chopped
450 g/1 lb pumpkin or
butternut squash flesh,
cubed
1 tbsp hot curry paste
300 ml/½ pint/1¼ cups
vegetable stock
1 large firm banana

400 g/14 oz can chickpeas,
drained and rinsed
salt and freshly ground
black pepper
1 tbsp freshly chopped
coriander/cilantro, plus
sprigs to garnish
rice or naan bread, to serve

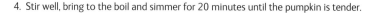

1. Heat 1 tablespoon of the oil in a saucepan and add the onion. Fry gently for 5 minutes until softened.

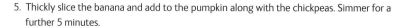

2. Add the garlic, ginger and spices and fry for a further minute. Add the chopped tomatoes and chillies and cook for another minute.

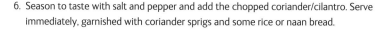

3. Add the pumpkin and curry paste and fry gently for 3–4 minutes before adding the stock.

4. Stir well, bring to the boil and simmer for 20 minutes until the pumpkin is tender.

5. Thickly slice the banana and add to the pumpkin along with the chickpeas. Simmer for a further 5 minutes.

6. Season to taste with salt and pepper and add the chopped coriander/cilantro. Serve immediately, garnished with coriander sprigs and some rice or naan bread.

Chocolate Rice Pudding

SERVES 6-8

65 g/2½ oz/⅓ cup
pudding rice
75 g/3 oz/⅓ cup
caster/superfine sugar
410 g/14 oz can
evaporated milk

600 ml/1 pint/2½ cups milk
pinch freshly grated nutmeg
¼ tsp ground cinnamon
(optional)
50 g/2 oz/⅔ cup dark/
bittersweet chocolate chips

25 g/1 oz/2 tbsp butter
freshly sliced strawberries,
to decorate
crème fraîche/sour cream,
to serve

1. Preheat the oven to 170°C/325°F/Gas Mark 3, 10 minutes before baking. Lightly butter a large ovenproof dish. Rinse the pudding rice, then place in the base of the buttered dish and sprinkle over the caster/superfine sugar.

2. Pour the evaporated milk and milk into a heavy-based saucepan and bring slowly to the boil over a low heat, stirring occasionally to avoid sticking. Pour the milk over the rice and sugar and stir well until well mixed and the sugar has dissolved.

3. Grate a little nutmeg over the top, then sprinkle with the ground cinnamon, if using. Cover tightly with kitchen foil and bake in the preheated oven for 30 minutes.

4. Remove the pudding from the oven and stir well to break up any lumps that may have formed. Cover with kitchen foil and return to the oven for a further 30 minutes.

5. Remove the pudding from the oven once again and stir to break up any more lumps. Stir the chocolate chips into the rice pudding and then dot with the butter. Continue to bake, uncovered, in the oven for a further 45 minutes–1 hour until the rice is tender and the skin is golden brown. Serve warm, with or without the skin, according to personal preference. Serve with a few sliced strawberries and a spoonful of crème fraîche/sour cream.

Onion Bhajis

SERVES 4-6

2 large onions, peeled
225 g/8 oz/2½ cups
  chickpea flour
small piece fresh root
  ginger, peeled and grated
½–1 small chilli, deseeded
  and finely chopped

½ tsp turmeric
½ tsp ground coriander
4 tbsp freshly chopped
  coriander/cilantro
freshly milled salt, to taste
125–150 ml/4–5 fl oz/½–⅔
  cup water

vegetable oil,
  for deep-frying

1. Finely slice the onions and place in a mixing bowl with the flour, spices and coriander/cilantro. Add salt to taste.

2. Slowly stir in the water and mix to form a thick consistency. Form into loose balls.

3. Heat the oil in a deep-fryer to a temperature of 180°C/350°F. Drop the bhajis, about 2 or 3 at a time, into the hot oil and deep-fry for 2–3 minutes until golden brown and crisp. Remove with a slotted spoon and drain on absorbent paper towels. Serve.

Lamb Passanda

SERVES 4-6

550 g/1¼ lb lean lamb, such as leg steaks
2 tbsp vegetable oil or ghee
1 tsp ground cumin
1 tsp ground coriander
1 tsp turmeric
½ tsp fenugreek seeds
3 green cardamom pods, cracked
1 cinnamon stick, bruised
3 whole cloves

5 cm/2 inch piece fresh root ginger, peeled and grated
1–2 green chillies, deseeded and finely chopped
2–4 garlic cloves, peeled and crushed
2 red onions, peeled and chopped
150 ml/¼ pint/⅔ cup natural/plain yogurt
250 ml/8 fl oz/1 cup water

85 ml/3 fl oz/⅓ cup coconut cream
1 green pepper, deseeded and cut into strips
50 g/2 oz/⅓ packed cup sultanas/golden raisins
3 tbsp ground almonds
25 g/1 oz/scant ¼ cup blanched almonds
25 g/1 oz/scant ¼ cup unsalted cashews, chopped

1. Discard any fat or gristle from the lamb, cut into thin strips and reserve. Heat the oil or ghee in a large frying pan, add the spices including the cinnamon and cloves and cook for 3 minutes.

2. Add the ginger, chillies, garlic, onions and meat and cook, stirring, until the meat is coated in the spices.

3. Stir in the yogurt, then spoon into a bowl, cover and leave to marinate in the refrigerator for 15 minutes.

4. Clean the pan and return the meat mixture to it together with the water. Bring to the boil, then reduce the heat, cover and simmer for 15 minutes. Pour in the coconut cream and add the green pepper and sultanas/golden raisins. Stir in the ground almonds. Return to the boil, then reduce the heat and simmer for 20 minutes, or until the meat is tender. Spoon into a warmed serving dish, sprinkle with the nuts and serve.

Chocolate Crepes

For the crepes:
75 g/3 oz/⅔ cup plain/all-purpose flour
1 tbsp unsweetened cocoa powder
1 tsp caster/superfine sugar
½ tsp freshly grated nutmeg
2 eggs
175 ml/6 fl oz/¾ cup milk

75 g/3 oz/⅓ cup (6 tbsp) unsalted butter, melted

For the mango sauce:
1 ripe mango, peeled and diced
50 ml/2 fl oz/¼ cup white wine
2 tbsp golden caster/unrefined superfine sugar
2 tbsp rum

For the filling:
225 g/8 oz dark/bittersweet chocolate
75 ml/3 fl oz/⅓ cup double/heavy cream
3 medium/large eggs, separated
2 tbsp golden caster/unrefined superfine sugar

1. Preheat the oven to 200°C/400°F/Gas Mark 6, 15 minutes before cooking. To make the crepes, sift the flour, cocoa powder, sugar and nutmeg into a bowl and make a well in the centre. Beat the eggs and milk together, then gradually beat into the flour mixture. Stir in 50 g/2 oz/¼ cup (4 tbsp) of the melted butter and leave to stand for 1 hour. Heat an 18 cm/7 inch nonstick frying pan and brush with a little butter. Add about 3 tablespoons of the batter and swirl to cover the base of the pan. Cook over a medium heat for 1–2 minutes, flip over and cook for a further 40 seconds. Repeat with the remaining batter. Stack the crepes, interleaving with greaseproof/waxed paper.

2. To make the sauce, place the mango, white wine and sugar in a saucepan and bring to the boil over a medium heat, then simmer for 2–3 minutes, stirring constantly. When the mixture has thickened, add the rum. Chill in the refrigerator while making the filling and baking.

3. For the filling, melt the chocolate and cream in a small heavy-based saucepan over a medium heat. Stir until smooth, then cool. Beat the egg yolks with the sugar for 3–5 minutes until the mixture is pale and creamy, then beat in the chocolate mixture. Beat the egg whites until stiff, then add a little to the chocolate mixture. Stir in the remainder. Spoon a little of the mixture onto each crepe, fold in half twice to form a triangle, brush with a little butter and bake in the preheated oven for 15–20 minutes until the filling is set. Serve hot or cold with the mango sauce.

Tarka Dhal

SERVES 4-6

2 green chillies
200 g/7 oz/1 heaped cup red split lentils
175 g/6 oz/1 scant cup yellow split lentils
2 onions, peeled and chopped

4 garlic cloves, peeled and sliced
2 tomatoes, chopped
1 tsp turmeric
1.25 litres/2¼ pints/1¼ quarts water
2 tbsp vegetable oil

1 tsp cumin seeds
1 tsp fennel seeds
2 tbsp freshly chopped coriander/cilantro

1. Deseed the chillies and chop. Rinse the lentils, then place in a large saucepan with the onions, 2 of the sliced garlic cloves, the chillies, tomatoes, turmeric and water. Bring to the boil, then reduce the heat, cover and simmer for 20 minutes. Remove the lid and cook for a further 5 minutes.

2. Heat the oil in a frying pan, add the seeds and remaining sliced garlic and cook for 1–2 minutes until lightly browned.

3. Place the cooked lentil mixture into a warmed serving bowl, stir in the chopped coriander/cilantro and sprinkle the toasted seeds and garlic on top. Serve.

Creamy Vegetable Korma

SERVES 4-6

2 tbsp ghee or
  vegetable oil
1 large onion, peeled
  and chopped
2 garlic cloves, peeled
  and crushed
2.5 cm/1 inch piece root
  ginger, peeled and grated
4 cardamom pods
2 tsp ground coriander

1 tsp ground cumin
1 tsp ground turmeric
finely grated zest and juice
  of ½ lemon
50 g/2 oz/½ cup ground
  almonds
400 ml/14 fl oz/1¾ cups
  vegetable stock
450 g/1 lb/4 cups potatoes,
  peeled and diced

450 g/1 lb mixed vegetables,
  such as cauliflower, carrots
  and turnip, cut into chunks
150 ml/¼ pt/⅔ cup
  double/heavy cream
3 tbsp freshly chopped
  coriander/cilantro
salt and freshly ground
  black pepper
naan bread, to serve

1. Heat the ghee or oil in a large saucepan. Add the onion and cook for 5 minutes. Stir in the garlic and ginger and cook for a further 5 minutes, or until soft and just beginning to colour.

2. Stir in the cardamom, ground coriander, cumin and turmeric. Continue cooking over a low heat for 1 minute, stirring.

3. Stir in the lemon zest and juice and almonds. Blend in the vegetable stock. Slowly bring to the boil, stirring occasionally.

4. Add the potatoes and vegetables. Bring back to the boil, then reduce the heat, cover and simmer for 35–40 minutes until the vegetables are just tender. Check after 25 minutes and add a little more stock if needed.

5. Slowly stir in the cream and chopped coriander/cilantro. Season to taste with salt and pepper. Cook very gently until heated through, but do not boil. Serve immediately with naan bread.

Chocolate Rice Pudding Brûlée

SERVES 6

2 tbsp cocoa powder (unsweetened)
75 g/3 oz/⅓ cup short-grain rice
600 ml/1 pint/2½ cups milk
1 bay leaf

grated zest of 1 orange
50 g/2 oz white chocolate, roughly chopped
1 tbsp golden caster/unrefined superfine sugar

4 medium/large egg yolks
250 ml/8 fl oz/1 cup double/heavy cream
½ tsp vanilla extract
4 tbsp demerara/turbinado sugar

1. Preheat the oven to 150°C/300°F/Gas Mark 2, 10 minutes before baking. Preheat the grill/broiler on high when ready to use. Gradually blend the cocoa powder with 3 tablespoons boiling water to form a soft, smooth paste. Place the rice and milk, bay leaf, orange zest and the cocoa powder paste in a saucepan. Bring to the boil, stirring constantly. Reduce the heat and simmer for 20 minutes, or until the rice is tender. Remove from the heat and discard the bay leaf, then add the white chocolate and stir until melted.

2. Whisk together the caster/superfine sugar and egg yolks until thick, then stir in the cream. Stir in the rice mixture together with the vanilla extract. Pour into a buttered shallow dish. Stand the dish in a baking tin/pan with sufficient hot water to come halfway up the sides of the dish. Cook in the preheated oven for 1½ hours, or until set. Stir occasionally during cooking, either removing the skin from the top or stirring the skin into the pudding. Remove from the tin and leave until cool.

3. Sprinkle the demerara/turbinado sugar over the surface of the pudding. Place under the preheated grill and cook until the sugar melts and caramelizes, turning the dish occasionally. Serve immediately or chill in the refrigerator for 1 hour before serving.

Vegetable Samosas

1 small potato, peeled
2–3 tbsp vegetable oil, plus
    extra for deep-frying
1 tsp mustard seeds
1 onion, peeled
    and chopped
1 tsp ground coriander

½–1 tsp garam masala
½ tsp turmeric
1–2 red chillies, deseeded
    and chopped
2 tbsp water
1 large carrot, peeled
    and grated

75 g/3 oz/½ cup frozen peas
75 g/3 oz/½ cup French/
    green beans, trimmed
    and chopped
250 g/9 oz/13 sheets
    filo/phyllo pastry dough

1. Cut the potato into small dice and leave in a bowl of cold water until required. When ready to use, drain thoroughly and shake dry.

2. Heat 2 tablespoons of the oil in a frying pan, add the mustard seeds and stir-fry for 1 minute, or until they pop. Add the onion and continue to fry for 5–8 minutes until softened. Add the remaining oil if necessary.

3. Add the spices, chilli and water and cook for a further 3 minutes, then add the potatoes, carrot, peas and beans. Stir, then cover and cook for 10–15 minutes until the vegetables are just cooked. Allow to cool.

4. Cut the pastry into 7.5 cm/3 inch strips. Brush a strip lightly with water and place a second strip on top. Place 1 tablespoon of the filling at one end of the strip, then fold the pastry over to form a triangle. Brush the pastry lightly with water. Continue folding the pastry, forming triangles to the end of the strip. Repeat with the remaining pastry and filling.

5. Heat the oil in a deep-fryer to a temperature of 180°C/350°F and deep-fry the samosas, in batches of about 2 or 3 at a time, for 2–3 minutes until golden. Remove with a slotted spoon and drain on absorbent paper towels. Serve hot or cold.

Aromatic Chicken Curry

SERVES 4

125 g/4 oz/⅔ cup red lentils
2 tsp ground coriander
½ tsp cumin seeds
2 tsp mild curry paste
1 bay leaf
small strip lemon rind
600 ml/1 pint/2½ cups chicken
   or vegetable stock

8 skinless chicken thighs
175 g/6 oz/¾ cup spinach
   leaves, rinsed and shredded
1 tbsp freshly chopped
   coriander/cilantro
2 tsp lemon juice
salt and freshly ground
   black pepper

To serve:
freshly cooked rice
low-fat natural/plain yogurt

1. Put the lentils in a sieve and rinse thoroughly under cold running water.

2. Dry-fry the ground coriander and cumin seeds in a large saucepan over a low heat for about 30 seconds. Stir in the curry paste.

3. Add the lentils to the saucepan with the bay leaf and lemon rind, then pour in the stock. Stir, then slowly bring to the boil. Turn down the heat, half-cover the pan with a lid and simmer gently for 5 minutes, stirring occasionally.

4. Secure the chicken thighs with cocktail sticks/toothpicks to keep their shape. Place in the pan and half-cover. Simmer for 15 minutes.

5. Stir in the shredded spinach and cook for a further 25 minutes, or until the chicken is very tender and the sauce is thick.

6. Remove the bay leaf and lemon rind. Stir in the coriander and lemon juice, then season to taste with salt and pepper. Serve immediately with the rice and a little natural yogurt.

Rice Pudding

SERVES 4

65 g/2½ oz/⅓ cup
  pudding rice
50 g/2 oz/¼ cup
  granulated sugar

410 g/14 oz can light
  evaporated milk
300 ml/½ pint/1¼ cups semi-
  skimmed/low-fat milk

pinch freshly grated nutmeg
25 g/1 oz/2 tbsp butter
jam/jelly, to serve

1. Preheat the oven to 150°C/300°F/Gas Mark 2. Lightly oil a large ovenproof dish. Sprinkle the rice and the sugar into the dish and mix.

2. Bring the evaporated milk and milk to the boil in a small pan, stirring occasionally. Stir the milks into the rice and mix well until the rice is coated thoroughly.

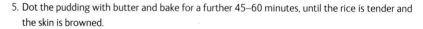

3. Sprinkle over the nutmeg, cover with kitchen foil and bake in the preheated oven for 30 minutes.

4. Remove the pudding from the oven and stir well, breaking up any lumps. Cover with the same kitchen foil. Bake in the preheated oven for a further 30 minutes. Remove from the oven and stir well again.

5. Dot the pudding with butter and bake for a further 45–60 minutes, until the rice is tender and the skin is browned.

6. Divide the pudding into four individual serving bowls. Top with a large spoonful of the jam/jelly. Serve immediately.

Carrot & Ginger Soup

SERVES 4

4 slices bread, crusts removed
1 tsp yeast extract
2 tsp olive oil
1 onion, peeled and chopped
1 garlic clove, peeled
   and crushed
½ tsp ground ginger

6 carrots, peeled and
   chopped
1 litre/2 pints/1 quart
   vegetable stock
2.5 cm/1 inch piece root
   ginger, peeled and
   finely grated

salt and freshly ground
   black pepper
1 tbsp lemon juice

To garnish:
chives
lemon zest

1. Preheat the oven to 180°C/350°F/Gas Mark 4. Roughly chop the bread. Dissolve the yeast extract in 2 tablespoons warm water and mix with the bread.

2. Spread the bread cubes over a lightly oiled baking sheet and bake for 20 minutes, turning halfway through. Remove from the oven and reserve.

3. Heat the oil in a large saucepan. Gently cook the onion and garlic for 3–4 minutes.

4. Stir in the ground ginger and cook for 1 minute to release the flavour.

5. Add the chopped carrots, then stir in the stock and the fresh ginger. Simmer gently for 15 minutes.

6. Remove from the heat and allow to cool a little. Blend until smooth, then season to taste with salt and pepper. Stir in the lemon juice. Garnish with the chives and lemon zest and serve immediately with the garlic croutons.

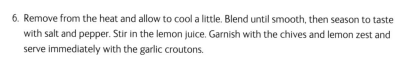

Vegetarian Spaghetti Bolognese

SERVES 4

2 tbsp olive oil
1 onion, peeled and
    finely chopped
1 carrot, peeled and
    finely chopped
1 celery stalk, trimmed
    and finely chopped
225 g/8 oz minced Quorn/soy
    meat substitute

150 ml/¼ pt/⅔ cup red wine
300 ml/½ pt/1¼ cups
    vegetable stock
1 tsp ketchup
4 tbsp tomato purée/paste
350 g/12 oz/4 cups dried
    spaghetti
4 tbsp half/reduced fat
    crème fraîche/sour cream

salt and freshly ground
    black pepper
1 tbsp freshly chopped
    parsley

1. Heat the oil in a large saucepan and add the onion, carrot and celery. Cook gently for 10 minutes, adding a little water if necessary, until softened and starting to brown.

2. Add the minced Quorn/soy meat substitute and cook for a further 2–3 minutes before adding the red wine. Increase the heat and simmer gently until nearly all the wine has evaporated.

3. Mix together the vegetable stock and ketchup and add about half to the Quorn mixture along with the tomato purée/paste. Cover and simmer gently for about 45 minutes, adding the remaining stock as necessary.

4. Meanwhile, bring a large pan of salted water to the boil and add the spaghetti. Cook until *al dente*, or according to the packet instructions. Drain well. Remove the sauce from the heat, add the crème fraîche/sour cream and season to taste with salt and pepper. Stir in the parsley and serve immediately with the pasta.

Baked Lemon & Sultana Cheesecake

275 g/10 oz/1⅓ cups
  caster/superfine sugar
50 g/2 oz/¼ cup
  (4 tbsp) butter
50 g/2 oz/½ cup self-raising
  flour
½ level tsp baking powder
5 large/extra-large eggs

450 g/1 lb/2 cups
  cream cheese
40 g/1½ oz/⅓ cup plain/all-
  purpose flour
grated zest of 1 lemon
3 tbsp fresh lemon juice
150 ml/¼ pint/½ cup crème
  fraîche/sour cream

75 g/3 oz/½ cup
  sultanas/golden raisins

To decorate:
1 tbsp icing/powdered sugar
fresh blackcurrants or
  blueberries
mint leaves

1. Preheat the oven to 170°C/325°F/Gas Mark 3. Oil a 20.5 cm/8 inch loose-bottomed round cake tin/pan with nonstick baking parchment.

2. Beat 50 g/2 oz/¼ cup of the sugar and the butter together until light and creamy, then stir in the self-raising flour, baking powder and 1 egg. Mix together lightly until well blended. Spoon into the prepared tin and spread the mixture over the base. Separate the 4 remaining eggs and reserve.

3. Blend the cheese in a food processor until soft. Gradually add the egg yolks and sugar and blend until smooth. Turn into a bowl and stir in the plain/all-purpose flour, lemon zest and juice. Mix lightly before adding the crème fraîche/sour cream and sultanas/golden raisins, stirring well.

4. Whisk the egg whites until stiff, fold into the cheese mixture and pour into the tin. Tap lightly on the work surface to remove any air bubbles. Bake in the preheated oven for about 1 hour until golden and firm. Cover lightly if browning too much. Switch the oven off and leave in the oven to cool for 2–3 hours. Remove the cheesecake from the oven. When completely cold, remove from the tin. Sprinkle with icing/powdered sugar, decorate with the blackcurrants or blueberries and mint and serve.

Cream of Spinach Soup

SERVES 4

1 large onion, peeled
  and chopped
5 large plump garlic cloves,
  peeled and chopped
2 medium potatoes, peeled
  and chopped
750 ml/1¼ pints/3¼ cups

cold water
1 tsp salt
450 g/1 lb spinach, washed
  and large stems removed
50 g/2 oz/¼ cup
  (4 tbsp) butter
3 tbsp flour

750 ml/1¼ pints milk
½ tsp freshly grated nutmeg
freshly ground black pepper
6–8 tbsp crème fraîche or
  sour cream
warm foccacia bread,
  to serve

1. Place the onion, garlic and potatoes in a large saucepan and cover with the cold water. Add half the salt and bring to the boil. Cover and simmer for 15–20 minutes until the potatoes are tender. Remove from the heat and add the spinach. Cover and set aside for 10 minutes.

2. Slowly melt the butter in another saucepan, add the flour and cook over a low heat for about 2 minutes. Remove the saucepan from the heat and add the milk, a little at a time, stirring continuously. Return to the heat and cook, stirring continuously, for 5–8 minutes until the sauce is smooth and slightly thickened. Add the freshly grated nutmeg to taste.

3. Blend the cooled potato and spinach mixture in a food processor or blender to a smooth purée, then return to the saucepan and gradually stir in the white sauce. Season to taste with salt and pepper and gently reheat, taking care not to allow the soup to boil. Ladle into soup bowls and top with spoonfuls of crème fraîche or sour cream. Serve immediately with warm foccacia bread.

Brown Rice Spiced Pilaf

1 tbsp vegetable oil
1 tbsp blanched almonds, flaked or chopped
1 onion, peeled and chopped
1 carrot, peeled and diced
225 g/8 oz/2 cups flat mushrooms, thickly sliced
¼ tsp cinnamon

large pinch dried chilli flakes
50 g/2 oz/½ cup dried apricots, roughly chopped
25 g/1 oz/2 tbsp currants
350 g/12 oz/1½ cups brown basmati rice
zest of 1 orange

900 ml/1½ pints/1 scant quart vegetable stock
2 tbsp freshly chopped coriander/cilantro
2 tbsp freshly snipped chives
salt and freshly ground black pepper
snipped chives, to garnish

1. Preheat the oven to 200°C/400°F/Gas Mark 6. Heat the oil in a large flameproof casserole dish and add the almonds. Cook for 1–2 minutes until just browning – be careful, as the nuts will burn very easily.

2. Add the onion and carrot. Cook for 5 minutes until softened and starting to turn brown. Add the mushrooms and cook for a further 5 minutes, stirring often.

3. Add the cinnamon and chilli flakes and cook for about 30 seconds before adding the apricots, currants, rice and orange zest. Stir together well and add the stock. Bring to the boil, cover tightly and transfer to the preheated oven. Cook for 45 minutes until the rice and vegetables are tender.

4. Stir the coriander/cilantro and chives into the pilaf and season to taste with salt and pepper. Garnish with the extra chives and serve immediately.

Poached Pears

SERVES 4

2 small cinnamon sticks
125 g/4 oz/⅔ cup
    caster/superfine sugar
300 ml/½ pint/1¼ cups
    red wine

150 ml/¼ pint/⅔ cup water
thinly pared rind and juice of
    1 small orange
4 firm pears
orange slices, to decorate

frozen vanilla yogurt or low-
    fat ice cream, to serve

1. Place the cinnamon sticks on the work surface and, with a rolling pin, slowly roll down the side of the cinnamon stick to bruise. Place in a large heavy-based saucepan.

2. Add the sugar, wine, water, pared orange rind and juice to the pan and bring slowly to the boil, stirring occasionally, until the sugar is dissolved.

3. Meanwhile, peel the pears, leaving the stalks on. Cut out the cores from the bottom of the pears and level them so that they stand upright.

4. Stand the pears in the syrup, cover the pan and simmer for 20 minutes, or until tender.

5. Remove the pan from the heat and leave the pears to cool in the syrup, turning occasionally.

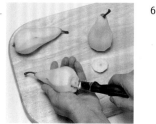

6. Arrange the pears on serving plates and spoon over the syrup. Decorate with the orange slices and serve with the yogurt or low-fat ice cream and any remaining juices.

Swede, Turnip, Parsnip & Potato Soup

2 large onions, peeled
25 g/1 oz/2 tbsp butter
2 carrots, peeled and
   roughly chopped
175 g/6 oz/1 cup
   swede/rutabaga, peeled
   and roughly chopped
125 g/4 oz/¾ cup turnip,
   peeled and roughly
   chopped

125 g/4 oz/¾ cup parsnips,
   peeled and roughly
   chopped
175 g/6 oz/1 cup potatoes
   peeled and roughly
   chopped
1 litre/2 pints/1 quart
   vegetable stock
½ tsp freshly
   grated nutmeg

salt and freshly ground
   black pepper
4 tbsp vegetable oil,
   for frying
125 ml/4 fl oz/½ cup
   double/heavy cream
warm crusty bread, to serve

1. Finely chop 1 of the onions. Melt the butter in a large saucepan and add the chopped onion, carrots, swede/rutabaga, turnip, parsnips and potatoes. Cover and cook gently for about 10 minutes, without colouring. Stir occasionally during this time.

2. Add the stock and season to taste with the nutmeg, salt and pepper. Cover and bring to the boil, then reduce the heat and simmer gently for 15–20 minutes, or until the vegetables are tender. Remove from the heat and leave to cool for 30 minutes.

3. Heat the oil in a large heavy-based frying pan. Finely chop the remaining onion, add to the frying pan and cook over a medium heat for 2–3 minutes, stirring frequently, until golden brown. Remove the fried onions with a slotted spoon and drain well on absorbent paper towels. As they cool, they will turn crispy.

4. Pour the cooled soup into a food processor or blender and process to form a smooth purée. Return to the cleaned pan, adjust the seasoning, then stir in the cream. Gently reheat and top with the crispy onions. Serve immediately with chunks of bread.

Baby Onion Risotto

For the baby onions:
1 tbsp olive oil
450 g/1 lb/18 baby onions, peeled, halved if large
pinch sugar
1 tbsp freshly chopped thyme

For the risotto:
1 tbsp olive oil
1 small onion, peeled and finely chopped
2 garlic cloves, peeled and finely chopped
350 g/12 oz/1½ cups risotto rice

150 ml/¼ pint/⅔ cup red wine
1 litre/2 pints/1 quart hot vegetable stock
125 g/4 oz/½ cup low-fat soft goats' cheese
salt and freshly ground black pepper
rocket/arugula leaves, to serve

1. For the baby onions, heat the olive oil in a saucepan and add the onions with the sugar. Cover and cook over a low heat, stirring occasionally, for 20–25 minutes until caramelized. Uncover during the last 10 minutes of cooking.

2. Meanwhile, for the risotto, heat the oil in a large frying pan and add the onion. Cook over a medium heat for 5 minutes until softened. Add the garlic and cook for a further 30 seconds. Add the risotto rice and stir well. Add the red wine and stir constantly until the wine is almost completely absorbed by the rice. Begin adding the stock a ladleful at a time, stirring well and waiting until the last ladleful has been absorbed before stirring in the next. It will take 20–25 minutes to add all the stock, by which time the rice should be just cooked but still firm. Remove from the heat.

3. Add the thyme to the onions and cook briefly. Increase the heat and allow the onion mixture to bubble for 2–3 minutes until almost evaporated. Add the onion mixture to the risotto along with the goats' cheese. Stir well and season to taste with salt and pepper. Serve with rocket/arugula leaves.

Chocolate, Orange & Pine Nut Tart

For the sweet shortcrust pastry:
150 g/5 oz/1 heaped cup plain/all-purpose flour
½ tsp salt
3–4 tbsp icing/ powdered sugar
125 g/4 oz/½ cup (8 tbsp) unsalted butter, diced

2 medium/large egg yolks, beaten
½ tsp vanilla extract

For the filling:
125 g/4 oz dark/bittersweet chocolate, chopped
65 g/2½ oz/scant ½ cup pine nuts, lightly toasted

2 large/extra-large eggs
grated zest of 1 orange
1 tbsp Cointreau
250 ml/8 fl oz/1 cup whipping cream
2 tbsp orange marmalade

1. Preheat the oven to 200°C/400°F/Gas Mark 6, 15 minutes before baking. Place the flour, salt and sugar in a food processor with the butter and blend briefly. Add the egg yolks, 2 tablespoons of iced water and the vanilla extract and blend until a soft dough is formed. Remove and knead until smooth, wrap in clingfilm/plastic wrap and chill in the refrigerator for 1 hour.

2. Lightly oil a 23 cm/9 inch loose-based flan tin/tart pan. Roll the dough out on a lightly floured surface to a 28 cm/11 inch round and use to line the tin. Press into the sides of the flan tin, crimp the edges, prick the base with a fork and chill in the refrigerator for 1 hour. Bake blind in the preheated oven for 10 minutes. Remove and place on a baking sheet. Reduce the oven temperature to 190°C/375°F/Gas Mark 5.

3. To make the filling, sprinkle the chocolate and the pine nuts evenly over the base of the pastry case/pie crust. Beat the eggs, orange zest, Cointreau and cream in a bowl until well blended, then pour over the chocolate and pine nuts. Bake in the oven for 30 minutes, or until the pastry is golden and the custard mixture is just set. Transfer to a wire rack to cool slightly. Heat the marmalade with 1 tablespoon water and brush over the tart. Serve warm or at room temperature.

Courgette & Tarragon Tortilla

5–6 potatoes
3 tbsp olive oil
1 onion, peeled and
  thinly sliced

salt and freshly ground
  black pepper
1 courgette/zucchini,
  trimmed and thinly sliced

6 eggs
2 tbsp freshly chopped
  tarragon
tomato wedges, to serve

1. Peel the potatoes and slice thinly. Dry the slices in a clean dishtowel to get them as dry as possible. Heat the oil in a large heavy-based pan, add the onion and cook for 3 minutes. Add the potatoes with a little salt and pepper, then stir the potatoes and onion lightly to coat in the oil.

2. Reduce the heat to the lowest possible setting, cover and cook gently for 5 minutes. Turn the potatoes and onion over and continue to cook for a further 5 minutes. Give the pan a shake every now and again to ensure that the potatoes do not stick to the base or burn. Add the courgette/zucchini, then cover and cook for a further 10 minutes.

3. Beat the eggs and tarragon together and season to taste with salt and pepper. Pour the egg mixture over the vegetables and return to the heat. Cook on a low heat for up to 20–25 minutes until there is no liquid egg left on the surface of the tortilla.

4. Turn the tortilla over by inverting it onto a saucepan lid or a flat plate, then sliding it back into the pan. Return the pan to the heat and cook for a final 3–5 minutes until the underside is golden brown. If preferred, place the tortilla under a preheated grill/broiler for 4 minutes, or until set and golden brown on top. Cut into small squares and serve hot or cold with tomato wedges.

Vegetarian Cassoulet

SERVES 6

125 g/4 oz/⅔ cup dried haricot/navy beans, soaked overnight
2 tbsp olive oil
2 garlic cloves, peeled and chopped
225 g/8 oz (about 9) baby onions, peeled and halved
2 carrots, peeled and diced

2 celery stalks, trimmed and finely chopped
1 red pepper, deseeded and chopped
175 g/6 oz/1½ cups mixed mushrooms, sliced
1 tbsp each freshly chopped rosemary, thyme and sage
150 ml/¼ pint/⅔ cup red wine

4 tbsp tomato purée/paste
1 tbsp dark soy sauce
salt and freshly ground black pepper
50 g/2 oz/1 cup fresh breadcrumbs
1 tbsp freshly chopped parsley
basil sprigs, to garnish

1. Preheat the oven to 190°C/375°F/Gas Mark 5, 10 minutes before baking. Drain the haricot/navy beans. Place in a saucepan with 1 litre/2 pints/1 quart fresh water. Boil rapidly for 10 minutes. Reduce the heat and simmer gently for 45 minutes. Drain the beans, reserving 300 ml/½ pint/1¼ cups of the liquid.

2. Heat 1 tablespoon of the oil in a flameproof casserole dish and add the garlic, onions, carrots, celery and red pepper. Cook gently for 10–12 minutes until tender and starting to brown. Add a little water if the vegetables start to stick. Add the mushrooms and cook for a further 5 minutes until softened. Add the herbs and stir briefly. Stir in the red wine and boil rapidly for about 5 minutes until reduced and syrupy. Stir in the reserved beans and their liquid, tomato purée/paste and soy sauce. Season to taste with salt and pepper.

3. Mix together the breadcrumbs and parsley with the remaining oil. Scatter this mixture evenly over the top of the stew. Cover loosely with kitchen foil, transfer to the preheated oven and cook for 30 minutes. Carefully remove the foil and cook for a further 15–20 minutes until the topping is crisp and golden. Serve garnished with basil sprigs.

Crème Brûlée with Sugared Raspberries

600 ml/1 pint/2½ cups fresh
   whipping cream
4 egg yolks
75 g/3 oz/⅓ cup
   caster/superfine sugar

½ tsp vanilla extract
25 g/1 oz/2 tbsp brown sugar
175 g/6 oz/1 generous cup
   fresh raspberries

1. Preheat the oven to 150°C/300°F/Gas Mark 2. Pour the cream into a bowl and place over
   a saucepan of gently simmering water. Heat gently, but do not allow to boil.

2. Meanwhile, whisk together the egg yolks, 50 g/2 oz/4 tablespoons of the caster/superfine
   sugar and the vanilla extract. When the cream is warm, pour it over the egg mixture, whisking
   briskly until it is completely mixed. Pour into six individual ramekin dishes and place in a
   roasting tin/pan. Fill the tin with enough water to come halfway up the sides of the dishes.
   Bake in the preheated oven for about 1 hour until the puddings are set. (To test if set,
   carefully insert a round-bladed knife into the centre. If the knife comes out clean, they
   are set.) Remove the puddings from the roasting tin and allow to cool. Chill in the refrigerator,
   preferably overnight.

3. Sprinkle the brown sugar over the top of each dish and place the puddings under a preheated
   hot grill/broiler. When the sugar has caramelized and turned deep brown, remove from the
   heat and cool. Chill the puddings in the refrigerator for 2–3 hours before serving.

4. Toss the raspberries in the remaining caster sugar and sprinkle over the top of each dish.
   Serve with a little extra cream, if liked.

Sweet Potato Crisps
with Mango Salsa

For the salsa:
1 large mango, peeled, stoned
   and cut into small cubes
8 cherry tomatoes,
   quartered
½ cucumber, peeled if
   preferred and finely diced
1 red onion, peeled and
   finely chopped

pinch sugar
1 red chilli, deseeded and
   finely chopped
2 tbsp rice vinegar
2 tbsp olive oil
grated zest and juice
   of 1 lime

**For the sweet potato
   crisps/chips:**
450 g/1 lb/⅔ cup sweet
   potatoes, peeled and
   thinly sliced
vegetable oil, for deep-frying
sea salt
2 tbsp freshly chopped mint

1. To make the salsa, mix the mango with the tomatoes, cucumber and onion. Add the sugar, chilli, vinegar, oil and the lime zest and juice. Mix together, cover and leave for 45–50 minutes.

2. Soak the sweet potatoes in cold water for 40 minutes to remove as much of the excess starch as possible. Drain and dry thoroughly in a clean dishtowel or absorbent paper towels.

3. Heat the oil to 190°C/375°F in a deep-fryer. When at the correct temperature, place half the sweet potatoes in the frying basket, then carefully lower into the hot oil and cook for 4–5 minutes until they are golden brown, shaking the basket every minute so that they do not stick together.

4. Drain the potato crisps on absorbent paper towels, sprinkle with sea salt and place under a preheated moderate grill/broiler for a few seconds to dry out. Repeat with the remaining crisps. Stir the mint into the salsa and serve with the potato crisps.

Pasta with Courgettes, Rosemary & Lemon

SERVES 4

350 g/12 oz/4½ cups dried
   pasta shapes, such
   as rigatoni
1½ tbsp good-quality extra
   virgin olive oil
2 garlic cloves, peeled and
   finely chopped
4 courgettes/zucchini,
   thinly sliced

1 tbsp freshly chopped
   rosemary
1 tbsp freshly
   chopped parsley
zest and juice of 2 lemons
25 g/1 oz pitted black olives,
   roughly chopped
25 g/1 oz pitted green olives,
   roughly chopped

salt and freshly ground
   black pepper

To garnish:
lemon slices
fresh rosemary sprigs

1. Bring a large saucepan of salted water to the boil and add the pasta. Return to the boil and cook until *al dente*, or according to the packet instructions.

2. When the pasta is almost done, heat the oil in a large frying pan and add the garlic. Cook over a medium heat until the garlic just begins to brown. Be careful not to overcook the garlic at this stage or it will become bitter.

3. Add the courgettes/zucchini, rosemary, parsley and lemon zest and juice. Cook for 3–4 minutes until the courgettes are just tender. Add the olives to the frying pan and stir well. Season to taste with salt and pepper and remove from the heat.

4. Drain the pasta well. Add to the frying pan. Stir until thoroughly combined. Garnish with lemon and fresh rosemary. Serve immediately.

Egg Custard Tart

SERVES 6

For the sweet pastry:
50 g/2 oz/¼ cup
  (4 tbsp) butter
50 g/2 oz/¼ cup white
  vegetable fat/shortening

175 g/6 oz/1⅓ cups plain/
  all-purpose flour
1 egg yolk, beaten
2 tsp caster/superfine sugar

For the filling:
300 ml/½ pint/1¼ cups milk
2 eggs, plus 1 egg yolk
2 tbsp caster/superfine sugar
½ tsp freshly grated nutmeg

1. Preheat the oven to 200°C/400°F/Gas Mark 6, 15 minutes before baking. Oil a 20.5 cm/8 inch flan tin/tart pan. Make the pastry by cutting the butter and vegetable fat/shortening into small cubes. Add to the flour in a large bowl and rub in until the mixture resembles fine breadcrumbs. Add the egg yolk, sugar and enough water to form a soft and pliable dough. Turn onto a lightly floured surface and knead. Wrap and chill in the refrigerator for 30 minutes.

2. Roll the dough out onto a lightly floured surface and use to line the oiled flan tin. Place in the refrigerator to chill.

3. Warm the milk in a small saucepan. Briskly whisk together the eggs, egg yolk and sugar. Pour the milk into the egg mixture and whisk until blended. Strain through a sieve into the pastry case/pie crust. Place the flan tin on a baking sheet.

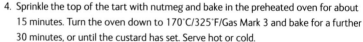

4. Sprinkle the top of the tart with nutmeg and bake in the preheated oven for about 15 minutes. Turn the oven down to 170°C/325°F/Gas Mark 3 and bake for a further 30 minutes, or until the custard has set. Serve hot or cold.

Smoked Salmon Sushi

175 g/6 oz/1 scant cup
  sushi rice
2 tbsp rice vinegar
4 tsp caster/superfine sugar
½ tsp salt

2 sheets sushi nori
65 g/2½ oz smoked salmon
¼ cucumber, cut into
  fine strips

To serve:
wasabi
soy sauce
pickled ginger

1. Rinse the rice thoroughly in cold water until the water runs clear, then place in a pan with 300 ml/½ pint/1¼ cups water. Bring to the boil and cover with a tight-fitting lid. Reduce to a simmer and cook gently for 10 minutes. Turn off the heat, but keep the pan covered, to allow the rice to steam for a further 10 minutes.

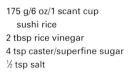

2. In a small saucepan, gently heat the rice vinegar, sugar and salt until the sugar has dissolved. When the rice has finished steaming, pour over the vinegar mixture and stir well to mix. Empty the rice out on to a large flat surface (a chopping board or large plate is ideal). Fan the rice to cool and to produce a shinier rice.

3. Lay one sheet of sushi nori on a sushi mat (if you do not have a sushi mat, improvise with a stiff piece of fabric that is a little larger than the sushi nori) and spread with half the cooled rice. Dampen the hands before doing this (this helps to prevent the rice from sticking to the hands). On the nearest edge, place half the salmon and half the cucumber strips.

4. Roll up the rice and smoked salmon into a tight Swiss-roll/jelly-roll-like shape. Dampen the blade of a sharp knife and cut the sushi into slices about 2 cm/¾ inch thick. Repeat with the remaining sushi nori, rice, smoked salmon and cucumber. Serve with wasabi, soy sauce and pickled ginger.

Teriyaki Turkey with Oriental Vegetables

1 red chilli, deseeded and
   thinly sliced
1 garlic clove, peeled
   and crushed
2.5 cm/1 inch piece root
   ginger, peeled and grated
3 tbsp dark soy sauce
1 tsp sunflower/corn oil
350 g/12 oz skinless turkey
   breast fillets, cut into
   thin strips

1 tbsp sesame oil
1 tbsp sesame seeds
2 carrots, peeled and cut
   into matchsticks
1 leek, trimmed and shredded
125 g/4 oz/1¼ cups small
   broccoli florets
1 tsp cornflour/cornstarch
3 tbsp dry sherry
125 g/4 oz/1 cup mangetout/
   snow peas, cut into strips

To serve:
freshly cooked egg noodles
sesame seeds, for sprinkling

1. Put the chilli into a small bowl with the garlic, ginger, soy sauce and sunflower/corn oil. Add the turkey and mix until well coated. Cover with clingfilm/plastic wrap and marinate in the refrigerator for at least 30 minutes.

2. Heat a wok or large frying pan. Add 2 teaspoons of the sesame oil. When hot, remove the turkey from the marinade. Stir-fry for 2–3 minutes until browned and cooked. Remove and reserve.

3. Heat the remaining 1 teaspoon oil in the wok. Add the sesame seeds and stir-fry for a few seconds until they start to change colour. Add the carrots, leek and broccoli and continue stir-frying for 2–3 minutes.

4. Blend the cornflour/cornstarch with 1 tablespoon cold water to make a smooth paste. Stir in the sherry and marinade. Add to the wok with the mangetout/snow peas and cook for 1 minute, stirring all the time, until thickened. Return the turkey to the wok and continue cooking for 1–2 minutes until the turkey is hot, the vegetables are tender and the sauce is bubbling. Serve the turkey and vegetables immediately with the egg noodles. Sprinkle with the sesame seeds.

Oaty Fruit Puddings

SERVES 4

125 g/4 oz/1⅔ cups
  rolled oats
50 g/2 oz/¼ cup low-fat
  margarine, melted
2 tbsp chopped almonds

1 tbsp clear honey
pinch ground cinnamon
2 pears, peeled, cored and
  finely chopped
1 tbsp marmalade

orange zest, to decorate
low-fat custard or fruit-
  flavoured low-fat yogurt,
  to serve

1. Preheat the oven to 200°C/400°F/Gas Mark 6. Lightly oil and line the bases of four individual pudding bowls or muffin tins/pans with small circles of greaseproof/waxed paper.

2. Mix together the oats, low-fat margarine, almonds, honey and cinnamon in a small bowl. Using a spoon, spread two thirds of the oaty mixture over the bases and around the sides of the pudding bowls or muffin tins.

3. Toss together the pears and marmalade and spoon into the oaty cases. Scatter over the remaining oaty mixture to cover the pears and marmalade. Bake in the preheated oven for 15–20 minutes until cooked and the tops of the puddings are golden and crisp.

4. Leave to cool for 5 minutes before removing the puddings from the bowls or tins. Decorate with orange zest and serve hot with low-fat custard or low-fat fruit-flavoured yogurt.

Curried Parsnip Soup

SERVES 4

1 tsp cumin seeds
2 tsp coriander seeds
1 tsp vegetable oil
1 onion, peeled and chopped
1 garlic clove, peeled
  and crushed

½ tsp turmeric
¼ tsp chilli powder
1 cinnamon stick
4 parsnips, peeled and chopped
1 litre/1¾ pints/1 quart
  vegetable stock

salt and freshly ground
  black pepper
fresh coriander/cilantro
  leaves, to garnish
2–3 tbsp natural/low-fat plain
  yogurt, to serve

1. In a small frying pan, dry-fry the cumin and coriander seeds over a moderately high heat for 1–2 minutes. Shake the pan during cooking until the seeds are lightly toasted.

2. Reserve until cooled. Grind the toasted seeds in a pestle and mortar.

3. Heat the oil in a saucepan. Cook the onion until softened and starting to turn golden.

4. Add the garlic, turmeric, chilli powder and cinnamon stick to the pan. Continue to cook for a further minute. Add the parsnips and stir well. Pour in the stock and bring to the boil. Cover and simmer for 15 minutes, or until the parsnips are cooked.

5. Allow the soup to cool. Once cooled, remove the cinnamon stick and discard.

6. Blend the soup in a food processor until very smooth. Transfer to a saucepan and reheat gently. Season to taste with salt and pepper. Garnish with fresh coriander/cilantro leaves and serve immediately with the yogurt.

Fish Lasagne

75 g/3 oz/¾ cup mushrooms
1 tsp sunflower/corn oil
1 small onion, peeled and
   finely chopped
1 tbsp freshly chopped
   oregano
400 g/14 oz can chopped
   tomatoes
1 tbsp tomato purée/paste

salt and freshly ground
   black pepper
450 g/1 lb cod or haddock
   fillets, skinned
9–12 sheets precooked
   lasagne verde

For the topping:
1 egg, beaten

125 g/4 oz/½ cup cottage cheese
150 ml/¼ pint/⅔ cup natural/
   low-fat plain yogurt
50 g/2 oz/½ cup grated
   Cheddar cheese

To serve:
mixed salad leaves
cherry tomatoes

1. Preheat the oven to 190°C/375°F/Gas Mark 5. Wipe the mushrooms, trim the stalks and chop.
   Heat the oil in a large heavy-based pan, add the onion and gently cook for 3–5 minutes until soft.
   Stir in the mushrooms, oregano and chopped tomatoes.

2. Blend the tomato purée/paste with 1 tablespoon water. Stir into the pan and season to taste with
   salt and pepper. Bring the sauce to the boil, then simmer, uncovered, for 5–10 minutes.

4. Remove as many of the tiny pin bones as possible from the fish and cut into cubes. Add to the
   tomato sauce mixture and stir gently, then remove the pan from the heat.

5. Cover the base of an ovenproof dish with 2–3 sheets of the lasagne verde. Top with half the fish
   mixture. Repeat the layers, finishing with the lasagne sheets.

6. To make the topping, mix together the beaten egg, cottage cheese and yogurt. Pour over the
   lasagne and sprinkle with the cheese. Cook the lasagne in the preheated oven for 35–40 minutes
   until the topping is golden brown and bubbling. Serve the lasagne immediately with the mixed
   salad leaves and cherry tomatoes.

Orange Curd & Plum Pie

SERVES 4

700 g/1½ lb plums,
   stoned and quartered
2 tbsp light brown sugar
grated rind of ½ lemon
25 g/1 oz/2 tbsp butter, melted
1 tbsp olive oil

6 sheets filo/phyllo pastry,
   plus 1 for decoration
½ x 411 g/7 oz jar luxury
   orange (or lemon) curd
50 g/2 oz sultanas/
   golden raisins

icing/powdered sugar,
   to decorate
Greek/plain yogurt, to serve

1. Preheat the oven to 200°C/400°F/Gas Mark 6. Lightly oil a 20.5 cm/8 inch round cake tin/pan. Cook the plums with 2 tablespoons of the light brown sugar for 8–10 minutes to soften them. Remove from the heat and reserve.

2. Mix together the lemon rind, butter and oil. Lay one of the sheets of filo/phyllo pastry in the prepared cake tin and brush with the lemon rind mixture. Cut four of the remaining pastry sheets in half and then place one half sheet in the cake tin and brush again. Top with the remaining halved sheets, brushing each time with the lemon rind mixture. Fold each sheet in half lengthways so that part of them lines the sides of the tin at the same time as the bottom to make a filo case.

3. Mix together the plums, orange curd and sultanas/golden raisins. Spoon into the pastry case/pie shell. Draw the pastry edges up over the filling to enclose. Brush the extra remaining pastry sheet with the lemon rind mixture. Cut into thick strips. Scrunch each strip of pastry and arrange on top of the pie.

4. Bake in the preheated oven for 25 minutes until golden. Sprinkle with icing/powdered sugar and serve with the Greek/plain yogurt.